MW00484187

POLAND'S NAVY

1918–1945

POLAND'S NAVY

1918–1945

MICHAEL ALFRED PESZKE

HIPPOCRENE BOOKS INC.
New York

Copyright©1999 Michael Alfred Peszke

All rights reserved.

ISBN 0-7818-0672-0

For information, address:
HIPPOCRENE BOOKS, INC.
171 Madison Avenue
New York, NY 10016

Printed in the United States of America

CONTENTS

PREFACE

The conference on the occasion of the 75th anniversary of the Polish Naval Aviation, which was held in Gdynia-Oksywie in 1995, was an opportunity to meet many interesting people— especially those dealing with the history of the Polish Navy. One of the most interesting figures, taking part in the conference, was Prof. Michael Alfred Peszke from the USA—son of Porucznik (lieutenant) Observer Alfred Bartlomiej Peszke, who was seconded to the Naval Aviation Wing in 1926.

It was then that I got to know the publications written by Prof. M. A. Peszke, *Polska Marynarka Wojenna w II Wojnie Swiatowej*, published as a supplement to the *Przeglad Morski* and translated by Andrzej Jablonski and Mieczyslaw Serafin, from the original 1989 publication, sponsored by the Polish Naval Association, London; and his *Battle for Warsaw 1939–1944* also published in 1995 of high historical importance.

After two years I have had an opportunity to study another book commemorating the heroic deeds of Polish seamen during WW II: *Poland's Navy, 1918–1945*.

I have been impressed by the contents of the book and wish to pay tribute to the author for his consistence and tenacity in historical investigations. The facts collected in this new publication have earned the author a good place in the group of historians dealing with the Polish Navy during World War II. To this group belong: J. Bartosik, Cz. Ciesielski, J. Dyskant, Zb. Flisowski, A Guzowski, B. Karnicki, E. Kosiarz, M. Kulakowski, J. Pertek, St. Piaskowski, J. Przybylski, B. Romanowski, Cz. Rudzki, E. Sopocko, B. Wronski, and many others.

It is timely that this book will be published on the 80th anniversary of the Polish Navy. It contains not only the evaluation of the historical background and conditions in which the Polish Navy was established but also an analysis of its development during the years of 1920–1939 and its wartime activities at the side of the Royal Navy. The whole work was divided into eleven chapters and was supplemented with eight appendices. Its structure testifies to the knowledge on constructing a historical work. It contains not only an analysis of facts. They were embedded in the concrete conditions under which the political views were formed and the naval views evolved.

M. A. Peszke created a monograph of enormous historical value, which comprises a huge number of facts and is a very rich source of knowledge.

Having many years of experience in teaching midshipmen-officer candidates, expected to do their service in the Polish Navy, I am pleased to underscore the fact that we have gained one more source of knowledge on the activities of our predecessors, which provide us with grounds for historical reflections.

Kontr-Admiral (Rear Admiral) dr. hab. Antoni Komorowski,
Professor and Commandant,
Polish Naval Academy Gdynia 15 Dec 1997

INTRODUCTION AND ACKNOWLEDGMENTS

There were many causes for the German attack on Poland on September 1, 1939. There were many reasons why the Poles resisted German blandishments and refused on October 24, 1938 to join the anticomintern pact which would have made Poland a German satellite, as was the case for Hungary or Slovakia. Poland's adamant, and in the West not well understood, refusal of a tacit acceptance of the German aim to incorporate the free city of Danzig into Germany was based on the conviction that this inexorably led to the loss of the Polish Pomeranian corridor and would again have separated Poland from the Baltic.[1] The creation of a Polish navy in 1918, and its continued national nourishment, was in many ways a symbolic act to affirm the strong bond of the Polish Government with a policy of enhancing maritime trade and presenting the Polish flag on all the oceans of the world.

In 1939 the Polish navy failed to protect the Polish coast, just as the Polish army failed to safeguard Polish land and its military aviation was unable to defend the skies against overwhelming odds and the subsequent treacherous attack by the Soviet Union on September 17, 1939. Yet the unremitting sea presence of the Polish navy continued to affirm Polish sovereignty and maintained the claim to the historically Polish Pomeranian lands, a viable economic access to the sea. In this determination not to give up their window to the world, the Polish navy and merchant marine played vital roles. In retrospect, the Polish navy had little more than a symbolic function, but that symbolism was important for the citizens of the Second Polish Republic and thus played a far greater role than its small size.

The Second Polish Republic was created on November 11, 1918, but the date of its demise is more controversial. Certainly, in September 1939, Poland was again invaded and occupied by its two neighbors, with a resulting fourth partition in

October 1939. But its constitutional government and its accredited officials (to say nothing of its armed forces) continued to function until July 5, 1945, when the Western Allies revoked their recognition of the Polish Government based in London. Thus, de jure and de facto, the Second Polish Republic existed for twenty-six years, one fifth of it in exile.

The Polish armed forces, however, existed until well into 1947, owing allegiance to a government that was recognized only by the Republic of Ireland and the Vatican. Even after the final demobilization of the forces, the government in exile existed. Finally, the last President in Exile, His Excellency Ryszard Kaczorowski, flew into Warsaw in 1992 and handed over the insignia of the presidency to Lech Walesa, the first freely elected president of Poland in over fifty years.

Poland was one of many German-occupied countries during the Second World War with governments in exile, located in London, and armed forces fighting the Germans. Prominent in this Allied coalition were the Norwegians, with a large merchant marine; the Free French, with not much more than the pride and ambition of de Gaulle; the Dutch, with a significant naval force (albeit primarily based and subsequently lost in the Pacific); and the Czechs, whose combat forces were limited to three air squadrons, all with a distinguished record.

The Polish contribution was easily the biggest of these Allied contingents which all came under British operational command.

The Polish Navy fought from September 1, 1939, to VE-Day on May 8, 1945. Except for a number of weeks in September 1939, when Polish surface and underwater units operated in the Baltic, the Polish naval war was fought from British bases in the United Kingdom and in the Mediterranean, by the side of the Royal Navy. While the Polish Navy was the smallest of the three Polish armed services in the Allied coalition against Germany (it comprised a mere 3 percent of the total manpower of the Polish service personnel in exile), it played a unique role, representing sovereign Polish territory. Its presence in so many ports of the world, uplifted the hearts of thousands of Poles who had been torn from their country by the war. It showed that the Polish state continued to exist in spite of the reign of terror visited on the Poles by the two occupiers, the Germans and the Russians. Its white and amaranth ensign in Allied ports, operations, and convoys affirmed that Poland was part of the United Nations in the war against at least one of the totalitarian oppressors of Europe. It constantly affirmed on all the seas and in all of the free world's ports that the Polish government had all the attributes of statehood, even though in exile. One of the more prosaic aspects was the fact that the Polish government in exile issued stamps that were used aboard Polish ships and carried letters marked *Poczta Polska* all over the world.

This is how the British First Lord of the Admiralty, Alexander, characterized the Polish Navy when opening an exhibition dedicated to Britain's Polish ally in London in the Spring of 1944:

> Whenever in the course of naval operations in this present world conflict at sea a great concourse of ships is gathered together, there is almost always to be seen one or more Polish ensigns, worn either by Polish warships or by vessels of the Polish Mercantile Marine, or by both. In view of its small size, the number of operations in which the Polish Navy has taken a part is almost incredible, especially bearing in mind that some of them are continuous. Amongst these operations are Narvik, Dunkirk, Lofoten Islands, Tobruk, Dieppe, attacks on shipping in the Channel, Sicily, Italy, Oran and patrols, notably in the Mediterranean, and convoy escorting. The recent work of the Polish ships in the Mediterranean has been especially brilliant.

I was too young to take an active part in the momentous events of the Second World War but old enough to have a clear memory of many of the events that took place. In the summer of 1941, I travelled from Lisbon to Gibraltar aboard a small British freighter, SS *Avoseta*, (which was subsequently sunk by the Germans with loss of life that included Polish families) and then from Gibraltar to the Clyde and Glasgow aboard the SS *Scythia*. While in Gibraltar, I saw the HMS *Ark Royal*, part of the famous Force H, but only later did I find out why the officers and the sailors exuded that typical British confidence and assurance—they had just taken a most prominent role in the sinking of the *Bismarck*.

During this Atlantic trip, in the middle of a large convoy, I observed the activities of the small escort warships, and the launching and landing of the *Swordfish* from the decks of the escorting carrier, HMS *Furious*, a converted battle cruiser with a most unusual profile. Our convoy underwent two enemy attacks, with no damage, which I was able to confirm many years later in the archives of the British Public Record Office by studying the pertinent logs of the Royal Navy's warships.

In that year of 1941, the allies lost over four million tons of shipping due to enemy action, while their shipyards were able to build a mere one and a half million tons. This was still the time of the German surface raiders, converted liners such as the *Atlantis* and *Thor* which preyed on allied merchantmen.[2] This was the beginning of the critical stage of the Battle of the Atlantic which was won by the Allies only in the second part of 1943, not least due to the expert decoding of German naval codes at Bletchley Park.[3]

After many years of researching the logs of the various warships that took part in the convoy, I learned that the cause for the ten-day voyage between Gibraltar and Glasgow on the Clyde was the fact that one or more of the German surface raiders was reported to be in the Atlantic, and the convoy was diverted to northern waters until it was reinforced by a Royal Navy battleship, *HMS Royal Sovereign*, with an escort of four destroyers.

The log of the British battleship for July 9, 1941 states: *"1838 [hours] Piorun reports vessels in sight bg. 210 degrees. At 1941 convoy sighted bg. 210 degrees."* It was late in the afternoon on that long summer day that I saw, for the first and last time during the war, a Polish destroyer. It was part of the escort of the battleship. The emotions I felt as it cut across our bow displaying the Polish white and amaranth ensign has stayed with me all my life. And in my mind, from that day on what I wanted to be was a Polish naval officer. This in spite of the fact that I had been born at Deblin, the Polish Aviation Officer's Academy, where my Father at that time was on the faculty; that I had always been in the American vernacular, an air force brat, surrounded by aviation people, and often, even in wartime, visiting air bases and fields. I suspect this was at least to some extent disappointing to my Father. The political situation at war's end, put a stop to my adolescent fantasies and I matriculated to Trinity College, Dublin, where I studied medicine.

Yet, it was not to be, and my only brief contact with the Polish Navy was to visit the two Polish museum warships, the ORP *Burza* and its successor, ORP *Blyskawica,* which had both played a gallant role throughout the war.[4] Finally, fifty years later, I achieved a symbolic closure to my ambitions when I was piped aboard the Polish destroyer, ORP *Warszawa*, while visiting the Polish Naval Academy in Oksywie in 1995.

This history is an expanded and much corrected version of my original short sketch written on behalf of the Polish Naval Association in London (1989) on the fiftieth anniversary of the outbreak of the Second World War, which was translated into Polish and published as a supplement to the *Przeglad Morski* (Naval Review) no. 4, 1995. The section on Polish naval aviation (Appendix D) is a translation of the paper given in Polish at the symposium on the seventy-fifth anniversary of Poland's naval aviation, organized jointly by the Polish Naval Academy (Komandor dr. hab. Antoni Komorowski) and the Command of the Brigade of the Polish Naval Aviation (Komandor dypl. pilot Jan Kania) in Oksywie in May 1995. This paper was published in Polish by *Przeglad Morski*, no. 66, 1995. My thanks also go to my host in Oksywie during that visit, the dean of social studies at the naval academy, Komandor dr. Wincenty Karawajczyk and his charming wife.

The assistance of the staff of the Polish Institute and, in particular, Andrzej Suchcitz and Elzbieta Barbarska, is most gratefully acknowledged. Crown copyright material in the Public Record Office is reproduced by permission of the Controller of Her Majesty's Stationery Office.

Excerpts from, *The Gathering Storm*, *Their Finest Hour*, *The Grand Alliance* and *Hinge of Fate* by Winston Churchill are reprinted by permission of Houghton Mifflin which has the copyright. The photographs come from a number of sources, some from my late Father, but I do wish to thank the Polish Naval Association in London, the Polish Library in London, the editors of *Morski Przeglad* and *Bandera*, and in particular, Marian Kluczynski who is responsible for the color plates.

I also need to extend a word of utmost appreciation to the late Komandor Bohdan Wronski, a distinguished Polish naval officer, a fine scholar, for many years the director of the Polish Institute and General Sikorski Museum in London, and author of many papers and books on the Polish military in general, and the Polish Navy, in particular. He extended his friendship and good counsel regarding Polish military history. Also to his wife, Mrs. Irena Wronska, who facilitated the publication of my first study of the Polish Navy.

I also wish to thank my son, Michael Alexander Peszke, graduate of Tabor Academy U.S. Naval Honor School and of the Massachusetts Maritime Academy, who went over this manuscript and attempted to help me with correct naval terminology. Thanks to him, I have stopped referring to maps and ropes, and I know a little more secondhand about a career that I would have liked to pursue and which I envy him. I wish him fair winds in his life.

My sincere thanks, appreciation and admiration go to Mr. Joe McCloskey, who proofread the manuscript. His comments improved the final version and his grasp of my historical intent was impressive. The whole editorial board of Hippocrene Books, Inc. were also most supportive, in particular Mr. Jacek Galazka and Ms. Carol Chitnis.

Finally I wish to thank the Kosciuszko Foundation (New York), particularly The Joseph B. Slotkowski Memorial Publishing and The William and Mildred Zelosky Funds of The Kosciuszko Foundation, Inc. whose generous grant has made publication of this book possible.

NOTES

1. Jedrzejewicz, Waclaw, ed. *Diplomat in Berlin, 1933–1939. Papers and Memoirs of Jozef Lipski. Ambassador of Poland*, Columbia University Press, 1968. pp. 453–454.
2. David Woodward, *The Secret Raiders. The Story of the German Armed Merchantmen in the Second World War*, New York, 1955. Between March 1940 and late 1943 ten of these German ships often disguised as neutral freighters, were responsible for the sinking of 775 thousand tons of allied merchant shipping and in

addition tied up valuable Royal Navy surface warships all over the South Atlantic, Indian Ocean and the Pacific.

3. Kahn, David, *Seizing the Enigma. The Race to Break the German U-Boat Codes, 1939–1943,* Boston, 1991.

4. *ORP* is the abbreviation for *Okret Rzeczypospolitej Polskiej,* or warship of the Polish Republic, being analogous to HMS, Her Majesty's Ship in the Royal Navy. Polish language differentiates between an *okret*, namely a warship, and a *statek*, which is a liner or freighter. A tanker would be *tankowiec.*

CHAPTER I
HISTORICAL BACKGROUND

FIRST POLISH CONTACTS WITH THE BALTIC IN THE ELEVENTH CENTURY

Archaeological research suggests that, well over a thousand years ago, there were Slavic tribes living on the shores of the southern Baltic, engaging in various maritime pursuits, such as fishing, coastal commerce, and of course the usual brigandage, pillage, and piracy. The tribes lived on the island of Rugia, worshiped the four-faced and all-seeing Slavic God, *Swiatowid,* and were recognized as a major Baltic power. This antedated the formation of the Polish state which became part of Western Christian civilization in A.D. 966, when the Polish king, Mieszko I, accepted baptism and initiated the Piast Dynasty, which would rule Poland for the next four centuries.

In the year 1000 the Holy Roman Emperor made a momentous visit to Poland, during which he acknowledged Poland's autonomy, which had until then been disputed. At the same time the Metropolitan See of Gniezno was created subject only to the Papacy in Rome. This has been Poland's prime see for nearly a thousand years and is the keystone of the Polish identity with the Western European tradition. With the creation of the Metropolitan See, the bishoprics of Kolobrzeg (Pomerania) and Wroclaw (Silesia) were then placed under its jurisdiction. These are the formal, legal, and historical foundations of Poland's claims to those territories.

After the death of Mieszko's son, King Boleslaw the Brave, in 1025, the Polish kingdom split up into a number of small dukedoms, each ruled by a Piast princeling. Central authority was reinstituted over most of the Polish territory by the kings of Malo-Polska with their capital in Krakow in the fourteenth century; while Silesia and Pomerania continued as autonomous duchies under Piast dukes.

EARLY NAVAL DEVELOPMENT AND CREATION OF THE MARITIME COMMISSION BY KING ZYGMUNT AUGUST IN 1568

Many historians accept 1456 as the first organized Polish naval effort. In that year, the burghers of Gdansk wrote letters of marque, on authority from the Polish king, to send thirteen armed Gdansk merchant ships to interdict a fleet of Dutch ships sailing with cargoes to Konigsberg on behalf of the Teutonic Knights. This powerful crusading order, mostly composed of German knights, was committed to the policy of converting the pagan peoples of the region, now known as the Baltic states. Its ethnic composition inevitably, if not by actual policy, helped to increase German influence in the south-central region of the Baltic.

In 1457, the Gdansk galleons fought and destroyed a Danish and Kurlandian fleet off Bornholm. Emboldened by such success the Gdansk masters followed the coastline, destroying and capturing ships in Lübeck, Rostock, and Stralsund. More such writs followed and in 1463, the king of Poland sent a Polish Royal Fleet to battle against the Danes, who were allied with the Teutonic Knights. The Poles broke the blockade imposed by the Danish fleet; of the forty-four enemy ships, only one, with the Grand Master of the Teutonic Knights aboard, survived. Eighteen hundred enemy soldiers and only two hundred sixty sailors escaped while the rest were either captured or perished.

This naval victory coupled with major land successes led inexorably to the decline of the Teutonic Knights. In 1466, the Treaty of Torun was signed returning Torun, Elblag, Olsztyn, and Malbork to Poland after almost one hundred years of subjugation by the Teutonic Knights.

In 1568, King Zygmunt August, the last of the Piast Dynasty, convened a Maritime Commission, headed by Jan Kostka with the authority to tax and the responsibility to protect the Polish coast. This *Commissio Maritima* in 1571 wrote the first set of instructions for Polish ship masters and in reality was Poland's first admiralty.

SEVENTEENTH CENTURY WARS AGAINST THE SWEDES

This battle, which has gone into Polish naval history as a memorable victory occurred on November 28 1627, off the lovely town of Oliwa, located between Gdansk and the modern city of Gdynia. The Polish Royal Fleet defeated a Swedish fleet which had attempted to blockade the Polish ports and interdict Polish trade.[1] Polish warships with magnificent names such as *Panna Wodna* (Water Maiden) and *Swiety Jerzy* (Saint George) won ever-lasting fame. It was many hundreds of years before other Polish warships, with names such as *Orzel* (Eagle) and *Blyskawica* (Lightning), also entered this Polish naval pantheon. In the seventeenth century, as in the twentieth, the ships sailed under the same ensign: an arm holding a cutlass on an amaranth field placed on a Maltese cross superimposed on the national Polish white and amaranth colors, as described in the Dutch manual *Niewe Hollandse Scheepsbouw* by A. Allard in 1695.

PARTITIONS

In the seventeenth century, as Polish fortunes declined, so did the Polish presence in the Baltic. This economic decline led to political decline and to progressive territorial losses with the third and final partition, and resulting extinction of Poland as an independent state in 1795. This in spite of the great efforts of the last king, Stanislaw Poniatowski and his *Sejm* (Parliament), which passed Europe's most progressive and liberal constitution on May 3, 1791.

NOTE

1. Eugeniusz Koczorowski, *Bitwa pod Oliwa* (The Battle of Oliwa), Gdansk, 1976; and *Flota Polska w Latach, 1587–1632* (The Polish Fleet in the Years, 1587–1632), Warsaw, 1973. Jozef Wieslaw Dyskant, *Oliwa, 1627*, Warsaw, 1993. Also see Ludwik Kubala, *Wojny Dunskie i Pokoj Oliwski* (The Danish Wars and the Oliwa Peace), Lwow, 1922, and Adam Szelagowski, *Walka o Baltyk, 1544–1621* (The Fight for the Baltic, 1544–1621), Lwow, 1904.

CHAPTER II
POLAND'S REBIRTH, 1918

RECREATION OF THE REPUBLIC IN 1918

In the close to one hundred and twenty years of alien rule from Moscow, Vienna, and Berlin, punctuated by a number of bloody and unsuccessful revolts, the events of 1918 were long awaited.[1]

The defeat of Imperial Russia by the Central Powers in 1917, to be followed shortly by their own defeat at the hands of the Western coalition of Britain, France, and the United States, was an event of historical serendipity, as much as the dramatic and wholly unexpected collapse of Soviet Communism seventy years later.

Jozef Klemens Pilsudski (1867–1935) was one of the main architects of Poland's re-emergence from over a century of captivity.[2] In his youth he had been in the forefront of the clandestine anti-Tsarist patriotic movement in the Russian-occupied sector of Poland, and at the outbreak of the Great War in 1914, he threw his small Polish all-volunteer force legion to the side of the Austrians against the Russians. But Pilsudski refused to go the next step, tying his policies and principles to the concept of subordinating Poland to the Germanic nations. Pilsudski was arrested by the Germans in 1917 for refusing to take an oath of allegiance to the Kaiser, and his legionnary brigade was disbanded and many of his officers and legionnaires imprisoned by the Germans. After the Armistice of November 11, 1918, the Germans released Pilsudski, and his return was greeted by the exuberant acclamation of the Warsaw populace. The Regency Council promulgated him head of state, or *Naczelnik Panstwa*, pending the writing of a constitution. Pilsudski became the second Pole to be given the title of *Naczelnik Panstwa*, the first being Tadeusz Kosciuszko, hero of two continents.[3]

PILSUDSKI CREATES THE MODERN POLISH NAVY ON NOVEMBER 28, 1918

On November 28, 1918, the anniversary of the victory off Oliwa, Pilsudski issued a short four-line executive order creating the Polish Navy:

> Rozkazuje utworzyc Marynarke Polska -mianujac jednoczesnie pulkownika marynarki Bogumila Nowotnego Szefem Sekcji przy Ministerstwie Spraw Wojskowych.
>
> "I order the creation of the Polish Navy and nominate Colonel of the Navy Bogumil Nowotny to be Section Chief in the Ministry of Military Affairs."

These words are engraved over the entrance to the Polish Naval Academy in Oksywie.

Perhaps this order left too much unsaid. On the other hand, it is a great example of decisiveness and succinctness to bureaucrats, who love to create mountains of paper.

But there was an embryonic Polish Navy before Pilsudski's order. On November 1, 1918, the General Officer Commanding of the Polish army in Galicia, General Boleslaw Roja ordered that all Vistula river monitors and gunboats which originally belonged to the Austrians, but were now located in Polish-controlled territories, be centralized in Krakow.

In this period of administrative chaos caused by the disintegration of Russian and Austrian authority in eastern central Europe, nationalistic forces were being spontaneously reawakened and the Poles were not the only national group seeking to establish local control. Often the nationalistic forces of other ethnic groups were at odds with Polish aspirations. After well over a hundred years under the foreign yoke, after a number of bloody and unsuccessful rebellions against the oppressor, the Polish nation was free to declare its sovereignty. But to declare independence was the easy step; to preserve its boundaries from the grasping hands of neighbors required further military effort. The Germans, Russians, Ukrainians, Lithuanians and even the Czechs all disputed Polish claims to areas perceived by the Poles as historically theirs or as essential to the Polish state and the viability of its economy.

A number of wars had to be fought, and a number of national uprisings endured, before the regions of Poznan, Silesia, and the western marches were secured by treaties. But it was the failure to gain Gdansk, and the British insistence that it be a Free City, coupled with the failure of Polish diplomatic steps to have East Prussia declared a demilitarized zone (as was the area west of the Rhine) that had the most deleterious effect for future Polish security.

THE FREE CITY OF GDANSK

Gdansk, known in medieval days as Dantiscum, is a historic Polish gateway to the outside world, whose history is a paradigm of Poland's fortunes. From its earliest days as a port in the kingdom of Mieszko I, to its heyday as the birthplace of the Solidarity union (*Solidarnosc*) in the turbulent days of 1980, Gdansk has been a barometer of Poland's sovereignty and independence. It was lost by the Poles to the Order of the Teutonic Knights in 1308, regained in 1466 after the defeat of the Order, and remained Polish until the second partition in 1793. This three-hundred-year period (1466–1793) was Gdansk's cultural and economic zenith. The combination of magnificent architecture and commercial prosperity made it the wealthiest and most populated city of the Polish kingdom. So affluent were the burghers of the city, that they dealt with the king and his ministers as equals. In fact the city often assumed a posture of complete autonomy in all matters relating to trade and maritime issues. When Polish kings were powerful, the city was subservient; when weak, its burghers often became arrogant, shamefully abetted by the Polish magnates, who feared any curtailment of the trade through Gdansk, as well as any political developments which might make the king more powerful and thus limit their own powers.

Gdansk's historic association with the Hanseatic League has led to both misunderstanding and confusion since many view that as a sign of German provenance, even though such cities as Norwich, Oslo, and Rotterdam were also members of this medieval trade association, an early paradigm for the common market. The Baltic was a major center of trade, in which a number of countries competed for a monopoly. Holland, England, France, and Spain's Hapsburgs all vied for trading ports in the Baltic. The Kings of Denmark, controlling the entrance to the Baltic, attempted to impose tariffs. For a time, the English had trading posts in Elblag in competition with Gdansk, and were tacitly supported by the Polish king who wished to weaken the burghers of Gdansk.

In 1919, the victorious Western powers, at the Versailles deliberations, declared Gdansk a Free City, placing it under the aegis of the League of Nations, but giving some economic rights, as well as a military transit facility (Westerplatte), to Poland. There was precedent for this in the short-lived period under Napoleon when it was a free city, garrisoned by French and Polish troops. While the majority of the citizens were German, there were fifty thousand Poles.

Gdansk was the focus and barometer of Polish-German diplomatic relations, and eventually the point of military strife.[4] The first shots of the Second World War were probably fired on the Polish fortifications of Westerplatte at the mouth of the Vistula near Gdansk.

THE POLISH-RUSSIAN WAR, 1919–1920

In the late months of 1920, the war against the Russians successfully drew to a close. It was a see-saw campaign which included Polish forces advancing to Kiev and then retreating all the way back to the Vistula.[5] The magnificent Polish victory under the command of Pilsudski at the northeast outskirts of Warsaw, called the Battle of Warsaw, in August 1920, stopped the Russians.[6] This was shortly followed by the crushing of the Russian armies in the Battle of Niemen and the ensuing armistice which led to the Treaty of Riga (1921) between Poland and the Russians.

The Polish Navy participated in this war by manning a small number of river gunboats and monitors on the complex of rivers flowing from the Polish town of Pinsk to the Ukrainian Dnieper. In the first stage of the Polish offensive against the Russians in early 1920, the Polish riverine flotilla units were successful and penetrated east to the Dnieper and as far south as Kiev. But as the Russians regrouped and counterattacked, the warships withdrew west to Pinsk. Then there were no more navigable waters to which they could retreat, and the boats had to be scuttled and the crews evacuated to Modlin, near Warsaw, where they were formed into infantry units and sent back into the fray. Many of the Polish naval officers, who in the Second World War commanded Polish warships, on the great oceans, won their battle spurs in the fighting on the Dnieper and its many tributaries. After hostilities ceased with the signing of the Armistice and the Peace Treaty of Riga, many of the scuttled warships were refloated.

With the signing of the Treaty of Riga, war with the Russians was successfully concluded; but the rancor was not erased and Soviet aggression of 1939 was payback from the Russians.

While the boundaries in the east were won in battle, those in the west with Germany were won by a combination of negotiations and plebiscites carried out during the most critical time in the new state's short-lived existence. The British did not endorse their French allies in supporting the Polish cause. The final result was that Poland only received a one hundred and forty kilometer strip of sandy beach, the small shallow-water fishing port of Puck and the beautiful peninsula of Hel, with its small fishing port.

Poland's access to the Baltic coast was through a long narrow corridor, which became known pejoratively as the "Polish Corridor." Having failed to get Gdansk, the Poles attempted to ensure that the German enclave of East Prussia became demilitarized, as was the case for Germany west of the Rhine. But once again the British policy of balance of power, which now feared French hegemony on the continent, stalemated the foreign policy of the nascent Polish state. The way the Poles were treated by the Western coalition was a bitter pill for the Poles. Even though much of the fighting in the Great War between the Russians and the Germans had been on Polish territory, and had led to horrible damage to Polish agriculture and industry, the Poles were denied war reparations. They were, in fact, made to assume obligations for debts undertaken by the partitioning powers, since as a successionist state they were deemed to be fiscally responsible. This kind of legalistic casuistry was infuriating to the Polish people. Finally

Poland was made to sign the Nationality Minorities Treaty which allowed the League of Nation ingerence into internal Polish affairs. Germany, a defeated enemy with many millions of ethnic Poles within its borders, was not subject to this provision. Many years later, the Polish Foreign Minister, Jozef Beck challenged the League of Nations to make this clause pertain to all members of the League. This was of course refused and the Polish government repudiated that provision of the treaty. This led to bitter recriminations implying that Poland was responsible for destroying the Versailles Treaty.

NOTES

1. Piotr Wandycz, *Lands of Partitioned Poland, 1795–1918*, University of Washington University Press, 1974.
2. Waclaw Jedrzejewicz, *Pilsudski: A Life for Poland*, New York, 1982.
3. Miecislaus Haiman, *Kosciusko: Leader and Exile*, New York, 1977, and *Kosciusko in the American Revolution*, New York, 1975.
4. Hans L. Leonhardt, *Nazi Conquest of Danzig*, University of Chicago Press, 1942. Also, the Polish position is well articulated by Szymon Askenazy, *Dantzig and Poland*, London, 1921.
5. Adam Zamoyski, *The Battle for the Marshlands*, East European Monographs, Boulder, CO, 1981.
6. Pilsudski, *Year 1920*, New York, 1970, and Viscount D'Abernon, *The Eighteenth Decisive Battle of the World*, Warsaw 1920; London, 1931.

CHAPTER III

POLISH NAVAL DEVELOPMENT, 1920–1939

THE FIRST YEARS

The Poles took possession of their Baltic shore on February 10, 1920. The first Polish warship commissioned and to fly the Polish ensign on the Baltic after many decades was the hydrographic survey vessel, ORP *Pomorzanin*. In late 1920, the Poles purchased a gunboat, ORP *Komendant Pilsudski*, followed by ORP *General Haller* in April 1921, both purchased in Finland. In 1921 the Poles also purchased a number of armed trawlers in Denmark and the ORP *Jaskolka*, ORP *Mewa*, ORP *Czajka*, and ORP *Rybitwa* became commissioned initiating the tradition of naming small warships after seabirds. These were replaced in the late thirties by Polish-built minesweepers. Polish hopes of receiving a significant number of the surrendered imperial German fleet warships, later scuttled at Scapa Flow, were essentially ignored since the British were most reluctant to give even a small number of the captured German warships to the fledgling Polish Navy. But eventually a number of torpedo boats were received in late 1921. They were named after denizens of various Polish provinces; ORP *Kaszub*, ORP *Krakowiak*, ORP *Kujawiak*, ORP *Mazur*, ORP *Slask*, ORP *Podhalanin*. But this was well after the Polish-Russian war was concluded in 1921.

The first years of Polish independence were difficult.[1] Three different areas of Poland, that had been administered by different partitioning countries with strikingly different legal and economic systems, had to be integrated. Investment capital was a mere trickle while the German Weimar Republic undertook a punishing customs war with Poland.[2]

Poland depended heavily on its French ally both for surplus war material as well as for capital loans; but the infusion of

foreign capital and French loans was inadequate, and the
plans for the growth of the navy, therefore, constantly confronted by fiscal realities.[3] The issues of an operational doctrine for the navy in a small landlocked sea, based on a minute
coastline, were the topic of heated debate among a small group
of individuals who were able to see further than the immediate
never ending crises confronting the country.

In the case of war against the Soviets, there was an excellent chance that even a small Polish naval force would be in a
position to protect the Polish coast, to give some assurance that
merchant ships from the west would be safely escorted, and
that even offensive operations against the Soviets might be successfully undertaken. In such an eventuality the Polish ports
and their hinterland, the Pomeranian corridor, would be safe
from air and land attack. This was certainly not the case in the
event of war with Germany. But in the first years of independence, the Versailles Treaty provisions limiting German military strength, in addition to the potential force of the French
alliance, dating from 1921, made Germany less of a threat
than the Soviet Union. In fact much German planning was initiated to prevent a feared Polish aggression.[4] It also led directly
to the clandestine collaboration between Germany and the
Soviets and the Rapallo Treaty of April 16, 1922.[5]

In the case of war with Germany, it was proposed and
debated that at the very least, the Polish Navy should have the
potential to interdict German sea movements between Germany
proper and East Prussia. One of the most prominent theoreti-
cians, who in the war years would cover himself with great dis-
tinction, was Marian Kadulski. He argued that the Baltic Sea
absolutely required a fleet of small torpedo boats and minelaying
submarines. The minelaying submarine option was quickly
accepted, but it has to be remarked with regret that it was only
in 1939 that the naval authorities signed contracts with British
shipyards for delivery of motor-torpedo boats which were only
delivered in the United Kingdom after the outbreak of the war.

This strategic equation began to change in the unstable
diplomatic era following Hitler's election to the post of Chan-
cellor of Germany and his march into the demilitarized zone
west of the Rhine in 1935.

It is undeniable that the Polish Navy lacked the bases or
the size to play an active part in Polish war plans against

Germany, and it is probably true in hindsight, as Admiral Jerzy Swirski said in England after the war, that the task of the Polish Navy was to create future naval cadres.

CONSTRUCTION OF THE SEAPORT OF GDYNIA

A number of individuals are forever associated with the first years of Poland's return to the Baltic and its endeavors to establish a maritime presence. Pride of place has to go to Admiral Kazimierz Porebski, who was nominated to the post of Chief of the Department of Maritime Affairs (*Department Spraw Morskich*) which entailed both naval and mercantile matters. In January 1922, he became Commandant of the Polish Navy. He was responsible for the creation in June 1920 of the Polish Merchant Marine Academy, initially in Tczew; and of the Polish Naval Officers' Academy in October, 1922 in Torun. Among his many organizational accomplishments were the instructions given to Tadeusz Wende, an engineer, to begin the plans for the creation of the port of Gdynia in May 1920.

The success of the Polish economy in this difficult period, where Germany actively carried out an economic tariff war against the Poles, was due to the growth of the port of Gdynia, which was built, with French capital loans. In the early twenties Gdynia was a small fishing hamlet, without a pier, where the fishermen pulled their thirty-foot boats onto the beach after fishing. In 1939, Gdynia was the busiest port in the Baltic.

BEGINNING OF THE MODERN NAVY

France was Poland's primary military ally and, for many years, the main source of military equipment and most of its investment capital. French World War One military surplus came to Poland in great quantity, though too frequently of inadequate or badly used quality, and it was French commercial loans that created Gdynia. It is natural that France being the source of the loans, the monies would have to be spent in France. So it was to France that the Poles turned for minelaying submarines. The first contract bids were sent out with specifications in late 1924. Polish plans, however, fell foul of

French internal corruption. The original plans for a fleet of nine submarines had to be scaled down, due not only to fiscal constraints but also to the fact that French politicians, lobbied by the various large industrial companies, demanded that the French loans, were to be distributed according to internal French needs, and not necessarily Polish strategic plans. Therefore, the number of submarines was scaled down to three and contracts for two surface warships (not sought by the Poles) were awarded to French shipyards: hence the sudden appearance of two French-built destroyers, quite outside of the Polish plans. The French-built destroyers were far from a success, but the submarines were plagued by problems from the first months of operation.

It was in 1932 that the first of the French-built submarines was commissioned in the Polish Navy and became operational. In time all three were worked up and formed the Polish Submarine Division, under the command of Kdr. ppor. Eugeniusz Plawski. The Poles planned thoroughly for the delivery of the boats. Polish officers and senior noncommissioned officers were seconded to the prestigious French *École de navigation sous-marine* in Toulon.

In the mid-thirties, the Poles turned to the British for two additions to the destroyer division. These British built destroyers, *Grom* and *Blyskawica,* modified for minelaying and strengthened for ice navigation, were among the largest and fastest destroyers in the world. Polish naval architects were planning to build two more such warships in Polish shipyards. These were to be called the *Orkan* and *Huragan.* The keel for the *Orkan* was laid on July 15, 1939, accompanied by a mass celebrated by the senior chaplain of the Polish Navy, Kdr. por. W. Miegon, the author's godfather. Polish shipyards had already designed and built a whole class of small coastal minelayers and minesweepers, the diesel-powered Jaskolka class. The two older French-built destroyers, *Burza* and *Wicher,* were to be modernized in Polish yards.

In addition to these surface warships, there was a large, minelayer (also French-built), which in peacetime functioned as the training ship *Gryf.*

In the mid-thirties, the Polish Naval Staff decided to build up the submarine division, and bids were issued for two oceangoing submarines. After another scandal with French shipyards, whose dubious specifications were discovered in time, the contracts went to the Dutch.

But while the Dutch built the submarines to excellent standards, many features were of Polish design. One of the most innovative was the watertight compartment for the forty-millimeter Swedish AA Bofors. This allowed the crew of the antiaircraft gun to be at battle quarters and ready to fire the instant the submarine surfaced.

ORP *Orzel* was launched in Holland on January 15, 1938, and arrived in Polish waters a full year later after exhaustive working up in the North Sea. Her sister submarine, ORP *Sep*, was launched on October 17, 1938. Then the pace of finishing work seemed to slow down. At first, the Poles suspected that the perceptible delay in the working-up process was because there were no more contracts being awarded to the Dutch and, thus, the shipyards had little incentive to finish the work. But the truth was different. It turned out that pro-German sympathizers were slowing the process. On April 2, 1939, Admiral Swirski issued orders that when *Sep* went out on its next shake-down cruise into the North Sea, it would be with a Polish commanding officer, kdr. ppor. W. Salamon, and that the boat would not return to the Dutch port. To assist the *Sep* in its voyage to Poland, the Polish destroyer *Burza* was dispatched to Oslofjord with extra personnel. The two Polish warships met, and on April 16, 1939, *Sep*, with many Dutch workers aboard, lowered the Dutch flag, hoisted the Polish ensign and proceeded to Gdynia, which it reached on April 18, after having had to be towed the last hundred miles because its bunker oil reserves were depleted. The drastic Polish action, which elicited a strong protest from the Dutch, was due to the serious situation caused by the German occupation of Prague on March 15, 1939. Polish Forces were placed on partial mobilization and the situation was clearly escalating.

Just before the war the Polish Navy signed a contract with the French shipbuilder Chantier Augustin Normand in Le Havre, for two more ocean-going submarines. In view of the previous bad experience with French dockyards, the award of such a major contract seems paradoxical. But while the Dutch built good submarines, they had too many German sympathizers; while the French were willing to give loans for military build-up by the Poles. Also the contract called for many component parts to be Polish-built, including Polish diesel engines from Rohn-Zielinski and communication equipment from Poland's Wytwornia Radiotechniczna or *Awa*.[6] It also called for Swedish Bofors guns and British torpedoes.

The *Orzel*-class submarines compared favorably in all aspects of performance with the German *U-37*- and British *Triumph*-class submarines. But these boats were built for waters other than the Baltic. For the cost of each of these large cruiser submarines, the Poles could have purchased at least two small submarines, better suited for Baltic operations. Later in the war, the Polish Navy commissioned two small British U-class submarines, which would have been ideal for such operations in a small, shallow sea such as the Baltic.

By September in 1939 the Polish Naval Force had much to be proud of, primarily in the well trained and highly professionalized officer and senior noncommissioned officer corps. Polish warships visited foreign ports and the Polish flag was being shown in many distant shores. The Polish Navy, as well as its Mercantile Marine, were in fact the country's best envoys.

The final comment on the pre–1939 Polish Navy might be these words written by Pilsudski, so often castigated as a man lacking technical expertise:

> If in our strange climate of megalomania, expressed in words which lack substance, if in our amusing mania for planning, which projects an elephant out of a mouse or at the very least a panther or tiger, we have some flowers in our army, then our unhappy navy leads the field in these great statements. For when ideas have no boundaries, where should one seek them if not in the oceans. In my opinion this is the worst problem of the navy, which is the most difficult to integrate into a comprehensive system of the nation's defense. In all my operational concepts I never go beyond the vital and achievable goal of controlling the sea lanes in the Gulf of Gdansk.

Pilsudski finished his sardonic comments with this final exhortation:

I specially urge that thought be given to motorboats which will be important for the defense of the coastline as well as for work on the rivers.[7]

POLISH MERCHANT MARINE

The Polish merchant marine also grew, and in 1939 had reached 135,000 BRT, for a total of close to forty seagoing ships. A number of the new liners, like MS (motor ship) *Pilsudski* and MS *Batory*, were built in Italy and paid for by Polish exports of coal, expedited through the modern coal wharfs of Gdynia, while MS *Sobieski* and MS *Chrobry* were built in the United Kingdom.

The liners were named after the most prominent Polish kings, and after the man who had helped recreate the Polish State, Jozef Klemens Pilsudski. All four were state-of-the-art ships, and were elegantly decorated with Polish art and furniture, serving as a Polish window to the Western world, as well as earning Western currency for the Polish economy. In 1938, Polish passenger and merchant ships earned over thirty million zloty for the Polish economy. As the new liners were introduced into the lucrative and very competitive Atlantic service, the older Polish passenger ships were relegated to the South American routes, or to the Mediterranean where they carried Jewish immigrants to Palestine until the British, out of their concern about oil—and thus deferential to Arab feelings— placed an embargo on such arrivals.[8]

NOTES

1. Neal Pease, *Poland, the United States and the Stabilization of Europe, 1919–1933*, Oxford University Press, 1986; Anna M. Cienciala and Titius Komarnicki, *From Versailles to Locarno*, University Press of Kansas, 1984; Titus Komarnicki, *Rebirth of the Polish Republic: A Study in the Diplomatic History of Europe, 1914–1920*, London, 1957.

2. Jozef Korbel, *Poland between East and West: Soviet and German Diplomacy Toward Poland, 1918–1933*, Princeton University Press,

1963; Harald von Riekhoff, *German-Polish Relations 1918–1933*, Johns Hopkins University Press, 1971; Joseph Rothschild, *Pilsudski's Coup d'Etat*, Columbia University Press, 1966.

3. Piotr Wandycz, *France and Her Eastern European Allies, 1919–1925*, Minnesota University Press, 1961, and *Twilight of French Eastern Alliances, 1926–1936*, Princeton University Press, 1988.

4. Citino, Robert, *The Evolution of Blitzkrieg: Germany Defends Itself Against Poland, 1918–1933*, New York, 1987.

5. Nekrich, Aleksander M., *Pariahs, Partners, Predators: German-Soviet Relations, 1922–1941*, University of Wisconsin Press, 1997.

6. This company was also responsible for the building of the Polish decoding machine, the *Bomba*. See, Gordon Welchman, "From Polish Bomba to British Bombe: The Birth of Ultra," *Intelligence and National Security*, 1986, 1: 70–110.

7. Kozlowski, ed., *Jozef Pilsudski w Opinii Politykow i Wojskowych*, Warsaw, 1985.

8. Laurence Weinbaum, *A Marriage of Convenience: The New Zionist Organization and the Polish Government, 1936–1939*, New York, 1993.

CHAPTER IV

1939
THE ONSET OF THE SECOND
WORLD WAR

PREPARATIONS FOR WAR

The impending war clouds were not ignored in Poland, and as early as 1935, a semiofficial Polish publication, *Polska Na Morzu*, devoted a whole chapter to the danger of German revisionism.[1] The German march into the remilitarized zone west of the Rhine in 1936, forced the French to become more vigilant and again to strengthen their traditional links in the east. It is a truism, however, that the French always sought allies in the east to stalemate Germany, without being prepared to actually assist them. The Maginot Line, much maligned but in 1940 impregnable, if not long enough, was the French answer to the impending danger of German militarism. The French had no plans for moving out of their protected fortifications. Belgium's answer to the German move was to declare neutrality.[2]

After the German move into the demilitarized area west of the Rhine, war with Germany became a possibility, though many Polish politicians, in particular the foreign minister, Beck, believed until the last moment that Germany was rational, and, if confronted by a determined stance in conjunction with the United Kingdom and France, would not engage in war, and certainly not in a war on two fronts.[3]

But both the British and the French, uneasy allies, vacillated between the idea of reviving the pre–1914 alliance with Russia (now the Soviet Union), or appeasing Germany at the expense of their eastern client states.

But in spite of diplomatic ambivalence, the French offered the Poles a generous loan for remilitarization during the 1936 visit of the Polish Inspector General (war time commander-in-chief) Marshal Edward Smigly-Rydz to France.

This loan of two and a quarter billion French francs was spread over four years. But only a fraction of the loan was assigned for direct military purchases. Some of it was for construction of indigenous Polish military-related industries and some was to aid the Polish Treasury cope with internal fiscal issues stemming from a very active mobilization budget.[4] The military budget from 1935 on was about thirty percent of the total state resources and grew from 938 million zloty in 1936 to a projected 1.34 billion for 1940. (The exchange rate in 1939 was 8.9 zloty to the U.S. dollar.) The budget was clearly unequal to the task of modernizing the Polish forces and there have been many condemnations in hindsight for its failure to provide motorized equipment and modern planes in sufficient quantity.[5]

The Polish Navy's share of the budget varied (depending on the source), from an estimated 2.5 percent to a generous 5 percent. It translated into an approximate annual transfer of 35 million zloty to the navy. Bearing in mind that the cost of a small Polish built minesweeper (*Jaskolka* class) was 1.3 million zloty, that a *Grom*-class destroyer was thirteen million, and that an *Orzel*-class submarine was 8.2 million zloty, the total Navy budget—which also had to pay for the maintenance of facilities, logistical infrastructure, quartermaster supplies, and salaries—did not go very far. As a prominent Polish strategist said of the Polish military planning, it was a doctrine based on poverty.

Admiral Swirski argued throughout the interwar period for an independent Ministry of Naval Affairs, assuming correctly that the guiding principles of the Ministry of Military Affairs, which had jurisdiction over the navy, would favor the land forces and their constituent military aviation service.

In 1938, Czechoslovakia was sacrificed on the altar of peace, but when in March 1939, the Germans reneged on their pledge to Chamberlain, and occupied the rump Czech state and its capital Prague, France and, in particular, Britain were concerned.

The events of 1938, followed by the German occupation of Prague, put the Polish General Staff and the Naval Command in a quandary. The Polish ports were not only surrounded by German territory on both sides, but the distance to Polish ports and naval bases from German bases was a mere thirty miles. It was obvious that a military attack could come from either German East Prussia or German Pomerania or from both. The Polish staff accepted the inevitability of the Polish coast being cut off from the rest of Poland in the first days of the war, as well as the fact that the small Polish Navy was no match for the Germans. It could neither protect the Polish coast nor escort Polish ships with supplies from the Western Allies.

There were also discussions on moving the Polish surface ships to ports in other Baltic countries, and on using these ports for the shipment of military and civilian cargo. Latvia connected to the Polish rail system through northeast Poland while in the south, Romania, lying on the Black Sea and thus relatively free of possible German naval interference, had a signed agreement with Poland for transit of war matériel through Galati on the Danube. In the first instance, Polish plans called for surface warships, as well as merchant ships, to stay in the Baltic; in the second, only merchantmen were to operate in the Black Sea.

BRITISH GUARANTEE TO POLAND, MARCH 1939

On March 30, 1939, the British gave Poland a guarantee of its independence. Simon Newman wrote; "Since the Chiefs of Staff advised that 'it was better to fight with Poland as an ally than without her' . . . we ought to take steps to ensure that Poland did resist German aggression."[6] The British guarantee changed the whole tenor of planning since Poland seemed now to be tied into an Allied coalition and the Polish Foreign Ministe Jozef Beck, was convinced that German logic would not allow them to engage in a two front war.[7] But the Polish Government was concerned lest the pacifist influences in both Paris and London prevail in case of limited German demands on revindication of the Versailles treaty, which had never been popular among the British. Beck insisted that *cassus belli* be decided by the Poles, and that the Free City of Gdansk with specific Polish rights was inviolate.

On the military side, a whole set of exchanges and discussions between the Poles, French, and British began in Paris and Warsaw respectively. It was obvious that the Polish coastal region would be quickly isolated from the rest of Poland in the event of a major war. In the staff-level discussions held in Warsaw during the summer of 1939, the Poles requested that British warships enter the Baltic and be based in the port of Gdynia. This was not considered feasible by the British, who in turn suggested that Polish surface ships sail to ports in the United Kingdom before they could be trapped and destroyed. The British representative in these naval negotiations was Royal Navy Commander Henry Bernard Rawlings. This plan was accepted by the Poles, and authority for issuing the order was exclusively reserved by Marshal Edward Smigly-Rydz (the Polish Inspector General of the Armed Forces and wartime designee as commander-in-chief). Those who describe the departure of the Polish warships as a flight are simply ignorant of the military discussions and agreements.

A number of Polish historians comment that Churchill, in his role as First Lord of the Admiralty, a position which he assumed on the outbreak of the war, argued for the so-called Catherine plan. This called for specially modified British battleships of the Royal Sovereign-class to enter the Baltic and interdict German trade with Scandinavia, particularly the transport of iron ore. All kinds of blockade of German bound goods was to be a major and justifiable preoccupation of the British throughout the early war years. It is argued that if Churchill considered this, then more could have been done to help the Poles in September or even prior to the outbreak of the war. The situation is complex, since the movement of a significant British fleet toward Polish ports could have convinced Hitler that the British were serious, which he doubted for many months even after the outbreak of the war. But it is also true that Churchill wanted to base his plans on the concept of home ports, either in the Soviet Union or in Sweden.

The fundamental answer to this lies in the question of British policy towards Poland, the Soviet Union, and Germany. The British wished to adhere to their traditional foreign policy of balance of power, and were more concerned about preventing

Poland from joining Germany in a political or military alliance than in protecting Poland. Simon cites a British prewar aide-mémoire: "The value of Poland lay not in the capacity of her army to launch an offensive against Germany, which was virtually nonexistent, but in her capacity to absorb German divisions. Above all she must not be allowed to supplement them by subordinating her foreign policy to Hitler's, or to allow them free reign in the west by maintaining an attitude of benevolent neutrality."[8]

There was another meeting in Warsaw in July of 1939 between the Poles and their Western allies, specifically between the representatives of the three intelligence services. The British were represented by Commander Denniston, Dillwyn Knox, and Colonel Stewart Menzies in disguise as an Oxford academic; the Poles, by Colonels Stefan Mayer and Gwido Langer. The Poles gave each of the Western allies a copy of the reconstructed German code machine, Enigma. Lewin wrote:

> "As the war ran on the Poles would work for the joint cause memorably—in fighter and bomber squadrons of the RAF; in besieged Tobruk; on the Italian heights of Cassino and the battlefields of Normandy. Nevertheless, their most distinctive achievement was their first. They had carried out impeccably the momentous peacetime decision of their General Staff: In case of a threat of war the Enigma secret must be used as our Polish contribution to the common cause of defense, and divulged to our future allies. They had made Ultra possible."[9]

MOBILIZATION OF THE FLEET

As a result of this heightened international tension, Poland began to make plans for the impending war. By March, 1939, many of the western Polish military districts had already been partially mobilized.

As early as 1936, Polish shipowners were obligated by the Polish Ministry of Commerce and Trade to ensure that whenever their ships entered docks for major refurbishing, their decks would be strengthened to accommodate artillery, as well as heavy machine guns.

On March 30, 1939, the Polish legislative body, the *Sejm,* enacted legislation requiring all shipowners to place their vessels at the disposition of the government in the event of war. In April, the Polish Naval Headquarters developed a special radio link for the merchant marine which was successfully used in late August to alert all ships to stay out of the Baltic, and to seek British, French, or neutral ports.

In May 1939, all shipowners were given instructions that ships returning to Gdynia have a minimum ten-to-fifteen day supply of bunker oil and food to allow for expedient departure.

In August, the whole Polish Merchant Marine and fishing fleet were placed on a state of alert, and all Baltic-bound ships were diverted or, if already in Polish ports, their departure was hastened. By the end of the month, instructions were given that only coded orders emanating from Warsaw were to be obeyed.

A small number of ships, about 9 percent of Poland's merchant marine tonnage, were deliberately left in the Baltic because the Poles planned on using them for shipping between the neutral ports of Finland and Sweden, on the one hand, and the disembarkation ports of Latvia and Estonia on the other. These merchantmen were not in Polish ports, but deep in the northern waters of the Baltic, and after the campaign, slowly made their way south, adhering to Swedish territorial waters. In October 1939, these three ships, SS *Slazak,* SS *Rozewie,* and SS *Poznan*, made a successful break for Britain.

At long last, the madness of Hitler had overcome the passivity and sophistry of the British Government, and the initiatives of March 1939, led to the Polish-British Treaty of Mutual Assistance signed on August 25, 1939. The British Parliament and the British people had come to the realization that the German menace had to be confronted.[10]

NAVAL AND COASTAL REGION COMMAND STRUCTURE IN 1939

A brief mention of the Polish Naval Command structure is in order. The Commandant of the Polish Navy, directly responsible to the Minister of Military Affairs in peacetime and to the commander-in-chief in wartime, was Kontr-Admiral Jerzy

Swirski. His headquarters were in Warsaw and his chief of staff was Kdr. K. Korytowski while his staff consisted of the following senior officers: Kontr-Admiral K. Czernecki (later murdered by the Soviets at Katyn along with forty other naval officers, along with many thousands of Polish army officers), Kdr. W. Zejma, Kdr.por. E. Plawski, Kdr.por. K. Durski-Trzasko, Kdr.ppor. Z. Dzienisiewicz and Kdr.ppor. K. Namiesniowski.

In the summer of 1939, as a result of the deteriorating situation with Germany and the heightened state of mobilization of the western garrisons, a decision was made to create a separate Coastal Defense Region under the command of Kontr-Admiral Jozef Unrug. This was then divided into land and sea defenses. The land defenses were primarily ground forces commanded by Colonel S. Dabek of the Polish Army; the sea component was commanded by Kdr. S. Frankowski. The fortified region of Hel, which had a battery of modern coastal 152-millimeter guns, was commanded by Kdr. W. Steyer and was to all intents and purposes a third defense component. The destroyer and submarine divisions were directly accountable to Admiral Unrug.

Just days prior to the war, Admiral Unrug moved his headquarters from Oksywie (a naval port next to Gdynia) to Hel. The ground defenses of the region of Gdynia and Oskywie were strengthened and consisted of two regiments of infantry, each consisting of two battalions, and a brigade of the National Guard, (a force falling somewhere between the American National Guard and the wartime British Home Guard). The ground forces defending the Hel peninsula were an elite battalion of the Polish Border Defense Corps (K.O.P. or *Korpus Ochrony Pogranicza).*

Hel peninsula had been built as a major defensive and naval base. A narrow gauge railroad that was well camouflaged and run by the navy, served to connect the many bunkers, oil storage tanks, artillery emplacements, and logistical support systems for the navy. It lacked the sophisticated repair facilities necessary for complete maintenance of submarines, but it would have been more than adequate to support small torpedo and motor gunboats, had they been in service.

The garrison at Westerplatte which was forced to capitulate on September 7, was nothing more than a reinforced infantry company.

The river flotilla, based at Pinsk in eastern Poland on the Pripet Marches, was commanded by Kdr. W. Zajaczkowski with Kdr.por. H. Eibel as his second in command, and an army officer, Major W. Szczekowski as chief of staff. This flotilla, which consumed a significant share of the state's resources, was an anachronism in 1939.

In addition to this relatively large flotilla, there were river craft on the Vistula whose purpose was to defend the bridges from enemy planes.

POLISH DEFENSE STRATEGY

A very brief word has to be said about the general strategy underlying Polish plans in September 1939. The Polish army was already partially mobilized as of March 1939, when Germany occupied Prague. It is too easily forgotten by critics of the Poles that the disposition of the Polish armies was dictated by two factors.

First, the Poles continued to hope that logic would prevail, and Germany would not undertake full-scale hostilities against enemies in the West and East. Therefore, there was concern about another Munich style appeasement with losses of Polish territory, such as Polish rights in Gdansk.

Secondly, the Poles were convinced that if there was a war, it would be a coalition effort and that while Poland might have to suffer heavy initial losses, in men and territory, initially the final outcome would be a decisive offensive in the West, leading to complete victory and the overthrow of Hitler. This to a great degree was based on the fame of the French army, and on the fact that the French had promised a ground offensive in the West on the fifteenth day of the war.[11]

From the first principle, fearing a last minute British wish to negotiate an armistice after the Germans were in possession of the disputed territories of Silesia and Pomerania, the Poles disposed their forces accordingly, on the long and tenuous borders, and even in the Pomeranian Corridor. The Poles wanted to ensure that the Germans be forced to deploy their full resources from the first day, and to wage war in the border regions.

Full mobilization of the Polish forces was ordered on August 30, but rescinded after an intervention by the British and French ambassadors, who thought that such a step might be perceived in the West as provocative.

Nonetheless, Poland's Military Aviation *(Lotnictwo Wojskowe)* was, in fact, placed on a full secret mobilization and dispersed well before the German attack, as attested by a German historian, Cajus Bekker, who wrote: "Despite all assertions to the contrary, the Polish Air Force was not destroyed on the ground in the first two days of fighting. The bomber brigade in particular continued to make determined attacks on the German forces up to September 16th."[12]

Three days after the German attack on Poland, both the United Kingdom and France declared war on Germany.

The naval balance seemed to favor the Western allies. The Royal Navy had twelve battleships and battle cruisers and eight aircraft carriers. The new King George class of five warships was yet to be commissioned. These capital ships were supported by fifty-eight cruisers in service.

The French had two modern battleships (*Strasbourg* and *Dunkerque*) and a number of excellent cruisers. Their two new battleships, *Richelieu* and *Jean Bart,* never saw service and they had one old aircraft carrier, *Bearn.*

The Germans only had two modern battleships, the *Gneisenau* and *Scharnhorst*, three "pocket battleships" and a small number of heavy and light cruisers, but no carriers. Their two super battleships, *Bismarck* and *Tirpitz,* were only completing their work up.

But the actual numbers were deceptive. The British and French were worried about the Italians and the Japanese, and many of the British warships were dispersed throughout the world. The Royal Navy's Home Fleet based at Scapa Flow, in the Scottish Orkney Islands, was much smaller than the above figures would suggest, limited to nine capital ships (all of World War I vintage) and five carriers.

Right from the first day of the war, the German surface commerce raiders forced the British to deploy their major warships in many different areas. In late 1939, the British had to commit six cruisers, one battleship, and a carrier to track down and destroy one German "pocket" battleship, the *Graf Spee.* In June 1940, after France withdrew from the war and Italy joined the Germans, the balance was razor-thin.

WAR IN THE BALTIC

The Polish destroyer division was on a heightened state of alert from March, 1939. One of the destroyers was always on patrol, keeping an eye on German shipping between the main German ports and the German enclave of East Prussia. All the Polish ships were also on a permanent state of air attack alert with antiaircraft crews at action stations. Leaves were either cancelled or only granted for the duration of the stand-down watch.

On August 30, 1939, ORP *Blyskawica,* the destroyer divisional leader, received the following order by semaphore from Polish Fleet Command: Execute PeKing. The sealed envelope was opened and read as follows:

> Destroyer division, consisting of *Blyskawica*, *Grom*, and *Burza* to sail for Britain, reaching position between Bornholm and Christians by sunset, passing Malmo at midnight. Departure immediate and arrival Britain during daylight.

The Division Commander, Kdr. por. R. Stankiewicz, chaired a brief meeting of his three destroyer captains: Kdr. por. W. Kodrebski *(Blyskawica)*, Kdr. ppor. A. Hulewicz *(Grom)* and Kdr. ppor. S. Nahorski *(Burza)*. At 1415 hours the Polish warships weighed anchor and departed, increasing speed to twenty-five knots. Bornholm was passed at 2140 and the Sund entered at 0010 on August 31. Danish radio enquiries demanding identification were ignored and at sunrise the destroyers were in the Kattegat. At 1530, while on a course for Scotland, a German plane was identified tracking the Polish warships. The course was changed to 315 degrees and at sunset back to 256 degrees.

At 0925 of September 1, a radio message was received reporting the German attack on Poland and the warships were placed on combat alert. Three hours later the Poles were met by two British destroyers and were escorted into Leith, Scotland.

Thus began an odyssey which was to last five years and see the amazingly return of two of these destroyers to Polish waters at war's end.

The three warships were preceded in western waters by two training ships: ORP *Iskra* and ORP *Wilia*. Among the trainees were naval officer cadets (midshipmen) who in the later war years supplied the growing Polish navy with well trained and highly motivated junior officer material.

Left behind in the Polish bases were a number of major surface ships, ORP *Gryf*, ORP *Wicher* and all the small minesweepers, gunboats, and trawlers, as well as the five-boat division of the Polish submarine squadron: ORP *Orzel*, ORP *Sep*, ORP *Zbik*, ORP *Wilk* and ORP *Rys*.

As the British welcomed the Polish crews and warships, Germany was unleashing its aggression against Poland. The first—but certainly not symbolic shots—were fired in the early hours of September 1, 1939, by the German training battleship, *Schleswig-Holstein*, against the Polish positions at Westerplatte, near the Free City of Danzig.

On the first day of the war, *Gryf* (commanded by Kdr. ppor. S. Kwiatkowski), a minelayer accompanied by the destroyer, *Wicher* (commanded by Kdr. ppor. S. de Walden) departed to lay a minefield southeast of the tip of Hel. A German air attack on the *Gryf* killed the commanding officer and the mission was aborted, the minelayer entering the harbor of Hel. On the other hand *Wicher* continued its night patrol, unaware that *Gryf* had turned back and observed a number of German ships operating just west of the German port of Pillau. A unique opportunity for carrying out a night torpedo attack against an unsuspecting enemy was foregone, since the commanding officer of *Wicher* was under strict orders not to jeopardize the primary mission of laying mines.

On September 2, *Wicher* returned to Hel, so as to be under the protection of land-based anti-aircraft artillery. On September 3, both ships, together with medium shore-based artillery, engaged two German destroyers and forced their retreat under a smoke screen. In the early afternoon hours, the Luftwaffe carried out a concerted attack on the two Polish ships and both were sunk. Because the water was shallow, much of the ship's artillery was salvaged and used in the subsequent defense of the Hel peninsula.

The only remaining surface ships left in the Baltic were the Polish-designed and built *Jaskolka* class combination minesweepers and minelayers. This division was commanded by Kpt. mar. T. Borysiewicz and fought in Polish waters until September 14. They engaged German ground units with artillery support for the Polish ground units and also carried out minelaying operations in the Polish waters. Enemy air superiority slowly took its toll, and the small ships were all eventually so badly damaged that they had to be beached. Some were salvaged by the Germans; a number of them returned to sail under the Polish flag at the conclusion of the war. So much for the Polish defense.

THE POLISH SUBMARINE DIVISION

The main offensive arm of the Polish Navy was the Submarine Division, commanded by Kdr. ppor. A. Mohuczy. The Polish Submarine Division, like all other warships, had been placed in a heightened state of readiness in March 1939. All leaves had been cancelled and personnel could not be away for more than a couple of hours unless they could be contacted by telephone. On August 24, 1939, the division was placed in combat readiness and fully mobilized. The crews and boats took on their full complement of supplies, torpedoes, ammunition and—for the three minelaying boats—mines. The operational plan was purely defensive. In fact it misled the Germans, who were concerned that the Polish boats would operate outside their immediate Baltic ports and disrupt all their Baltic sea trade. The three boats with minelaying capability were to lay mines in areas of the bay of Gdansk. The task for the division was to interdict the passage of German transports and troop ships between Germany proper and the isolated territory of East Prussia, a much more limited tactical goal than that feared by the Germans. Some thought was given to attacking the German battleship, *Schleswig-Holstein*, which was shelling Westerplatte, but nothing came of that option. The boats all operated independently but their fortunes had a common denominator.

Their operating orders, and the shallow and limited operational area, as well as the international conventions precluding attacks on civilian shipping without a fair warning and good cause, all made the final result disappointing. While the Poles adhered to the spirit as well as the letter of the convention, the Germans, as early as September 3, sank the British liner, *Athenia*, in the Atlantic with the loss of a hundred twelve passengers.

The Polish government was under great pressure from the Western allies to avoid any act which could be perceived as provocative; therefore, while the Polish boats left port with mines, the decision to actually lay them was reserved by the commanding officer of the submarine division and given only two days after the British and French declared war on Germany. This was clearly a delayed military decision based on political factors.

In the first five days, the Polish submarines carried out very local operations, observing German naval activity, but were unable to carry out torpedo attacks of any note. In turn they were often reconnoitered and attacked by German air and naval units involving intensive depth-charging. On two occasions German U-boats attacked the Poles with magnetic torpedoes which exploded before hitting their target. But the Germans, unaware of this technical flaw, heard the explosions and assumed that the targets had been sunk. German claims of Polish submarines sunk grew.

On September 5, 1939, the order to lay mines was radioed and was carried out by all three minelaying boats, after which all five boats departed for the northern Baltic near Gotland to get a brief respite from enemy attacks. Each of the Polish boats had some damage, the worst having been suffered by *Sep*.

On September 7, new division orders were issued. All the submarines were to return to the central Baltic region, and were assigned sixty-mile-wide sectors running north from the German shore to Sweden. The most westerly was just east of Bornholm. But the sad state of the boats made the orders difficult to implement. Only *Wilk* made a bona fide effort to sail west and quickly realized the lack of German shipping activity, in other words, no targets, in that region.

Between September 7 and 19, all but *Wilk* (which had been authorized due to bunker oil shortage to proceed to the United Kingdom on September 11) operated in the Baltic and forced the Germans to continue their antisubmarine activity and divert their merchantmen into Swedish neutral waters. The Germans were convinced by September 12, that they had sunk three of the Polish boats.

On September 14, the commanding officer of the Submarine Division radioed the following message to all subordinates:

Carry out patrols and interdict enemy shipping as long as possible. When unable to operate further break out for the United Kingdom. If that is impossible seek internment in Sweden. When approaching Great Britain contact Rosyth on 133 kilocycles and rendezvous thirty miles off May Island in the Firth of Forth.

After September 19, the submarines began to operate as local conditions and the state of each boat allowed. On September 19, German land forces captured Gdynia.

The following is a short summary of the naval action of the individual submarines.

ORP *Sep* (Commanding Officer Kdr. ppor. W. Salamon) made one submerged torpedo attack on a German destroyer on September 2. The torpedo missed but the ensuing depth charge attack resulted in serious hull damage; water entered and the boat became heavy. The noise of the pumps led to a second depth-charge attack and the commanding officer decided to sail to the vicinity of Gotland to recharge batteries and to make emergency repairs. *Sep* was able to make some repairs and carried out passive patrolling without noting any enemy shipping (which had been expected as Gotland lay in the shipping routes between many Swedish and German ports.) The submarine was so badly damaged, however, that it took fifteen minutes to submerge and the boat was a sitting duck, deprived of its one major asset, the cover of the sea On September 14, *Sep* was given the option of breaking for the United Kingdom or seeking Swedish ports. Crossing the Sund required the submarine to be able to submerge, but the damage was such as to interfere with keeping a set depth and the commanding officer decided to seek internment.

ORP *Rys* (commanding officer Kdr. ppor. A. Grochowski) was one of the three French-built boats adapted for mine-laying. *Rys* also carried out a torpedo attack and then on surface engaged a German motor-torpedo boat. On September 3, the damage caused by a German plane (or planes) led to a persistent seepage of oil which betrayed her position and prejudiced further patrolling. *Rys* entered Hel and remained partially submerged with her conning tower camouflaged. Repairs were done and the crew given a brief respite.

On September 7, *Rys* again departed harbor and patrolled its allotted sector. After laying its mines, the commanding officer decided to change his patrolling area to the vicinity of Gotland. The CO also radioed that he had observed some German ships but the orders remained the same, namely, that attacks were only to be carried out against armed shipping. On September 17, the crew received the demoralizing news of the Soviet invasion of Poland. In view of the serious damage, the CO decided that breaking out for the British Isles was impossible and instead tried to enter Sweden to carry out repairs. On entering Stavnas, he was advised that repairs could not be carried out in the internationally mandated period of twenty-four hours and the boat was interned.

ORP *Zbik*, (commanding officer Kdr. ppor. Z. Zebrowski), after carrying out its assigned patrols with no incidents, laid mines on September 5. On September 17, the CO concluded that it was pointless to continue patrolling in the Baltic given his orders to adhere to international conventions, After twenty-five days of patrolling, the CO sought internment in Sweden, having heard from neutral sources that the Sund was mined.

More than two hundred Polish naval personnel were thus interned in Sweden. The Polish warships remained the legal property of the Polish state and the Polish Naval Command in Paris (and later in London) were attentive to the continued maintenance of the boats, and ordered all the crews to stay in Sweden, hoping for some political or military development which would allow the Poles to have the three boats fully operational again in the Baltic. This situation persisted until December 1944, when the Polish Naval Headquarters authorized the evacuation of some of the Polish officers and non-commissioned officers to the United Kingdom.

ORP *Wilk* (CO Kpt. mar. B. Krawczyk) had a much luckier conclusion to her initial patrol. *Wilk* had also attempted to torpedo a German destroyer, on September 2, and also received a punishing depth-charge attack in retribution. The operational zone for *Wilk*, was well in the Gdansk Bay, and the international political constraints and ramifications allowed the Divisional Commander to order mine laying on September 3.

The second in command was Por. mar. B. Karnicki, who, in his memoirs (*Marynarski Worek Wpsomnien*), describes the gallant effort of the crew in laying mines under close enemy surface and air scrutiny. Apart from the danger of enemy attack, the actual feat of laying mines in underwater was difficult and demanded the greatest expertise from the crew. As the mines were ejected from special flooded tunnels, the boat had to be constantly trimmed by adjusting the flooding ballast tanks. Karnicki wrote that, later in the war, French and British skippers received high decorations for their minelaying in Norwegian waters, but all three Polish boats accomplished their mission in shallow waters close to enemy bases.

Karnicki also mentioned how on one occasion, after many hours of enemy depth-charge attacks, the submarine was in a silent mode on the bottom; the air became stale and difficult to breathe because the air filters, driven by electric motors, were switched off to minimize noise. The submarine was at a depth of eighty-seven meters.

Krawczyk finally decided that the boat had to surface and did so, after preparing his artillery section and machine-gun operators for a surface battle. However, on surfacing there were no enemy ships in the vicinity.

The Polish crew realized that oil was leaking and leaving a deadly trail for the Germans. It also convinced the Germans that the Polish submarine had been destroyed.

By September 10, Krawczyk estimated that he only had ten days of bunker fuel. After one more day of patrolling in her sector, *Wilk* was given specific permission to sail for the United Kingdom. *Wilk* sailed through the Danish passage on the surface and encountered no problems, arriving in Rosyth on September 20. Karnicki wrote that prior to the war, Polish submarines exercised the navigational skills of passage through the Sund to the North Sea.

After the crew was feted by the British and the oil replenished, *Wilk* went on to Scapa Flow. Karnicki describes the entrance into the Royal Navy's Home Fleet base as one that brought tears into the eyes of the Polish crew. As the Polish submarine dieseled past the ranks of the world's largest and proudest fleet, all the Royal Navy warships, from majestic battleships to small destroyers, had their crews on deck and each ship's crew gave a caps off three cheers for the *Wilk*.

Komandor ppor. Krawczyk became the first Polish officer during the war to receive the prestigious British Distinguished

Service Order. Later on he also received Poland's highest military decoration, the *Virtuti Militari.*

ORP *ORZEL*

The fifth submarine was the *Orzel* and hers is as fine a tale as any, one which even a proud maritime nation like Britain would be proud to tell.

Orzel had a unique role in the operational plan, code-named *Worek* (Sack). While two of the three minelaying boats were placed outside of the Gdansk bay, *Orzel* was left in reserve, in the bay of Puck, protected by the coastal artillery in Hel. Its role was to lay in wait for the German battleship, *Schleswig-Holstein,* as it departed from its alleged courtesy visit to the Free City of Danzig. But the German battleship was busy pounding away at the Polish defenders in Westerplatte, and since the Poles stubbornly held out for seven days, the *Orzel* waited in vain. Finally, new orders were cut by the Commanding Officer of the Submarine Division, Kdr. Aleksander Mohuczy, whose headquarters were in Hel and the boat left the shallow bay, contemptuously, but correctly called by the Polish submariners, the pond.

Kdr. ppor. H. Kloczkowski endured the same initial days of frustration and anxiety as his boat was depth-charged while patrolling in its sector. When enemy ships were sighted, they were either going too fast or were clearly unarmed merchantmen and thus immune to attack. Discouraging news from the home front tested the morale of the crew. On September 9, the CO became sick and decided to enter a neutral port to seek treatment, a decision universally condemned and which led subsequently to a court-martial and loss of his commission. Rather than enter the harbor in a small inflatable boat, or proceed to a Swedish or Finnish port, as instructed in his discretionary options, Kloczkowski took *Orzel* into Tallinn, a port and the capital of Estonia, which, although formally neutral, was actually sympathetic to Germany. On September 15, Kloczkowski was taken to a hospital and Kpt. mar. Jan Grudzinski assumed command. By September 15, it was obvious that not only was the Polish Campaign lost, but the Western Allies were merely paper tigers and it was Germany that was to be feared, more than the British, and certainly more than the Poles. Under a pretext fabricated under German pressure, the Estonians told the Polish CO that *Orzel* could not leave harbor within the specified twenty-four hours, since a German freighter was departing. This was a legitimate interpretation of the international convention, written to protect unarmed merchant ships from being followed and stalked when departing a neutral port. After twenty-four hours had elapsed, the Poles were advised that they had exceeded the permissible twenty-four hours allowed by convention for an armed belligerent warship to stay in a neutral port, and the submarine would therefore be interned. Armed guards were posted and the boat began to be systematically disarmed.

There are two reports in the British Public Record Office on the escape of *Orzel*, the longer of seven pages is captioned ISHMAEL, and is cited here in full. The author has always been assumed to be Captain S. W. Roskill, RN, who is also the author of the official history of the Royal Navy in World War Two.

They put into port of Tallinn on 15th September. It is a small basin about a quarter of a mile square. There are two entrances thirty yards apart. The centre of the harbour is a mass of rocks and ships can only lay alongside the wharf. They found two German oil tankers, an Estonian gunboat and five destroyers and two submarines alongside three sides of the basin, and was berthed between the gunboat and the destroyers. Their reception was most cordial. The submarine was secured alongside by four wires to the jetty, by another to a destroyer and a sixth held his bow to an anchor in the harbour. The sick captain was landed and the first Lieutenant, Lt. Cdr. John Grudzinski, took command. One of the two German merchant ships was to leave shortly so the Estonian authorities refused permission for the Orzel to proceed for another 24 [48] hours. At the end of this time officials arrived on board with the astonishing announcement that as Orzel had exceeded the time allowed in a neutral port to belligerents by International Law, the submarine was under arrest. They were asked for no parole but the breech locks of the guns were removed, all charts and small arms taken out of the ship, and preparations made to hoist the torpedoes with a crane. Two guards were mounted, one in the Control Room on board and the other on the jetty ashore. The remaining oil tanker had in the meanwhile hoisted the German flag and their crew watched proceedings from the rail, shaking their fists and shouting abuse. By Sunday afternoon, fifteen torpedoes had been hoisted out. By that time the second in command, whose name is Piasecki, had contrived unseen by the guard to file through the wire of the hoisting apparatus. It broke, leaving five torpedoes on board. The unsuspicious Estonian decided to call it a day and to hoist out the remainder the following day. In the meanwhile the Captain was unobtrusively busy with a hack saw cutting the wires, until only a single strand held them to the jetty.

The second engineer, Pierzchlewski, had been promoted to navigator. The only aid to navigation left on board was a list of light-houses and light-ships in the Baltic. He got a piece of squared paper and contrived to plot their approximate positions on it, and so reconstructed a crude chart of the Baltic. These activities could only be conducted in odd moments when the guard climbed on deck to smoke a cigarette or talk to his confrers on the jetty. They chose these moments to plan the details of their escape. It was decided that when midnight came they would over-power the guards, break the strands of wire that secured the submarine and get away as quickly as they could. The chief difficulty was the gyroscopic compass, which has to be run for some hours before it is serviceable. To drown the hum of the gyro they increased the speed of the ventilating fans, complaining to the guard that they were being deprived of fresh air. Then they all turned in. At midnight two burly members of the crew went on deck on the plea that they wanted a smoke. The guard ashore had been joined by a friend who stayed chatting with him. At intervals the Polish sailors returned to the upper deck. The Estonians had an overhead searchlight shining down on the submarine and jetty. There was also a telephone within reach of the guard. At 2 AM the visitor left. The two Polish sailors offered the guard a cigarette, which he declined. To attract him nearer to the gangway they drew his attention to a peculiarity of their gun mounting. This appeared to interest him and he approached the side of the jetty. The next instant he was seized, gagged and bound, and bundled into the submarine. At the same time his confrers below was seized, and the engineer lieutenant Floryan Roszak, ran ashore and cut the wires of the search light and telephone. Before they managed to gag the guard on the jetty he had let out several lusty bellows for help. There were answering shouts from the destroyers. The stranded wires that held them to the wharf were quickly cut and they brought the bow wire, to the capstan to haul their bow out. The sound of the capstan revealed their intentions and the destroyers switched on searchlights and opened fire on them with rifles. They made for the entrance, blinded by searchlights, with bullets spattering all round them. They refrained with difficulty, out of respect for international law, from torpedoing the German tanker, and just short of the entrance they grounded on some rocks. Men were now firing at them from the mole at almost point-blank range. There was a general fusillade from every direction. They blew their tanks, went full speed astern and slid off the rocks. Then they went ahead again and this time succeeded in slipping through the entrance, thirty yards wide. Out into the night and freedom. There is a fringe of small fortified islands outside Tallin. In half an hour searchlights began to sweep the surface. They were seen and fired on by heavy artillery which drove them under water, and presently they heard the propellors of destroyers and motor in pursuit of them. All night they fled submerged, steering blindly with no chart to give them soundings, and at dawn they lay down on the bottom. During the ensuing day heard the hunters passing to and fro over them. Depth charges burst round them, some near, some far, till they lost count of the explosions. About 9 PM there was a lull, and at midnight they rose cautiously and had a look round. They judged themselves to be at the entrance to the Gulf of Finland and there was nothing in sight. It must be remembered that their sole armament was five torpedoes. Their guns were out of action, and they had no rifles or revolvers.

The captain decided to cruise the Baltic in search of Russian or German ships as long as his torpedoes lasted and then to make for England. The first necessity was to find a sanctuary where he could lie undetected on the surface and charge his batteries; the second to capture a German merchant ship and compel her captain to sell them charts as a preliminary to sinking her. Accordingly he made for the Aland Islands at the entrance of the Gulf of Bothnia. Here he charged his batteries. He also ran ashore about five times on shoals and rocks, getting more and more damaged. By this time they were getting tired of their prisoners who kept up a ceaseless lamentation and speculation on how their families were faring. They learned from the German wireless—which was the only news they had—that they were being denounced to the world as murderers of their guards. Accordingly they turned south and one fine night in flat calm they stopped off the island of Gotland; they launched their berthon boat, put the two Estonians into it with money, cigarettes and a bottle of whisky, and watched them row to the shore a mile and a half away. Then these men who had lost their country and their families made a wireless signal to announce that the Estonians were safe so that their relations might have no further anxiety. This was on the 22nd day.

For a fortnight they cruised in the Baltic, watching the shipping creep backwards and forwards inside territorial neutral waters, protected from their torpedoes by International law. Every night they were hunted to prevent them from charging batteries. By day they cruised submerged, never knowing when they would strike a rock, or lay on the bottom. By this time their water was running low. For a fortnight they had not washed or used water for cooking. The cook had a scratch on his hand that was causing blood poisoning. He was the their first casualty, and on the 38th day they

decided to make their way out of the Baltic through
the Sund and try to reach England. From Bornholm
where there was a light they recognized they made for
the Swedish coast and turned up into the entrance to
the Sund, where they sighted a flotilla of German
destroyers patrolling the entrance. They sounded and
found there was seven fathoms of water, which was too
shallow for them to attack with any hope of escape.
They went down to the bottom and lay there, listening
to the propellers of the patrol destroyers passing to and
fro near by. When it was dark they rose to periscope
depth and went ahead. Soon afterwards they grounded.
They rose till their conning tower was awash and
grounded again. They came right up onto the surface
and swung round and missed them by a few yards as
they lay stranded. Backwards and forwards it went,
always just missing them; then realized that they had
floundered again grounded. A searchlight from one of
the destroyers into a channel so shallow that the Germans did not bother to search it with their lights. In
desperation they blew all their tanks and the submarine floated. They crept away on their motor, heading
up the Sund, and came again to deep water. But now
they began to experience difficulty in getting correct
trim, owing to the varying densities of the water. She
was trimmed for the Baltic and here in Kattegat they
were encountering streams, at different levels of partly
fresh water from fiords. To force her under with the
hydroplanes, going full speed ahead on the diesels, they
made too much noise; immediately there was a hue and
cry of searchlights and the destroyers were after them.
They contrived to reach the bottom and lay there
motionless for two hours while the hunt went to and fro
above them.

Finally the sounds died away. They rose to the surface and continued their journey, going to the bottom
again for a sleep when day began to break. They were
getting thirsty by now and the cook's symptoms were
grave. They decided to try and set a course for England. [following is scratched out by pen: make the Skaw
light the following night]. Their wireless apparatus had

been damaged by rifle fire; they had no recognition signals; once in the North Sea every man's hand was against them: they were fair game for German and British alike, menaced from the air, by surface patrols and by submarines. But the First Lieutenant Andrew Piasecki, could speak English. Early in the morning (on October 14, at 6 AM) a faint message on imperfect transmission reached a British shore W/T station. "Supposed position from 0630 on appointed place for Polish Navy. Beg permission entrance and pilot. But have no chart. Orzel". A few hours later a British destroyer found them and led them triumphantly into harbour. They learned then that their sister submarine was also safe. They only had three requests: to land the sick cook, to replenish their water supplies and to be given breech blocks for their guns. They were then prepared to go to sea forthwith on whatever patrol it pleased the British Navy to employ them. (P.R.O. ADM 171/9971)

Orzel was the longest-operating combat unit of the Polish September campaign. By the time *Orzel* reached port and safety in the United Kingdom, Polish naval units that had reached the British shores on the first day of the war, had already undertaken their first combat patrols.

Kapitan mar. Jan Grudzinski, commanding officer of the *Orzel* became the first Pole of the Second World War to be decorated with the highest Polish decoration for bravery, the Virtuti Militari, joining such heroes as Tadeusz Kosciuszko. He also received the prestigious British decoration, Distinguished Service Order.

LAST STAND IN THE BALTIC

It is very easy to make harsh judgments on the disposition and activities of the Polish naval units. The narratives of frustrating and regrettably uncoordinated activities mask some tactical success. The Germans in spite of their overwhelming superiority in naval assets, and complete and undisputed control of air space, failed to sink any of the Polish submarines, though many such claims were advanced. The presence of the Polish

submarines forced the Germans to take many active and passive measures. German merchant shipping was rerouted into
Swedish territorial waters because the Germans had no idea of
where the Polish submarines were operating.

The small *Jaskolka*-class warships continued to be effective
until the middle of September, and their small but surprisingly
effective artillery supported the Polish ground forces at Gdynia
and Hel. The Polish coastal artillery batteries, commanded by
Kapitan mar. Zbigniew Przybyszewski, kept the German warships from sailing into the bay of Gdansk and from giving their
artillery support to the German attacks.

Had the Poles implemented their prewar plans to position
heavy 320-millimeter coastal artillery and to commission ten
fast motor-torpedo-gunboats, then indeed the situation would
have been quite different. It is unfortunate that the doctrine
propounded by Kadulski was only followed in regard to the
submarines. A fleet of ten small torpedo boats would have
been invaluable. Also, the excellent qualities of design of the
ORP *Orzel* and ORP *Sep* nowithstanding—they were without
parallel in that era—Poland would have been better served by
small coastal submarines, like the British U-class. It is also a
pity that having positioned a number of merchantmen in the
Baltic, the naval command failed to station a number of small
trawlers in the northern regions of the Baltic with basic supplies, oil, and extra crew to give logistical support to the submariners. Piaskowski writes that after the onset of hostilities,
such a plan was considered but allegedly failed due to lack of
money to contract with foreign shipping.

When on October 1, the Polish Forces on Hel capitulated,
the whole naval garrison went into captivity. Only the small
motor patrol boat *Batory* was able to break through the
German blockade and reach Sweden.

NOTES

1. Targa, J.T., ed., *Polska Na Morzu*, Glowna Ksiegarnia Wojskowa, Warsaw, 1935.
2. Brian Bond, *France and Belgium, 1939–1940*, University of Delaware Press, 1975.
3. Gordon Craig and Gilbert Felix, *The Diplomats, 1919–1939*, Atheneum, New York, 1971, Chapt. 19, "The Diplomacy of Colonel Beck" by Henry L. Roberts, pp. 579–614; Gerhard L. Weinberg, *World in the Balance: Behind the Scenes of World War II*, Univerity Press of New England, 1981; Philip V. Cannistraro, Edward D. Wynot Jr, and Theodore P. Kovaaleff, eds., *Poland and the Coming of the Second World War: The Diplomatic Papers of A.J. Drexel Biddle Jr., United States Ambassador to Poland, 1937–1939*, Ohio State University Press, 1976.
4. For Polish prewar military budgets see, Kazimierz Krzyzanowski, *Wydatki Wojskowe Polski w Latach, 1918–1939* (Polish Military Expenditures, 1918–1939), Warsaw, 1976. The only English language reference to above is in Michael Alfred Peszke, *Battle for Warsaw, 1939–1944*, Boulder, CO, 1995, pp. 16–21.
5. Michael Alfred Peszke, "The Forgotten Campaign: Poland's Military Aviation in September, 1939," *Polish Review*, 1994; 39: 51–72.
6. Simon Newman, *March 1939: The British Guarantee to Poland: A Study in the Continuity of British Foreign Policy*, Oxford University Press, 1976.
7. Anna M. Cienciala, *Poland and the Western Powers: A Study in the Interdependence of Eastern and Western Europe*, University of Toronto Press, 1968.
8. Simon Newman, op.cit. David E. Kaiser, *Economic Diplomacy and the Origins of the Second World War: Germany, Britain, France and Eastern Europe, 1930–1939*, Princeton University Press, 1980.
9. Ronald Lewin, Ultra *Goes to War*, New York, 1978.
10. In addition to Simon Newman, op. the following give interesting accounts of the vicissitudes of British foreign policy. Taylor, AJP, *The Origins of the Second World War*, New York, 1985; Donald Cameron Watt, *How War Came: The Immediate Origins of the Second World War, 1938–1939*, New York, 1989; and, the memoirs of the British ambassador to Germany, Henderson, Sir Neville, *Failure of a Mission: Berlin 1937–1939*, New York, 1940.
11. General Sir Edmund Ironside, the British Chief of the Imperial Staff in that period, visited Poland in July 1939 and in his diaries,

published after the war wrote on July 26, 1939 "The French had lied to the Poles in saying that they are going to attack. There is no idea of it." *Time Unguarded: The Ironside Diaries, 1937–1940*, New York, 1962 p. 85.

12. Cajus Bekker, *The Luftwaffe War Diaries*, New York, 1968.

CHAPTER V
AT THE SIDE OF THE ROYAL NAVY, 1939–1940

CONSEQUENCES OF THE SOVIET INVASION OF EASTERN POLAND ON SEPTEMBER 17, 1939

Seventeen days after the German attack, on September 17, 1939, without declaration of war and contrary to existing treaties of nonaggression, the Soviet Union invaded eastern Poland, implementing the infamous Molotov-Ribbentrop Pact. The initial reasons were clouded in obscurity and it led Marshal Smigly-Rydz to promulgate an order to avoid combat with Soviet forces, unless attacked. Some Polish units obeyed this order while many fought. The units of the Pripet Flotilla scuttled their ships and their crews joined the land forces in the final battles against the Germans. But a large group of naval personnel were surrounded by the Soviets at Mokrana and taken prisoner: over thirty commissioned and noncommissioned officers were murdered on the spot.

The Polish armies by that date had been badly mauled by the Germans, and the Polish commander-in-chief had already made a decision to regroup in southeastern Poland, with their back's to Poland's border. It was hoped that existing agreements would allow supplies from the West to be transported through the Black Sea and the Danube River port of Galati in Romania, which had direct rail connections to Poland.

The Soviet invasion forced the Polish government and those military units that were based in the southeastern region to cross into Romania and Hungary.

But the Polish campaign was no easy walkover for the Germans, whose material losses precluded operations in the West, an opportunity squandered by the French. Zaloga and Madej wrote in their monograph that

> . . . the Polish Army fought for nearly five weeks against the full weight of the Wehrmacht and later the

Red Army, even though it was substantially outnumbered. In contrast, the British, French, Belgian and
Dutch armies, which outnumbered the Wehrmacht in
men, tanks and aircraft, and which did not suffer from
a precarious strategic encirclement as Poland did, held
out for only a few weeks more.[1]

THE CONSTITUTION IS PRESERVED

The Polish government was interned by the Romanians, though
Marshal Edward Smigly-Rydz shortly thereafter escaped
through Hungary to German-occupied Poland, where he attempted to play a part in the Polish underground army. He died
shortly of a heart attack.

The interned Polish president, Ignacy Moscicki, in accor-
dance with the Polish constitution, named a distinguished Polish
statesman, Wladyslaw Raczkiewicz, who was already in Paris, to
be the next president of Poland. In turn, Raczkiewicz nominated
General Wladyslaw Sikorski to the position of commander-in
chief, as well as Prime Minister and Minister of Military Affairs
(a ministry renamed the Ministry of Defense later in the war).
Sikorski formed a coalition government in which all of Poland's
political parties, except the Communists, were represented. The
Polish government, located in Paris, and recognized by all the
major democracies as the legitimate de jure constitutional government of Poland, set about rebuilding the Polish armed forces
in France and the United Kingdom.[2]

POLES REGROUP IN FRANCE

For the Polish government, for its military, and for Poles in general, the September campaign, however tragic, was merely the
first campaign of the war. It was firmly believed by all—the edu-
cated and sophisticated as well as the masses—that the war
would be won by the Western powers and that the Poles would
return to their country as victors. Sikorski, the Polish prime minister and commander-in-chief, in his radio address on January
23, 1940 to the Polish nation and Polish National Council (representing all Polish political parties), thus affirmed Poland's policy:
"The re-creation of the Polish Army to its maximum size is the

most important and essential goal of the Government." The Polish government in France and all its official agencies, such as embassies, sought to build up the Polish forces from the assets of citizens outside the occupied homeland, primarily from the large group of Polish immigrants in France estimated at close to 120,000 and from the approximately seventy thousand military personnel interned in Romania and Hungary. This last required a clandestine evacuation which was successfully expedited by a variety of means: by rail directly to France and also by ship from Romania and Greece to the Levant.

Among the chartered ships utilized in the evacuation were Polish liners that had been kept out of the Baltic prior to the first of September, and which continued to operate under the Polish flag throughout the war. The old Polish liner, SS *Warszawa,* relegated prior to the war to the Levantine route, played a major part in expediting Polish evacuation.

POLISH DESTROYER DIVISION
SEPTEMBER 1939–MAY 1940

Even before the city of Warsaw capitulated on September 26, 1939, and before the Polish government was driven out of the country by the Soviet invasion on September 17, 1939, the Polish Navy based out of British ports was back in action.

On September 4, one day after the British declared war on Germany in support of Poland, the commanding officer of the Polish Destroyer Division, Kdr. por. Stankiewicz, was invited to meet the First Lord of the Admiralty, Winston Churchill, as well as the First Sea Lord, Admiral of the Fleet, Dudley Pound. The Poles were advised that the British proposed to use the Polish warships in the western approaches, off the west coast of Ireland.

On September 6, the Polish Destroyer Division sailed around the north of Scotland and according to some reports made a visual contact with a German submarine and carried out a depth charge attack. There were conflicting reports whether an oil slick that was claimed to have been seen signified success. On September 8, the Poles passed through the Minches on the way to Milford Haven in Wales, and carried out a second depth-charge attack. On September 9, *Blyskawica* was ordered to escort the British ship, SS *Lassall* which carried war materials destined for Poland through Romanian ports. On arrival at Gibraltar on September 22, the situation in Poland had deteriorated to the extent that the mission was aborted. In October 1939, the two *Grom* class destroyers, which had been found too top-heavy in the Atlantic swell, were docked and their top weight reduced.

On October 22, the Polish destroyer division was in full combat operations, patrolling the western shores of Ireland. The resurgence of IRA activity in the British Isles led to some speculation, possibly based on intelligence data, that the German submarines were about to use the small bays and inlets of the rugged and unpopulated western shore of Ireland for refueling and provisioning the their U-boats. The Poles were used for this task since a transgression of Irish neutrality by the Polish naval units was less likely to have serious political repercussions in the United States with its strong, endemically anti-British, Irish lobby.

On October 28, the Poles again made a periscope sighting and carried out a depth-charge attack.

There was great continuity in the operations of the Polish Navy, bearing in mind that the Polish naval units fought in the Baltic, albeit somewhat symbolically until about October 12, (ORP *Orzel*), and that the Polish warships in the west had begun operations on September 6. It is no mere accident that Winston Churchill, who was now in the British Cabinet as the First Lord of the Admiralty, wrote, "the young Polish Navy had distinguished itself," and the "escape of the ORP *Orzel* was an epic."[3] Churchill also wrote in his memoirs that the British were singularly short of fleet destroyers and, by the end of 1940, only expected to commission nine more. We know the price the British paid a year later to receive the hundred old and decrepit American destroyers. The arrival of three fully operational and manned warships, two of them state-of-the-art, had to be a worthwhile addition to their forces.

The continuity of naval operations between the Polish warships based in the Baltic and those operating out of the United Kingdom may have had little military significance, but it was highly symbolic of the continued Polish effort in spite of their losses in the first campaign.

Finally, the Treaty of Mutual Assistance called exactly for that; and the assistance in the first month given the British by the Poles, well exceeded the assistance delivered by the British.

THE POLISH–BRITISH NAVAL AGREEMENT

In November 1939, the Polish government in Paris and the government of the United Kingdom signed the first of a number of military agreements which pertained to the Polish Navy. The consequence of this was the transfer of the Polish naval headquarters with its commandant, Kontr-Admiral Jerzy Swirski, to London from Paris. The Polish Army and Air Force headquarters remained in Paris, as did the Polish government, until June 1940, when the French capitulation led to the transfer of all Polish governmental agencies to Britain. (For the comprehensive text of this agreement, see Appendix A.)

INTERNED POLISH SUBMARINES

The desirability of getting the three Polish submarines out of benign Swedish internment was a matter of pressing concern for the Polish naval authorities. As early as October 4, 1939, the Polish naval attaché in London, Kmdr. por. Tadeusz Stoklasa, in a formal démarche to the British Admiralty enquired whether the interned Polish boats, should they succeed in escaping from Swedish ports, were to operate in the Baltic interdicting German shipping, or make for British ports. It should be noted that this was after the escape of *Orzel* but before its arrival in the United Kingdom.

The British response was cool, since they were more interested in preserving Swedish neutrality than in obtaining three additional submarines. But the dramatic arrival of the *Orzel* in the United Kingdom on October 14, 1939, made such an escape more feasible and the British, through their naval attaché in Stockholm, Commander John Poland, RN, considered whether such an escape would be consistent with their policies.

The Polish submarines were in fact being provisioned and certain emergency repairs carried out, as well as some spare parts ordered and installed. This was being done with tacit Swedish collaboration since the Swedish government realized that their own professed neutrality was precarious and German intentions far from clear. Commander Poland also expressed some reservations about the morale of two of the commanding officers but also felt that the junior officers and sailors were keen and inspired by the successes of *Wilk* and *Orzel*. But the passage through the Danish straits was considered insuperable, while escape could only be contemplated if the Swedes were sympathetic.

The outbreak of the Finnish-Russian winter war (November 1939–March 1940) again brought the issue to the fore in Polish plans. It needs to be remembered that Poland was in a de facto state of war with the Soviets and that the French were considering sending a Polish infantry brigade (the *Podhalanska*) and a Polish fighter wing to assist the Finns. The British were again concerned and urged restraint, but the Poles obtained from the French charts for the western Baltic with intelligence reports regarding the location of Allied and identified enemy minefields. The Poles also correctly pointed out that the Polish-British Naval Agreement did not cover the command of the interned Polish submarines, which remained strictly an internal Polish question and over which the British Admiralty had no jurisdiction.

The German invasion of Norway again brought the issue of the Polish submarines to the attention of all three governments. The British would be more supportive of Polish plans if the Swedes were to surrender, as had the Danes, or be invaded, and resist as did the Norwegians. But the British Admiralty still opined than an escape from the Baltic was impossible, that the Polish submarines ought to interdict enemy shipping in the Baltic, and that, if Swedish bases became unavailable, they should enter the only remaining neutral ports in Finland. With British support, the Poles now flew in Kpt. mar. Boguslaw Krawczyk, the CO of the *Wilk*, to assume command of the *Sep*. It was thought that the command of such a distinguished naval officer, who had already made his way through the Danish Straits to the United Kingdom, would reassure the junior officers and inspire all ranks. The command of *Rys* went to the first officer, Kpt. mar Rekner.

In the final outcome, the Germans did not attack Sweden, which managed to preserve its neutrality, and the Polish plans became moot. The Polish submarines remained in interment, and Kpt. mar. Krawczyk flew back to the United Kingdom to resume command of *Wilk*. The crews of the interned submarines were given orders to stay with their boats and not to escape. These orders were only lifted in the final months of the war. It is not surprising that the only officer from the interned crews who returned to Poland after the war was the demoralized commanding officer of *Sep*.[4]

"THE PHONEY WAR"

The period of October 1939 through April 1940 is invariably described as the *"phoney-war"* or *"sitzkrieg."* While undoubtedly true for the ground forces—and less so for the air forces of the combatants—it was anything but true for the naval units which were deployed in a grand game of hide-and-seek over the oceans of the world. The strategy was simple. The British and French attempted to institute a blockade of Germany, an endeavor doomed to failure since shipping went to Germany from neutral Sweden and through the Soviet Union. The Soviet Union also allowed German U-boats to provision in its Arctic ports.

On the other side, by using their large oceangoing U-boats and disguised surface raiders, the Germans attempted to choke British maritime trade. The menace of the German submarines, the infamous U-boats, is well known, but what is now forgotten is the danger to Allied shipping from the many German surface ships. In January 1940, Allied shipping losses went above 200,000 tons, then abated only to reach a critical high of 585,496 tons in June 1940. These high losses continued and reached a new peak of 679,632 tons in February 1941. German losses in U-boats throughout this early period averaged about four boats per month.

From the early days of the war until the middle of 1941, it was the German surface ships that took a heavy toll of British shipping, but also tied up many British warships on fruitless patrols. *Admiral Graf Spee*, one of Germany's so-called pocket battleships, sank over 50,000 tons of Allied shipping in its seventy days in the South Atlantic and the Indian Ocean. In November and December of 1940 alone, the German surface raiders—occasionally battleships, but more often disguised liners—sank a total of fifty-nine ships of 203,000 tons. This campaign went on through most of 1941. In early 1941, the German surface raider *Pinguin* sank 137,000 tons of Allied shipping, while the *Atlantis* sank 146,000 tons. In 1939, these German naval operations had been merely a nuisance though the Germans inflicted some humiliating reverses on the British when their battleship HMS *Royal Oak* was sunk in protected waters of the main base of the Home Fleet at Scapa Flow in the Orkney Islands, while the aircraft carrier HMS *Courageous* was torpedoed in the Bristol Channel.

ENFORCING THE BLOCKADE OF GERMANY NOVEMBER 1939–APRIL 1940

On October 29, 1939, the British must have decided that the Poles had passed their test of seamanship, since the Polish destroyer division was seconded to the Royal Navy's First Destroyer Flotilla in Harwich, arguably the most difficult area of naval operations in late 1939 and early 1940. The Polish division operated as a Polish group, carrying out intensive patrols and minelaying operations in the North Sea. Constant air attacks and the danger of negotiating waters that were often strewn by enemy mines made this dangerous and tiring work. Further-more, the North Sea was a navigational challenge with strong tidal currents, scattered shoals, prone to fog and violent storms. During this time the Germans also began to deploy their new magnetic mines. The danger from magnetic mines was well illustrated on November 21 when HMS *Gipsy*, a mere three hun-dred yards from ORP *Burza*, blew up with grievous loss of life. On October 26, 1939, Poland's pride, the liner *SS Pilsudski,* was in fact sunk by one of these secret and very lethal weapons.

The task of the First Destroyer Flotilla was to patrol off the shores of Belgium and Holland, both countries pitifully holding on to their proclaimed neutrality, and thus trading with Germany. The task of the flotilla was to implement the next to useless blockade by inspecting merchantmen heading in the direction of Germany and also to lay mines in German waters. The crews were at constant alert, with four hours notice at best, for departure. On November 7, *Blyskawica* (CO Kpt. mar. T. Gorazdowski) and *Grom* (CO Kdr. ppor. A. Hule-wicz) were attacked while on patrol off Dogger Bank by two Heinkel-115s which launched a torpedo. Evasive action pre-vented any damage.

On December 12, destroyers of the flotilla, including the Polish division commanded by Kdr. por. R. Stankiewicz, left harbor to intercept a German destroyer group purported to be near Texel. The flotilla sailed at full speed through a dark and foggy night, at times through British minefields, but no contact was made. It should be remarked that small ships like destroyers in those early days of the war did not have shipboard radar, and even as late as 1941, only a small number of major warships were equipped.

On December 17, 1939, *Blyskawica* (under commanding officer Kdr. ppor. J. Umecki) participated in minelaying operations near Emden. These operations were repeated again in January of 1940. On January 16, *Blyskawica* arrested a Latvian ship (*Raznov*) with cargo for Germany and brought it under escort to Dover. On February 20, *Burza* (under CO Kdr. ppor. W. Francki) depth-charged a German submarine. In March, the Polish ships participated in minelaying operations and escorted the French submarine tender *Jules Verne*. On April 1, all three Polish destroyers took part in a sweep off Heligoland.

The main focus of attention now began to shift to Norwegian waters. The Germans were using Norwegian territorial waters to move their ships in from the open Atlantic, to say nothing of the heavy trade in Swedish iron ore that was being shipped through Norwegian ports. The proof that the Norwegians had lost all control of their waters, or had decided to look the other way, occurred on February 16, 1940, when a British destroyer (HMS *Cossack*) under the command of the soon to be famous Captain Vian, boarded a German transport, *Altmark*, in Norwegian waters, and liberated hundreds of British sailors taken prisoner from sunk by the surface raiders. Needless to say the British action was against all international conventions, but it was obvious that the Norwegians should never have allowed German ships to carry prisoners through Norwegian waters, and their failure to exercise jurisdiction over their territory certainly justified the British action. London was jubilant, Churchill triumphant. "The navy is here" was the rallying cry of the country. Both sides were now eyeing Norway as the locus for control of the blockade or as a window onto the Atlantic waters.

POLISH SUBMARINES IN BRITAIN, DECEMBER 1939–1940

Two Polish submarines had broken out of the Baltic. *Orzel* was a modern boat, but minus the breech for its gun, which had been removed by the Estonians, and thus not completely up to snuff. *Wilk* was a relatively old boat, its performance hampered by frequent mechanical problems. But both boats had full crew complements, and had achieved more than most other Allied submarines at that time. After major refits, both were assigned to the Royal Navy's Second Submarine Flotilla based in Rosyth, Scotland. By the end of the year *Wilk* managed to accomplish two combat patrols out of British ports, but continued to be plagued by frequent breakdowns, and was finally placed in dry dock for a major refit, which was not completed until June 1940.

Orzel sailed out on her first patrol from British bases on December 29. Four patrols were accomplished in a very uneventful fashion. They averaged fourteen days and were the classic mixture of reconnaissance and interdiction of enemy shipping. The region patrolled was usually south of Norway and the island of Heligoland.

But in April 1940, the pace accelerated dramatically as the Germans, sensing that the British might place their troops in Norway, implemented a very successful combined ground, air, and naval operation directed at Denmark and Norway.

The first step, the occupation of Copenhagen, was simple beyond expectation. A German squad arrived, hidden in a barge as if it were a Trojan horse, and disembarked while the Danish foreign office was given an ultimatum: destruction of Copenhagen or the country placed under German protection. The second alternative was accepted by the Danes, who had been beaten by the Germans earlier in the century. They were now offered a continued independent existence with their own government, armed forces, legislature, and the continuation of their monarchy: the very model of a "benign" German protectorate.

The invasion of Norway was bloodier for all sides. The Germans were aided by a small group of pro-German senior officers and politicians led by Quisling, whose name was to become the synonym for treacherous collaboration. Some Norwegian units fought hard against the Germans, some were given confusing instructions, and some were pro-German and anti-British. The Germans moved their troops into Norway by ship and by air. But the British and French also reacted quickly and moved their forces to confront the Germans. The British wished to prevent German access to Swedish iron ore and, if possible, to benefit from it themselves.

One of the first harbingers of this German invasion occurred on April 8, 1940, when ORP *Orzel* (under Kpt. mar. Jan Grudzinski) while on her fifth patrol was near the south coast of Norway. On April 8, 1940, at 0945 hours, *Orzel* observed a ship at the entrance of Oslofjord. The captain ordered an intercept course while submerged, and at 1100 hours logged that the ship was not showing a flag. A few minutes later, the name of the ship was read as *Rio de Janeiro,* registered by Deutscher Lloyd as a 9,800-ton passenger vessel out of Hamburg.

At 1103 hours, *Orzel,* still adhering to the prewar London agreements, surfaced approximately 1,200 meters from the suspect vessel, and ordered it to stop and for the captain of *Rio de Janeiro* to come aboard *Orzel* with papers. The ship stopped, but no ship's boat was launched. At 1112 hours, *Orzel* fired a machine-gun burst at the ship. A boat was then launched, but simulated rowing made no headway. At 1120 hours, Grudzinski gave an order for the suspect vessel to be abandoned within fifteen minutes, and at 1145, torpedoes were launched after one more warning. Hours later, the Poles observed numerous floating bodies in German army uniforms. The sunken ship was one of the armada of German vessels that was in the process of sailing into Norwegian ports without declaration of war.

The Polish skipper scrupulously and punctiliously adhered to international conventions even as they were being flouted by the Germans.

NORWEGIAN CAMPAIGN, APRIL 1940–MAY 1940

The sinking of *Rio de Janeiro* marked the beginning of what became known as the Norwegian campaign.[5] In addition to Polish naval units, the Poles sent in their recently formed Podhalanska Brigade from France, which took part in the Allied operations around Narvik. This five-thousand-man brigade was the first of the Polish land forces to enter combat after the September campaign.

The Polish destroyer division, commanded by Kdr. por. S. Hryniewiecki, and consisting of, *Burza* (under CO Kdr. ppor. W. Francki), *Blyskawica* (CO Kdr. ppor. S. Nahorski) and *Grom* (CO Kdr. ppor. A.Hulewicz) sailed for Scapa Flow on April 4 from Harwich.

These Polish warships and a number of troop transports (prewar luxury liners) battled in the icy waters of the Norwegian fjords at the side of the Royal Navy until the end of the Norwegian campaign.

The Polish destroyers were engaged in operations between Narvik and Lofoten Islands, at times transporting Allied units, at times providing them with escort and anti-aircraft protection. On May 3, *Burza* landed French Alpine troops in Graatangend Fjord. From May 4, she was naval officer in charge of Skaaland. In addition, the Allied warships also engaged enemy ground positions, their artillery giving support to the ground troops. On May 3, *Grom* fired five-thousand shells against German positions. *Blyskawica* also engaged the enemy with all its armament and her artillery officer, Kpt. mar. Bohdan Wronski, received the Virtuti Militari for his splendid work and self-sacrifice.

Sadly, on May, 4, 1940, *Grom* was the target of a concerted German air attack and was sunk. Her CO kdr. por. Aleksander Hulewicz, many months later in Devonport, received the British Distinguished Service Order directly from King George VI.

The German navy suffered a series of crippling defeats at the hands of the Allies. One of the battles entered history as "the massacre of the German destroyers," which occurred from the guns of the Royal Navy's battleship HMS *Warspite*.

The severe losses did not predispose the Kriegsmarine to take on the Royal Navy in the future without clear air superiority. This undoubtedly led to the postponement of the invasion of the British Isles in late 1940, when the Luftwaffe failed to wrest control of the air during the Battle of Britain. But when the Germans were able to get local air superiority, Allied losses were serious. *Grom*, as well as the Polish liner SS *Chrobry* carrying British troops, were both lost due to German air attacks.

Norway was really lost because of events in Western Europe and Allied strategic ineptitude, as much as German prowess.

The inability of the Allies to control the air played a major tactical role. The decision to abandon Norway was tragic, and led to the overthrow of the Chamberlain Government and the formation of the British Coalition Government. The British Conservatives had a majority in the House of Commons and the rank and file Tories would have much preferred Lord Halifax as Prime Minister. At the insistence of the British Labour Party, who made it a condition of joining the coalition, hoiwever, the position went to Winston Churchill who was called to Buckingham Palace and asked to form the government that would lead the United Kingdom in the war against Germany.

The Allied decision to abandon Norway flies in the face of all long-range strategic principles. Possession of the northern Norwegian ports gave the Germans an opening onto the Atlantic which they lacked up to that time. It also opened the iron ore traffic to German control.

The Allied fleets were withdrawn, the remaining two Polish destroyers sailed for Scapa Flow and, by May 14, had reached Harwich to begin the long naval operations which culminated with the final evacuation of all British and remnant Polish forces from the continent.

GERMANY INVADES HOLLAND, BELGIUM, AND FRANCE

The "Phoney War" in Western Europe came to an abrupt end on May 10, 1940, when the Germans invaded Holland and Belgium, taking no heed of their proclamations of neutrality. In a modified von Schlieffen maneuver, they attacked north of the Maginot Line, and went on to defeat the combined Dutch, Belgian, French, and British armies in less than six weeks.[6]

Two Polish infantry divisions and a Polish armored brigade, as well some fighter units, fought in the French campaign. The two remaining Polish surface warships also took part in the bloody battles off the coast of Dunkirk, famous for the evacuation of the British army from France.

On May 21, ORP *Burza* sailed to Calais and shelled German troop concentrations. Later that same day, attacked by at least a geschwader of Junker-87s, *Burza* was hit, while her companion HMS *Wessex* was sunk and HMS *Vimiera* was badly damaged and dead in the water. *Burza* was able to make it back to Dover under her own steam and then was towed to Plymouth for repairs. *Blyskawica's* experiences were similar: patrols out of Harwich, enemy air attacks, and the constant, pervasive danger of mines. On May 29, she towed the disabled Royal Navy destroyer, *HMS Greyhound*, to Dover. *Blyskawica*, commanded by Kdr. ppor. S. Nahorski, endured six days of this for which a number of crew received Poland's second-highest award for bravery, the *Krzyz Walecznych* or Cross of Valor. A commentator wrote that it would be difficult to imagine more difficult situations. There were the very strong tidal currents, for which the Channel is famous; the shoals were an added navigational hazard, compounded by poor visibility from the smoke of burning towns; exploding ships; enemy air attacks, and even German E-boat attacks. On June 7, *Blyskawica* finally departed for Portsmouth for a refit.

FRANCE SEEKS ARMISTICE WITH GERMANY

On June 22, 1940, the French signed an armistice which allowed the Germans to occupy the entire Atlantic coast of France. The new French Government under Pétain was located in Vichy, since Paris was directly occupied. This gave rise to an infamous chapter in French history, that of Vichy France. The British were very concerned that the famed French fleet not fall into German hands, and entreated the French naval commander, Admiral Darlan, to order his warships to North American ports, which were still neutral. Darlan refused but ostensibly obtained German assurances that the French warships would be based in Vichy French–controlled ports like Toulon, and not be allowed to fall under German control.

The British were loath to accept these assurances. This led to one of the great tragedies of the Second World War: a French squadron that refused to comply with British options was attacked off Mers el-Khébir and many warships were sunk with great loss of French lives. As a result, Pétain broke off relations with the British. Within a couple of weeks, the British relationship with France went from that of active ally to tacit enemies.[7]

The British were now on their own, with an impending German invasion. In June 1940, Italy threw in its lot with Germany, changing the naval balance decisively to the disadvantage of the United Kingdom. The United States was still firmly committed to a policy of neutrality; while British resources were stretched to the breaking point.

In the summer and fall of 1940, Britain was fighting for its life. Churchill represented Britain at her best. He resisted Hitler's offers and blackmailed a willing Roosevelt into helping Britain. His message was quite simple, logical, and blunt. Were Britain to be defeated, America alone would confront alone the might of Germany and Japan, assisted by both Italy and the Soviet Union. He made it clear in his secret messages to the United States president, Franklin Delano Roosevelt that, as long as he was prime minister, Britain would fight and, if invaded and occupied, her fleet would be moved to Canada. He also dropped a strong hint, no doubt correct, that were he to be thrown out of his premiership (like Chamberlain before him), then he could not guarantee that the new government would not accommodate Germany just like Pétain. In those circumstances the British fleet might fall into German hands.

This cold and realistic outline of the future allowed the British to begin obtaining American supplies, ultimately led to the Lend-Lease Act and to the procurement of a hundred small destroyers, which, while worthless as fighting ships, were useful as escort vessels.

THE EVACUATION TO BRITAIN AND POLISH LOSSES IN THE FRENCH CAMPAIGN

The sudden collapse of the French front, the disintegration of the French army's morale, and the resulting French government crisis in France caught the Polish government by surprise. Sikorski, a lifelong Francophile, lived in denial of this reality for longer than most members of his government and military staff. He recovered quickly, however, and accepted Churchill's invitation to fly to London to arrange the evacuation of the Polish forces from France to the United Kingdom.[8] He was assisted, in this endeavor, to a degree often unappreciated, by the Polish ambassador in London, Count Edward Raczynski. As a result of Raczynski's contacts and diplomacy, the solid staff work of the Polish naval commandant, Admiral Swirski, and Churchill's goodwill, the British facilitated and aided the Poles in their commitment to continue the war. The goodwill of the British Admiralty was striking. In the initial moment of crisis, the British Foreign Office was most reluctant to endorse the evacuation of the Polish military to the United Kingdom.

One can speculate whether this was due to the fact that there were elements in the British Foreign Office, who were more than inclined to follow the French lead to a general accommodation with Germany. But the Royal Navy asserted from the beginning that all Poles who wished to be evacuated would be welcome.

But most of the Polish military formations, ground and air, were intermixed with French units, and many were not aware of the imminent crisis. Churchill allowed Sikorski the use of the British Broadcasting Corporation (BBC) to make a speech in Polish to all Poles in France, to break off and seek transport to the United Kingdom. The same courtesy was shown to De Gaulle. The speech of the leader of the Free French is histori-cally better known, but the numbers of Poles who followed Siko-rski, as opposed to the numbers of French, are like day and night. The total number of Poles (ground and aviation) evacu-ated was nineteen-thousand, representing a mere twenty-three percent of the Polish military in France. Of this number, five-thousand six- hundred were moved aboard Polish ships; the liners *Batory, Sobieski*, MS *Lechistan*, SS *Chorzow*, SS *Kmicic,* SS *Wilno* and two fishing trawlers, *Korab* and *Delfin*. Close to eight-thousand were officers and men of the Polish Air Force.

Of the twenty-five thousand foreign ground troops in the United Kingdom in July 1940, fourteen-thousand were Poles and two-thousand Free French.

The British sent their cruiser, HMS *Arethuse*, and boarded the Polish government and the Polish president, who were warmly greeted by King George VI on arrival in London.[9]

Not all the Poles in France heard Sikorski's address, how-ever, and not all were in a position to follow his instructions.

In the French disaster, the Poles lost most of the ground troops that they had so assiduously and painfully assembled, namely, two infantry divisions comprising 75 percent of the effective strength of their ground forces. Only a small number of land army units joined the successful evacuation of the majority of the Polish Air Force personnel. Close to seventy-thousand Polish soldiers were lost. The bloodiest losses were suffered by the grenadier division. The whole of the Second Fusilier Division was forced to cross into Switzerland and was interned. There were thousands of Polish stragglers from the various training centers located all over France, or as the British called them "*evaders,*" who had been unable to adhere to their commander-in-chief's orders to evacuate to Britain and who were not prepared to sit out the war in France. They made their way through various ways to North Africa or attempted to cross Spain to get to Portugal. The Poles interned in Switzerland were in fact ordered to stay put, since they represented a cohesive, integrated force. But some individuals became impatient and escaped.

POLISH NAVAL LOSSES AND ADDITIONS

The months of May and June were the nadir of Polish naval fortunes. The Polish submarine ORP *Orzel* carried out its sixth and uneventful patrol between April 28 and May 11, 1940. She failed to return from her seventh patrol and was posted missing and presumed lost on May 23. Her entire crew, including her CO Jan Grudzinski, five officers, one ensign, and fifty-eight crew members were lost. The loss was indeed tragic, because it was most likely due to British mines, of which the Polish commander had not been informed in time.

The other submarine, *Wilk*, continued to carry out combat patrols from the ports of Rosyth and Dundee, all in the direction of Skagerrak. The boat continued to be plagued by mechanical problems and finally it was decided, toward the end of the year, to place her in the training squadron and give the Poles a new submarine. During the period of her last six patrols, *Wilk* was commanded either by her old skipper, B. Krawczyk (now promoted to Komandor pod-porucznik), or by Kpt. mar. B. Karnicki, who later achieved fame commanding the famous ORP *Sokol* in the Mediterranean. The reason Karnicki doubled for Krawczyk was that the latter had been ordered to Sweden when it looked like Hitler, having conquered Norway and forced France to a humbling capitulation, might invade Sweden. Krawczyk's missions were to plan a breakout of the interned Polish submarines and to keep the Polish crews alerted.[10] However, in one of their very few sound diplomatic decisions, the Germans realized that a neutral Sweden was more profitable than an occupied one. Polish plans became moot.

While the losses were painful, the majority of the crews were saved and in the two training ships in western waters at the outbreak of the war, the Polish Navy possessed well trained cadres and reserves. This allowed for new warships to be taken over by the Polish Navy.

The British, now aware of Polish proficiency and their trained crews in short supply, signed an auxiliary agreement with the Poles for the loan of warships to the Polish Navy. On May 3, 1940, Poland's Constitution Day, the Polish flag was run up the British destroyer HMS *Garland* in Malta. This is believed to be the oldest name in constant usage in the Royal Navy, and the Poles decided to keep the name. Thus the ship entered Polish service as ORP *Garland.* The first commanding officer was Kdr. ppor. A. Doroszewski. Before proceeding to reinforce the defense of the British Isles, *Garland* escorted a passenger ship with Polish military evacuees from the Balkans. On September 26, 1940, *Garland* was assigned to Plymouth and was shortly joined by the other Polish destroyers in the Royal Navy's Fifth Destroyer Flotilla, whose main task was to guard the Western Approaches.

The mission of the Royal Navy's Western Approaches Command was to protect coastal convoys and to be ready for the expected German invasion. Constant patrols were carried out in waters where air and surface control was being challenged by the Germans.

It was also in the summer of 1940 that the Polish flag was hoisted on the first of ten fast motor-torpedo boats. Long awaited by the Poles, and in fact originally contracted with British yards, they were initially taken over by the British under the provision of the war exigencies. The first was *S-2* (*Wilczur*) and the second *S-3* (*Wyzel*) and their respective skippers were Ppor. E. Wcislicki and Ppor. A. Jaraczewski. On October 15, a third motor-torpedo boat was taken over by the

Poles as *S-1* (*Chart*) and commanded by Por. J. Sokolowski. There is some dispute whether the names were official, but the first three of the ten were more often than not called by these names, while subsequent boats were exclusively known by their number

THE BATTLE OF BRITAIN AND PREPARING FOR A GERMAN INVASION

After their evacuation from France, Polish ground troops were based in Scotland, where they formed the Polish First Corps commanded by Lt. General Marian Kukiel. Polish Air Force personnel were quickly integrated into Royal Air Force (RAF) fighter squadrons or all-Polish fighter and bomber units, and one Army co-operation squadron assigned to work with the Polish First Corps. All the resources of Britain were directed at preparing to fend off the expected German invasion. RAF bomber squadrons, including the Polish 300 and 301, bombed German shipping and invasion barges in the north ports of occupied France. Anti-invasion coastal forces were formed and patrolled the approaches to the beaches of Britain.

But to invade, meant not only to land ground troops, but required the ability to maintain the invading force. To accomplish this, the Germans had to achieve air superiority over southern England. This led to the greatest air battle of all times, the *Battle of Britain*. Polish airmen were now to make the name of the Polish wings resound around the world as the Polish fighter squadrons entered combat. Len Deighton wrote of the Polish airmen who fought in that aerial battle, that

> The Poles were the most numerous, and also made the greatest contribution. They deeply resented the *canard* that their air force had been wiped out in the first hours of the German invasion in September 1939, for some of them had flown and fought until the bitter end. They were much more highly-trained than most British pilots of the period, although they had no experience of high-performance monoplanes, they were also most remarkable marksmen. In a Fighter Command

gunnery contest early in 1941, three Polish squadrons took the first three places with scores of 808, 432 and 193. The best British squadron came fourth, with 150.[11]

Clearly Deighton's initial remark clearly refer to the participation of pilots of foreign nations as well.

The aerial battle was won by the Royal Air Force Fighter Command, splendidly commanded by Air Chief Marshal Sir Hugh Dowding. The victory denied the Luftwaffe control over the Channel, precluding any possibility of a German seaborne invasion.

REPLACEMENTS FOR THE POLISH NAVY

In June and July of 1940, a number of warships were abandoned in British ports by their French and Belgian crews, who opted to return home to families and homes under German occupation after their governments capitulated in June 1940. Some of these warships were handed over to the Polish Navy. Twelve such ex-Belgian trawlers, crewed by Polish naval personnel, operated out of Dartmouth in southwest England, on anti-invasion patrols. Initially their sole armament was one rifle each. This level of firepower was comparable to the British Home Guard, whose volunteers were armed with walking sticks and the occasional shotgun. These anti-invasion patrols continued until February 6, 1941.

The Poles also took over two modern French submarine chasers, each armed with a 75-millimeter gun and heavy machine guns. The warships retained their French numbers: *Ch-11* (CO Kpt. mar. J. de Latour) and *Ch-15* (CO Kpt. mar. A. Waciega, followed shortly by Kpt. mar. S. Pohorecki). These two warships carried out a total of forty-six and thirty-eight combat patrols respectively in the Channel until they were returned to the Free French Navy.

Two large French patrol ships were also temporarily placed under the Polish flag. These were the *Medoc,* which was torpedoed and sunk by a German U-boat on November 26, 1940, with the loss of its commanding officer, Kdr. por. R. Stankiewicz, and two Polish enlisted men, and the *Pomerol,* which was quickly handed over to the Royal Navy but continued to be commanded by Kpt. mar. R. Tyminski. *Pomerol* flew three flags: the French, Polish and Union Jack.

Finally, the relative surfeit of well trained Polish crews made possible the takeover of the French destroyer *Ouragan*. This was an old French destroyer, built by the same shipyard and to the same specifications as the Polish *Burza*; hence it was assumed to be familiar to the Poles. This ship was in a very bad state of repair and had actually been towed to Britain when France capitulated. The Polish flag was run up on July 18, 1940, with Kdr. por. E. Plawski as CO, succeeded by Kpt. mar. T. Gorazdowski. Plagued by mechanical problems, during its nine months under Polish command, she spent thirty days at sea, sixty days in harbor, and one hundred ninety-four days in dockyards. She was returned to the Free French on April 4, 1941.

In October 1940, the Poles commissioned a brand new fleet destroyer of the Javelin Class, HMS *Nerissa*, and renamed her ORP *Piorun*. This was part of the continued implementation of the Polish–United Kingdom agreements for the loan of ships to the Polish Navy during wartime. The first commanding officer was Kdr. por. E. Plawski.

NOTES

1. Steven Zaloga and Victor Madej, *The Polish Campaign, 1939*, New York, 1985.
2. Jozef Garlinski, *Poland in the Second World War*, MacMillan, London, 1985; Sarah Meiklejohn Terry, *Poland's Place in Europe*, Princeton University Press, 1983.
3. Churchill, *The Gathering Storm*, Boston, 1948.
4. Teresa Skinder-Suchcitz, *"Proby Uwolnienia Okretow Podwodnych z Internowania w Szwecji: Wrzesien 1939–Czerwiec 1940"*. *(Efforts to liberate the submarines from Swedish internment, September 1939–June 1940), Zeszyty Historyczne*, No. 115, 1996: pp. 59–72.
5. Francois Kersaudy, *Norway 1940*, New York, 1987. Also, Donald Macintyre, *Narvik*, New York, 1960.
6. Telford Taylor, *The March of Conquest*, New York, 1958, and Militargeschichtliches Forschunsamt, ed. *Germany and the Second*

World War, Vol. II: Germany's Initial Conquests, Clarendon Press, Oxford, 1991.

7. Charles W. Koburger, *The Cyrano Fleet: France and Its Navy, 1940–42*, Greenwood, 1989.

8. Keith Sword, ed. *Sikorski: Soldier and Statesman. A Collection of Essays*, London, 1990.

9. There is a historical enigma associated with the way that the Polish president and government were evacuated from France. There were no Polish warships available for the Polish authorities to board and it made more sense from a safety point of view to have them on a warship than on a freighter, or one of the Polish liners that were being used in the evacuation. A plane could also have been used. The unexplained fact is that for three entire days the Polish party was aboard a British warship, unable to communicate with London or its own troops in France under bombardment. The logs of the British warship do not explain this paradox. (PRO ADM 53/111412)

10. Teresa Skinder-Suchcitz, op.cit.

11. Len Deighton, *Battle of Britain*, London, 1980.

CHAPTER VI
THE BATTLE OF THE ATLANTIC BEGINS, 1940–1941

THE ONSET OF THE BATTLE
OF THE ATLANTIC

After the war, Churchill wrote, "The only thing that ever really frightened me during the war was the U-boat peril."[1]

Having failed to establish air supremacy over the south of England during the Battle of Britain in the summer of 1940, and thus losing the possibility of a successful invasion across the Channel, the Germans embarked on ever more threatening surface and underwater warfare against British shipping. The punishing daylight bomber raids of 1940 now became night attacks which continued throughout the spring of 1941.

The two ports that became crucial in this struggle as Britain's gateway to the free world and the crucial life line for all supplies, were Glasgow on the Clyde and Liverpool on the Irish Sea. All convoys heading to or from North and South America and Africa originated and terminated in one of these ports. Oceangoing ships were unloaded and then coastal ships distributed the cargoes to such ports as London, Bristol, and Newcastle. While Glasgow was at the extreme range of German bombers; Liverpool, Plymouth, Portsmouth, and—particularly London continued to be at the receiving end of severe German Luftwaffe attacks and suffered accordingly. Coastal convoys were vital since the British lacked sufficient rail capacity to move all the cargo necessary to sustain civilian life and the military effort.

The Polish destroyers were now moved to Greenock (near Glasgow) for convoy duty, initiating the long and exhausting period of naval activity in the Battle of the Atlantic, a fight waged over, under, and on the waters of the Northern Atlantic with changing fortunes, but always with Britain's (and the

Poles always assumed Poland's), future at stake. This battle went on for four years, without respite. Yet dangerous as the Germans always were, the danger from the Atlantic gales, the frequent fog and squalls which cut down on visibility, and the pervasive cold all sapped the energy of the crews, Allied a well as German. This was a formidable enemy, "The Cruel Sea," as brilliantly described by Nicholas Monsarrat.

For the small destroyers, the heavy Atlantic swell led to damage, men overboard and near to impossible navigational challenges. This was before satellite navigation and a clear sky were essential for accurate celestial navigation. Otherwise ships navigated by dead reckoning, which was hindered by the constant course changes and the variety of zigzag procedures adopted to minimize enemy submarine attacks. On approaching friendly shores, the Allied ships faced the danger of enemy mines, even of friendly minefields which may have shifted or were approached due to navigational error. There was frequent congestion of sea traffic, particularly when convoys were being formed and there was an ever present danger caused by the precautions of blackout, which made collisions another major hazard. In the Atlantic, however, two dangers were absent: there were no enemy mines and the German Luftwaffe was not the threat that it was in the southern regions of England.

During the winter of 1940–41 the Polish warships were to suffer the ravages of the Atlantic. In November 1940, *Burza*, while escorting, suffered storm damage and had to return to port. In that same month *Garland* (a British-built warship and designed for these kinds of sea conditions), suffered the loss of two men overboard and damage to her superstructure while sailing as escort to the battleship HMS *Revenge*.

Blyskawica, after completing her refitting, left the Clyde on December 4 but ran straight away into a powerful Atlantic storm, and when her steering jammed, returned to port for another two months of repairs. On February 11, 1941, she again put to sea, with HMS *Arrow* and HMS *Mistral* on convoy duty, but again experienced damage to her steering, in the heavy Atlantic winter storms, and returned for an extended refit, which included a change of her artillery to the British dual-purpose 4-inch caliber guns, as well as the installation of radar. Today, when most medium-size yachts have radar, it is important to remember that no ships had radar at the beginning of the Second World War, and that it became fairly ubiquitous only in the latter part of 1942.

By contrast, in October 1940, in one of the more felicitous episodes of its history, *Burza* sailed to the rescue of the large liner SS *Empress of Britain* and took on board more than two hundred fifty survivors.

POLISH PERSONNEL SHORTAGES

The Polish armed forces, re-created in the West after the lost September 1939 campaign, suffered from a constant and at time critical shortage of manpower. This was understandable in view of the fact that the Polish homeland was occupied and, unlike the German occupied states of Western Europe, landlocked with all adjacent territories under hostile control. The French, Belgians, and Norwegians could, if they had a mind, sail off on their numerous fishing trawlers to the British Isles. Agents could also be easily picked up from these adjoining countries by single-engined aircraft like the Lysander, which had the capability of landing and taking off from small fields.

That the Poles were able to build up their forces in France in 1939–40 speaks to the organizational ability of the Polish state, recreated in France. This effort was destroyed in June 1940, and had to be repeated once again in Britain. It demonstrated the high motivation, patriotism, and morale of the Polish military, who sought honor and not safety.

This shortage of suitable manpower affected the Polish Air Force in particular, since the crew losses of the four Polish bomber squadrons in the bombing offensive against Germany exceeded the number of available trainees. This shortage also plagued the Poles in their efforts to muster a fully motorized, two-divisional corps in Scotland. Only one armored division was finally formed, and that with great difficulty.[2]

This led to a continuing effort to bring out Poles from the occupied continent and in this the Polish Navy assisted. This was the function of the Polish Naval Mission based in Gibraltar. (This is developed in Chapter VII.)

The Polish Navy was initially in a very healthy state regarding manpower, the most satisfactory of the three services. At the onset of hostilities in September 1939, two Polish training ships (*Iskra* and *Wilia*), with a cadre of instructors and midshipmen, were in western waters. The Polish warships that reached British waters all had full complements. Many of the merchantmen also had naval reserve personnel who volunteered and, in many instances, were voluntarily enrolled or conscripted into the navy. As the war progressed the Polish Government tended to protect the merchant-marine seamen and saw such service as the equivalent of military service.

NAVAL ADMINISTRATION AND GROWTH

The Polish naval headquarters came to London in early 1940, well before the French capitulation, as a result of the signing of the Polish-United Kingdom Naval Agreement of November, 1939. Thus, when the French debacle of June 1940 occurred, the commandant of the Polish Navy and his small staff (as well as the Polish Navy Officer School) were all firmly ensconced in the United Kingdom and played a part in the evacuation of the Polish troops from France.

Responsible to the commandant were a number of primarily training centers, including the officer's cadet school (midshipmen) which commissioned its first class on September 3, 1941. The commandant was also responsible for a number of training centers ranging from such highly specialized skills as electronics and engineers to the mundane, but still essential, as cooks. There were also a number of rest and rehabilitation centers for officers and sailors, so that seagoing personnel could have a chance of getting some rest. It might be forgotten that the Polish naval personnel did not have families close by, nor their own houses or apartments. When not aboard ship, they required a relaxed setting to get what Americans later called "R and R," or rest and recuperation. This could only be found in special boarding houses purchased or rented for the personnel.

The last time that the Poles had sailed as a cohesive Polish Destroyer Division was during the Norwegian campaign. The loss of *Grom*, in Norwegian waters, and the unusual degree of damage inflicted on both *Blyskawica* and *Burza*, which mandated extensive refitting, followed by subsequent assignments of the newly commissioned Polish warships to various escort duties in different regions, inevitably led to the decision to disband the destroyer division. However, two administrative divisions were created: the North Command, based in Greenock, Scotland, and commanded by Kdr.por. W. Kodrebski; and the South Command, based in Plymouth, England, and commanded by Kdr. por. K. Namiesniowski.

These men were the original commanding officers. During the war, officers rotated between staff and administrative duties; between training assignments, and sea time. Also the more distinguished or politically adroit were rotated through the London-based Polish Naval Command and the Polish Officers' School, where they served as faculty. In some instances the senior officers were seconded to foreign posts as naval attachés.

The Polish commands were responsible for all matters of discipline, rotation of crews, health and training, and acted as liaisons with their British colleagues. In their official correspondence, the British referred to the Polish commanding officers as, "Senior Polish Naval Officers." Later in the war, a third command was created in the Mediterranean, first in Gibraltar, and finally in Bari, Italy, by that time in Allied hands.

In early 1941, the Poles took over a brand new British built U-class submarine which was named ORP *Sokol* which, in September 1941, undertook a number of patrols off the German-occupied coast of France. Subsequently it was seconded to the Royal Navy's Tenth Submarine Flotilla based in Malta, a British island colony strategically located between the boot of Italy and Libya (then an Italian colony and the location of the major campaign between the British Eight Army and the combined Italian and German forces). This was a period of drastically varying fortunes for the British in the North African campaign.

In the spring of 1941, the Polish Navy also commissioned two escort-class Hunt destroyers and renamed them ORP *Kujawiak* and ORP *Krakowiak*. This harked back to the tradition of naming small warships after the denizens of Poland's many historic provinces. The ships were seconded to the Royal Navy's Home Fleet base in Scapa Flow, in the windswept, desolate Orkneys, aptly described by Bartosik as the ideal penal colony because of their isolation. Then they were assigned for work up with the Royal Navy's Destroyer Flotilla in Plymouth in the south of England. The ships undertook the monotonous and dangerous work of escorting coastal convoys in the southern English waters.

THE NAVAL WAR CONTINUES

Polish ships sailed mostly on escort missions, then returned to port to be refitted and modernized. Personnel went on retraining courses, leave, and "R and R." Surface warship officers went through Royal Navy training in destroyer command, navigation, communications, artillery, antisubmarine tactics, and radar. Submarine officers attended appropriate courses to hone their skills.

The *Piorun*, after completing her work up as a Polish-manned ship at Scapa Flow, was assigned on December 5, 1940, to escort duty between Belfast, the Clyde, and Londonderry. One of its many missions included escorting the Royal Navy carrier HMS *Formidable*, a cruiser and in company with nine other destroyers on a hunt for German raiders. On December 28, *Piorun* once again left for the wintry hell of Scapa Flow.

On January 25, 1941, *Piorun* became part of the Seventh Destroyer Flotilla and participated in the escort of the British battleships, *Rodney*, *Nelson*, and *Repulse*. The operation's mission was to intercept or at least prevent the German battleships *Scharnhorst* and *Gneisenau* from breaking out into the Atlantic and threatening Allied convoys. Once again the heavy North Atlantic seas caused damage to both the Polish *Piorun* and the Royal Navy's *Repel*, and both had to return to port.

On January 22, 1941, the *Garland* sailed for Canada and her commanding officer was the senior officer for the convoy. *Ouragan*, while still in Polish service, escorted convoys to Iceland, but its dilapidated condition resulted in frequent breakdowns and limited its range in Northern Ireland and the Minch in the Hebrides off the west coast of Scotland.

After completing her refit on February 15, 1941, *Burza*, CO Kdr. ppor. Zygmunt Wojewodzki, undertook escort duties in the Irish Sea between the Clyde, Belfast, Liverpool, and Cardiff.

But at times longer operations were called for, such as escorts north to the Faroe Islands and Iceland, or south to Portsmouth. On July 30, 1941, *Burza* sailed as part of a large escort to Iceland and returned on August 7. On September 27, *Burza* was sole escort of a troopship to the Faroes, and on October 8, escorted the battleship HMS *Resolution* to Plymouth.

On March 24, 1941, *Piorun* was part of an escort of two Royal Navy battleships, *Revenge* and *Nelson*. Aboard the *Revenge* was the Polish commander-in-chief and prime minister, General Wladyslaw Sikorski, on his first visit to the United States.

This account, abbreviated as it is, and monotonous as it could easily become, gives a fair account of the work of the Polish warships, which paralleled the efforts of the overwhelming majority of the vessels of the Royal Navy. It was tiring, dangerous and boring, yet vital. The danger was from the sea more than from the enemy, who was seldom seen and, even more seldom, engaged in battle, except for the activity of the German Luftwaffe.

A major break in this kind of escorting activity was the fortune of *Piorun* (CO Kdr. por. E. Plawski), which left the Clyde on May 22, 1941, with the Royal Navy's Seventh Destroyer Flotilla. On May 25, the destroyers received orders to join the main body of the Home Fleet, which was tracking the German battleship *Bismarck. Piorun* became an integral part of Captain Vian's Fourth Destroyer Flotilla. The story of the pursuit and the sinking of the *Bismarck* is a story worth telling and has been well told.[3] The German colossus, in company with the heavy cruiser *Prinz Eugene*, had already sunk the pride of the Home Fleet, HMS *Hood*, and had managed to escape into the northern waters. Unbeknownst to the British Admiralty, the *Bismarck* had also been hit by the artillery of the British battleship, HMS *Prince of Wales*, and was a damaged ship, with an inadequate reserve of bunker oil. Vian's destroyers met the carrier *Ark Royal*, which was accompanied by the cruiser *Sheffield,* and proceeded to take part in the hunt. The role of the British cruiser was vital. It facilitated both the air torpedo attack and the destroyer attack.

The *Bismarck* was sighted by the *Piorun*, on the port side att 2237, May 25, 1941, just after the last shadowing plane returned to the *Ark Royal*. The destroyer flotilla was ordered to take up stat shadowing; at 2242 *Bismarck* opened heavy fire on *Piorun*, who made a spirited reply of firing three salvoes as a salute to Poland, before turning away under smoke cover. The visibility was so bad during the night because of squalls that when the Swordfish torpedo planes from the *Ark Royal* carried out their attack, they mistook the Royal Navy cruiser *Sheffield* for the enemy on their first sortie, but luckily missed!

Piorun's part in the night action was acknowledged in the official Admiralty report, which described the torpedo attack by the Fourth Destroyer Flotilla commanded by Captain Vian:

> The Commanding Officer of the Piorun had not worked with the Fourth Destroyer before and he therefore decided to wait until the last to deliver his attack, as he did not wish to interfere with the flotilla and was not conversant with their methods. He had drawn *Bismarck*'s fire for an hour during the period of dusk hoping that this would assist the other destroyers to get in their attack but after dark he retired to a distance of some 6 to 8 nautical miles to wait for them to finish. He had not succeeded in regaining touch when at 05.00 he was ordered by the Captain (D) Fourth Destroyer Flotilla, to proceed to Plymouth to fuel if not in contact with the enemy. The Captain (D) Fourth Destroyer Flotilla, knew that Commander Plawski, would certainly attack the enemy as soon as he could find him. Conditions as light came would not be easy and the Captain (D) was concerned lest a valuable ship and a fine crew be lost without need. The Piorun continued the search until 0600 and left an hour later.
>
> The conduct of the night operations by these five destroyers under Captain (D) Fourth Destroyer Flotilla was a model of its kind. In heavy weather frequently under fire, they hung on their prey with utmost determination, hit her with torpedoes and delivered her to me next morning without suffering damage, other than splinters, to any of their ships.[4]

Piorun returned to its home base at Greenock on the Clyde on May 30. Poland gained marvellous public media exposure and even some adulation. The famous *London Illustrated News* carried a feature, showing various facets of shipboard life on the *Piorun*, with a grinning Plawski, captioned "Poland's Navy in the Vanguard. Piorun finds the Bismarck." (June 1941). Plawski received the British Distinguished Service Cross for his part in the chase.

Piorun resumed convoying work, often being accompanied by the *Garland*. This frequently involved the escorting of fast liners, converted to troopships, which were on their way around the Cape of Good Hope, to reinforce British forces in the Middle East.

After a long and basic overhaul, *Blyskawica* (CO Kdr. ppor. Francki) resumed combat operations in the western approaches on December 2, 1941.

PUBLIC RELATIONS SUCCESSES

The first half of the year 1941 was the height of Polish political fortunes. Polish fighter squadrons had won acclaim in the Battle of Britain and were now grouped in three all Polish wings. The Polish Carpathian Brigade was earning glory in the defense of Tobruk as the *"rats of Tobruk."* These Polish contributions to Allied military endeavors, whether on land in the siege of Tobruk, in the air over Britain, or in the Battle of the Atlantic, had generated a feeling of sympathy among the British.

The Polish military were visited by many prominent personalities. His Majesty, King George VI, and Queen Elizabeth visited the Polish forces in Scotland as well as the Polish Air Force squadrons and naval establishments. Among the latter was a prominent visit to the Polish Naval Officers' Academy. Churchill visited the Poles, though he did not mention this when writing his memoirs. One of the more interesting commentaries from that time was the statement by Dalton, the first Minister of Economic Warfare, who wrote in his memoirs about his speech in December 1940, to the units of the Polish First Corps guarding the Scottish coast, "I tell them that on the day of victory Poland, as the first nation to stand up to Hitler, while others have been grovelling on their bellies, should ride in the van of the victory march".[5] Polish negotiations with Benes of the Czechoslovak government in exile for a postwar confederation of the two neighbors, concluded in January 1942, had enhanced the Polish prime minister General Wladyslaw Sikorski's personal prestige in the United Kingdom. In Scotland, with the assistance of the SOE (Special Operations Executive), the Poles created a parachute brigade cadre, whose first major airdrop exercise on August 23, 1941, posited the capture of an airfield in German occupied Poland to receive Polish air units flying from the United Kingdom.[6] The success of the first courier flight in November 1941, from the United Kingdom to Poland,[7] contributed to a sense of optimism and growing confidence among the Poles in the United Kingdom.

Britain had survived, and the outcome of the war would be an Allied victory. This esteem was capped by two events. Towards the end of 1941, two senior Polish officers, Major General Stanislaw Ujejski, the Inspector General of the Polish Air Force, and Kontr-Admiral Jerzy Swirski, the Commandant of the Polish Navy, were both awarded the prestigious British Order of the Bath, Military Class. This was in recognition of the excellence of the work of the two Polish services.

On Poland's national holiday, the third of May, the anniversary of the signing of Poland's historic progressive constitution, Churchill gave this eloquent speech to the Polish nation over the BBC:

> Tonight I am speaking to the Polish people all over the world. This is the hundred-and-fiftieth anniversary of the adoption by your Parliament of the Constitution.
>
> You are right to keep this day as a national holiday, because your Constitution of 1791 was a pattern, when it was framed, of enlightened political thought. Your neighbours in those bygone days saw in the adoption of this system the beginning of the regeneration of Poland. They hastened to perpetrate the partition of your country before the Polish nation could consolidate its position.
>
> The same tragedy, the same crime was repeated in 1939. The Germans became alarmed at the success achieved by the Polish nation in setting its house in order. They saw that their aggressive designs would be thwarted by the growth of a strong, independent

Polish State. At the time of the brutal German attack in September, 1939, your country had in the face of tremendous difficulties achieved notable progress during the twenty years of its revived national existence.

To complete this work of national reconstruction, you needed, and you hoped for, a similar period of peaceful development. When the call came, Poland did not hesitate. She did not hesitate to risk all the national progress she had made rather than compromise her national honour; and she showed in the spontaneous response of her sons and daughters that spirit of national unity and of self-sacrifice which has maintained her among the great nations of Europe through all her many trials and tribulations.

I know from talks I have had with Poles now in this country how magnificently the mass of the Polish nation answered the appeal to duty in the hour of need. I have been deeply moved by what I have heard of the inhabitants of Warsaw during the three weeks of the siege, and their continued strenuous resistance to the alien oppressor who now occupies their city. We in this country who are conscious that our strength is built on the broad masses of the British nation appreciate and admire the Polish nation for its noble attitude since the outbreak of the war. Mainly for geographical reasons, personal contacts between our two peoples have been restricted in the past; and fighting as we are at two ends of Europe against our common foe, this war has not yet provided an opportunity for personal contacts on any large scale between you and my own countrymen. The fortunes of war have, however, brought to these shores your President, your Government and many thousands of brave Polish soldiers, airmen, sailors and merchant seamen. Their bearing has won them universal admiration in this country and cast further lustre, if that were possible, upon the proud, heroic traditions of Poland. It has been my privilege to come to know your Prime Minister and Commander-in-Chief, General Sikorski, whose leadership, energy, and unfaltering confidence are a source of great encouragement to all who meet him. I have visited your soldiers in Scotland while they were waiting to repel the invader, and while they were longing in their hearts above all to carry back the flag of freedom to their fellow countrymen at home. I have seen your pilots, who have by their prowess played a glorious part in the repulse of the German air hordes. Meanwhile, your sailors have been earning the respect and high regard of their comrades in the Royal Navy and Merchant Marine, with whom they are sharing the task of maintaining those contacts with America and with the outside world through which will come the liberation of your country. The presence here of your Government and armed forces has enabled us to get to know each other better, and to build a foundation for Anglo-Polish relations after our common victory and the restoration of your freedom.

Our thoughts go out tonight not only to those valiant exiled Poles whom we have learned to like and respect in the British islands and who stand armed in the ranks of the armies of liberation, but even more to those who are gripped at home in the merciless oppression of the Hun.

All over Europe, races and States whose culture and history made them a part of the general life of Christendom in centuries when the Prussians were no better than a barbarous tribe, and the German Empire no more than an agglomeration of pumpernickel principalities, are now prostrate under the dark, cruel yoke of Hitler and his Nazi gang. Every week his firing parties are busy in a dozen lands. Monday he shoots Dutchmen; Tuesday Norwegians; Wednesday, French or Belgians stand against the wall; Thursday it is the Czeches who must suffer. And now there are the Serbs and the Greeks to fill his repulsive bill of executions. But always, all the days, there are the Poles. The atrocities committed by Hitler upon the Poles, the ravaging of their country, the scattering of their man-power, exceed in severity and in scale the villianies perpetrated by Hitler in any other conquered land.

It is to you Poles, in Poland, who bear the full brunt of the Nazi oppression—at once pitiless and venal—that the hearts of the British and American Democracies go out in a full and generous tide. We send you our message of hope and encouragement tonight, knowing that the Poles will never despair, and that the soul of Poland will remain unconquerable.

This war against the mechanised barbarians, who, slave-hearted themselves, are fitted to only to carry their curse to others—this war will be long and hard. But the end is sure; the end will reward all toil, all disappointments, all suffering in those who faithfully serve the cause of European and world freedom. A day will dawn, perhaps sooner than we now have a right to hope, when the insane attempt to found a Prussian domination on racial hatred, on the armoured vehicle, on the secret police, on the alien overseer, and on the still more filthy Quislings, will pass like a monstrous dream. And in that morning of hope and freedom, not only the embattled and at last well-armed Democracies, but all that is noble and fearless in the New World as well as in the Old, will salute the rise of Poland to be a nation once again.[8]

This was a formal salute to the Polish people from the leader of the Allied coalition. But there were many informal and even more moving gestures of sympathy to the Poles. Polish naval officer cadets (midshipmen), were often seconded to British warships. S.T. Olszowski describes his experiences on May 3rd, 1941 while aboard HMS *King George V.* He and the other Polish cadets from all the other ships at Scapa flow were personally invited by Admiral J. Tovey to join him for a glass of wine. They also had the opportunity to listen to the BBC carry the Churchill speech to the Polish nation. Admiral Tovey also ordered all ships of the Home Fleet at Scapa Flow to fly flags to honor the Polish ally.

The Polish Naval Academy commissioned its first crop of young officers in exile, and the Polish services initiated their own Staff College, a continuation of the prestigious Warsaw-based *Wyzsza Szkola Wojskowa*.

CULTURAL AND ACADEMIC INITIATIVES

It was already common knowledge, in early 1941, that the Germans had closed all Polish Universities, were destroying or removing Polish libraries and museum artifacts with an articulated goal of eradicating all Polish culture and all vestiges of Polish civilization. To begin building for the future and to counteract the German policy, the Polish Government undertook a number of initiatives.

The first, and most practical, with great help from the British and considerable assistance from the Polish-American community, was the creation of a Polish Medical School and the Ignacy Paderewski Hospital both in Edinburgh. The British named it the Polish Faculty of Medicine at Edinburgh.

A Polish School of Architecture at Liverpool University followed and the third was Polish Faculty of Law at Oxford University. Finally, a Polish University College in London was also created. A major library, still in existence in London, was also formed. Many newspapers, representing most of the political parties, were also started.

GERMANY ATTACKS THE SOVIET UNION

On June 22, 1941, the whole dynamic of the war was changed when Germany attacked the Soviet Union. Suddenly one of Poland's two enemies became an overnight ally of Britain. The attack had in fact been predicted by Polish intelligence services and the information was passed on to the British, who in turn warned Stalin.

The British were ecstatic, seeing in this a near miracle. The futility of all previous policies to have Germany face a war on two fronts, was created for them by Hitler himself. But the situation of their first ally and their newfound ally, demanded swift diplomatic action. The British brokered an agreement between the Polish government in London and the Soviets.[9] This agreement failed to protect the integrity of Poland's pre–1939 borders, since the Soviets would agree only to stipulate that the Molotov-Ribbentrop Agreement of August 1939, which had partitioned Poland, was null and void. The Soviet government continued to insist that the referendum, held in early 1940 under their administration of terror, was the legal grounds for the incorporation of the Polish eastern territories into the Soviet Union. This referendum had the classic Soviet 99 percent turnout: all voters enthusiastically supported the incorporation.

There was one immediate benefit from this development, namely the release of many thousands of Polish military and civilians who had been deported in inhuman conditions to work in the cold hell of Siberia. These men, women, and even children of whom many were orphans, finally wound their way to the British-controlled Middle East. The men, and thousands of women, formed the famous Polish 2 Army Corps that, under the command of General Anders, fought its way up the Italian peninsula as part of the British 8th Army, and won everlasting fame in the storming of Monte Cassino in 1944.

This release of prisoners also resulted in a small infusion of men (and ultimately of women) for the Polish navy. These were primarily volunteers but there were also some officers (though few in number) and sailors from the Pripet Riverine Flotilla, captured in 1939 by the Russians. After the war, Churchill wrote:

> The British Government were in a dilemma from the beginning. We had gone to war with Germany as the direct result of our guarantee to Poland. We had a strong obligation to support the interest of our first ally. At this stage in the struggle we could not admit the legality of the Russian occupation of Polish territory in 1939. In this summer of 1941, less than two weeks after the appearance of Russia on our side in the struggle against Germany, we could not force our new and sorely threatened ally to abandon, even on paper, regions on her frontiers which she had regarded for generations as vital to her security. There was no way out.[10]

Polish fortunes ebbed.

JAPANESE ATTACK ON PEARL HARBOR BRINGS THE USA INTO THE WESTERN COALITION

The Japanese naval air attack on Pearl Harbor on December 7, 1941, brought the United States into the war and led to the bizarre declaration of war by Hitler on the United States. Hitler had solved Roosevelt's predicament. The isolationists and pacifists, and the small core of pro-German sympathizers in the United States, were silenced. The miniscule American communist party, which had actively opposed all aid to Britain, but had changed its policy after the German attack on the Soviets, was now in the forefront of patriotic groupings.

The entry of the United States in the war only increased the tonnage of shipping that had to be escorted. In addition to the food, war matériel, oil, and munitions that were being brought over from the New World to the embattled island of Britain, there was now an increasing number of American military who were being shipped to Africa and the United Kingdom. The Americans would eventually invade North Africa and participate in the invasion of Italy and, finally, of France—both in Normandy and shortly thereafter in the south of France.

NOTES

1. Winston S. Churchill, *Their Finest Hour*, op.cit. p. 598.
2. The Polish Air Force in 1941 had reached its wartime maximum strength. It consisted of four bomber and eight fighter squadrons, and one Army Co-operation attached to the Polish First Army Corps. The Polish First Army Corps numbered close to twenty-five thousand men and was responsible for the defense of much of the Scottish shore north of Edinburgh. Its primary component was the Armored Division in process of training. There were also a number of cadre units, one of which became the Polish Parachute Brigade. There was a Polish Infantry Brigade (the Carpathian) which was fighting in North Africa as part of the British 8th Army.
3. Russell Grenfell, *The Bismarck Episode*, NY, 1949; and Ludovic Kennedy, *The Chase and Sinking of the Battleship Bismarck*, New York, 1974.

4. PRO ADM 199/1187. It turned out later that there had been no torpedo hits. Captain Vian commanded the following Royal Navy Tribal-class destroyers: *Cossack, Sikh, Zulu, Maori* and of course the Polish (Javelin class) *Piorun.*

5. Ben Pimlott, ed. *The Second World War Diary of Hugh Dalton,* London, 1986, p. 133.

6. The SOE was formally created in the weeks after Dunkirk with the famous enjoinder by Churchill, "*set Europe ablaze*", but was preceded by two groups dedicated to fomenting psychological and material sabotage, MI 6 working for the Foreign Office, and MI R working for the War Office. (P.R.O. HS 4/155 and Polish Archives, London LOT AV II/1a and LOT AV II/1b.) For a general history of the SOE see M.R.D. Foot, *SOE: The Special Operations Executive, 1940–1946,* University Publications of America, 1984. In the early formative years as Foot wrote, "the twigs of early resistance were still too damp outside of Poland, which the S.O.E. could hardly reach, to do more than smolder." p. 30; see also, David Stafford, *Britain and European Resistance, 1940–1945: A Survey of the Special Operations Executive with Documents* (University of Toronto Press, 1983). Peter Wilkinson and Joan Bright Astley, *Gubbins and SOE,* London, 1993. Jozef Garlinski, *Poland, SOE and the Allies,* London, 1969. Also Michael Alfred Peszke, *Battle for Warsaw, 1944,* Boulder, CO, 1995.

7. Robert Jackson, *The Secret Squadrons: Special Duty Units of the R.A.F. and U.S.A.A.F. in the Second World War,* London, 1983.

8. This speech is cited in *The Unrelenting Struggle: War Speeches by the Right Hon. Winston S. Churchill, C.H., M.P.,* Boston, 1942.

9. For a detailed analysis of the July 30, 1941 Agreement, see Anna M. Cienciala, "General Sikorski and the Conclusion of the Polish-Soviet Agreement of July 30, 1941: A Reassessment," *The Polish Review* 1996; XLI: 401–434.

10. Winston S. Churchill, *The Grand Alliance, op.cit.* p. 378; George Kacewicz, *Great Britain, the Soviet Union and the Polish Government in Exile, 1939–1945,* The Hague, 1979; and Hanson Baldwin, *The Crucial Years, 1939–1941,* New York, 1976.

CHAPTER VII
THE MEDITERRANEAN, 1941–1942

THE IMPORTANCE OF THE MEDITERRANEAN

That Polish warships fought in the Baltic, the North Sea, the Irish Sea and the Atlantic made logical sense in view of where Polish warships were based at the beginning of the war, the ensuing Polish-British naval agreements, and the obvious Polish geopolitical interests. But many Polish surface ships and submarines also fought in the Mediterranean. Much of the European war was conducted in the Mediterranean region. This was partly a function of the Italian and German thrust to capture the Suez Canal, penetrate the Middle East, join up with the pro-German nationalistic movements in countries like Iraq and, finally, to link up with the German offensive in the Caucusus. If this German strategy had succeeded, then the whole future of the war might have turned out differently, since it would have placed the richest oil fields of the world in German control and, thus, deprived the allies of their oil.[1]

It was a very close call. In April 1941, pro-Axis forces staged a coup in Iraq and the Vichy French in Syria, with significant land and air assets, facilitated the move of German air transport to Iraq. Much has been written about the disasters suffered by the British, both in Greece and soon afterward in Malaya and Singapore. Too little is known of the tenacity with which the British managed to keep control of the Mediterranean, in spite of being outnumbered on the sea by the Italians, and in the air by the combined air forces of the Italians and Germans. Most of this credit has to go to the tradition and spirit of the Royal Navy officers and other ranks who refused to accept the obvious, that they were beaten. In addition, they were superbly commanded by Admiral Andrew Browne Cunningham also known as ABC, who later succeeded Sir Dudley Pound as First Sea Lord and received a highly deserved peerage.[2]

93

The soft underbelly of Europe was a tantalizing strategic goal for Churchill and this was also strongly endorsed by the Poles, who saw the Balkans as not only the quickest and most direct route to Poland, but also the only strategic plan that offered any hope of liberating at least part of Poland by Western allies, rather than Soviet forces. Churchill was also obsessed with the idea of bringing Turkey into the Allied coalition and expanded much effort in the Aegean Sea towards that goal. Turkey remained neutral—but depending on the tides of fortune of the belligerents—bent its neutrality like all neutrals to stay in the good graces of the possible winner.

The Americans objected to this strategy, relentlessly argued for, and, finally, prevailed in their idea of an offensive at the most direct route against Germany, namely through France. But the concept of secondary fronts was accepted; the invasion of North Africa, followed by an invasion of Italy, was planned and executed. The Allied success in North Africa led the Vichy French forces to changing sides, while the invasion of Italy led to the overthrow of Mussolini and, shortly thereafter, the capitulation of the Italian forces.

MALTA

Right in the middle of the landlocked Mediterranean, nearly equidistant between the British stronghold of Gibraltar and the British bases in Egypt (Alexandria) and Lebanon (Beirut)—and a mere forty miles from Italy—lies the island of Malta, now independent, but then a British Crown Colony and peacetime home of the famous British Mediterranean Fleet.

Malta defied attacks and sieges through history, the most famous being the victory of the Order of the Knight Hospitallers of Saint John under the command of its Grand Master, La Vallete (after whom the capital of the island is named), over the Turks. This was also the high watermark of the last Moslem effort to conquer the Western world. Many years later Malta came under French rule and, in turn, was captured by the British during the Napoleonic wars.

Malta was never successfully used as a staging point for attacks against the Italian mainland, but it seems that the Axis Powers never fully appreciated the significance of this bastion, lying athwart their main lines of communication between Italy and North Africa. The pounding that the island endured is a matter of historical record as are the losses endured by the British in supplying the island. Malta was so short of supplies that two British minelaying submarines, *Cachalot* and *Rorqual* were modified to bring in emergency supplies.[3]

Each convoy to Malta had to run the gauntlet of enemy planes, which were based very close by in southern Italy and of the Italian fleet, which had a large number of modern submarines. This effectively checkmated many attempts to push through convoys with supplies. The large and modern Italian surface fleet also posed a potential threat to the British.

The two defeats inflicted on the Italian fleet by the British on November 11, 1940, at Taranto and on March 28, 1941, off Cape Matapan cooled the ardor of the Italians, who were also handicapped by shortages of bunker oil. The Royal Navy's Fleet Air Arm attack on the Italian fleet in the port of Taranto, launched from the carrier HMS *Illustrious,* was the first ever such operation and preceded the more famous Japanese attack on Pearl Harbor.[4]

Yet, in the circumstances, each Malta-bound convoy was still a risk and had to be heavily protected; each one suffered serious losses, primarily from air attacks.

FIRST POLISH NAVAL OPERATIONS IN THE MEDITERRANEAN

The first Polish warship to serve in the Mediterranean was the *Garland*, which was, in fact commissioned by Poles at Malta in 1940. It was transferred to the Western Approaches in late 1940, and it was 1942 before Polish surface warships sailed into the Mediterranean. They were not based in the Mediterranean but participated in Allied operations and interventions, initially to succor Malta and, subsequently, in the invasion of North Africa and eventually in convoy duty. Once these operations were accomplished, the Allied warships (including, of course, the Poles), sailed back to Gibraltar, or even to the United Kingdom where the convoys originated.

In the later stages of the war, during the invasion of Italy, and particularly in the Dodecanese operations, Polish surface warships operated in the Mediterranean for extended periods of time and were based in British ports of Beirut or Alexandria.

The main effort of the Polish warships was in the Atlantic and the Western Approaches, but Polish surface ships frequently ventured into the Mediterranean as part of Allied operations. In 1941, *Garland* took part in the Spitzbergen operation in the Arctic Ocean, while *Piorun* escorted the British battleship *HMS Prince of Wales* during the attempt to break the Italian blockade of Malta. On September 21, the task force was reinforced by the battleship *HMS Rodney* and two more cruisers and six destroyers. After departing Gibraltar on September 26, 1941, the task force was further strengthened by Force H, consisting of the battleship *HMS Nelson* and carrier *HMS Ark Royal.*

Piorun was Senior Officer of the escort for the *Nelson,* and was paired off with the Dutch *Isaac Sveers. Garland* had rejoined the *Piorun* as part of the escort for the *Rodney, Prince of Wales* and *Ark Royal,* formed as Force X, whose task was to screen the convoy from the Italian surface ships which, however, avoided a direct engagement.

The congregation of such an armada and its departure could not escape the prying eyes of German spies and sympathizers both in Spain and North Africa. The air attacks commenced on September 27, and were pressed home repeatedly.

The convoy reached Malta on September 28, but *HMS Nelson* suffered damage from enemy air attacks and departed back to Gibraltar escorted by *ORP Piorun* and *ORP Garland* plus a Royal Navy destroyer.

On September 30, the Polish ships departed for the Clyde and home, meeting a homebound convoy which included the Polish liner, SS *Sobieski.* After this short but bloody venture into the sunny Mediterranean, the Polish ships operated between Greenock and Nova Scotia.

THE POLISH FELUCCAS

The capitulation of France in June, 1940, placed the Polish Government and its accredited consular and embassy agencies and officials in Vichy France in a very ambiguous position. While General Sikorski made extensive efforts to collaborate with the London-based Free French Committee of General Charles de Gaulle, he also made an effort not to sever ties with the French Government of Marshal Pétain. (It needs to be pointed out that the Government of the United States continued to have diplomatic relations with Vichy France until 1943.)

By October 1940, the Germans had prevailed on the French to close all Polish consulates, which often continued to operate in a very clandestine fashion with active assistance of Polonophile Frenchmen.

The sudden collapse of France also placed the British in a quandary, since they had few intelligence assets in what had once been their closest ally. The Poles now placed their own very active and well-established intelligence network at British disposal, initiating a very warm collaboration with the British Special Operations Executive or SOE.[5]

There were also many thousands of Poles stranded in France. They had been based in many different places, and had either not heard Sikorski's radio appeal or had no means of making their way expeditiously to the ports before the evacuation was concluded. The Polish government, through its agencies in France, and its consular offices in Spain and Portugal, did all they could to facilitate the evacuation of these men, in order to save them from potential German incarceration, as well as to add to the manpower of the Polish forces in the United Kingdom. Some of these men had been able to get to French North Africa where they were now stranded.

In March 1941, a young Polish navy officer, Marian Kadulski was seconded to Gibraltar to organize a clandestine sea evacuation of these men, both from Metropolitan France and form its North African territories. Kadulski already had a very distinguished career in the Polish Navy and, prior to the war, had written in professional journals advocating the development of a large fleet of small torpedo boats. He had been aboard the *Blyskawica* in the Norwegian campaign and had carried out a number of assignments at the Polish naval attaché offices in Copenhagen and Antwerp. He was obviously judged to be an experienced and skilled officer, familiar with secret duties.

Within a very short time, he purchased a number of small feluccas which began to sail the Mediterranean disguised as fishing vessels, but always returning with a number of Polish personnel. It was inevitable that he would begin to be involved with an intelligence agency, Agency Africa, run by a Polish officer by the name of Slowikowski.[6]

The British SOE also began to show an interest since, amazing as it may sound, they had no similar operation in the Mediterranean. In 1941, Captain F.H. Slocum, who carried the title of Deputy Director Operations Division, (Irregular) or DDOD(I) brought in a second Polish naval officer, Jan Buchowski, to Gibraltar to duplicate the Polish achievement, there for the SOE. Thus, officially, Kadulski worked for the Polish Navy, delegated to the Polish Gibraltar Mission; while Buchowski worked for the Polish Navy being delegated to the British SOE.[7]

These distinct roles were not always clear, and the degree of collaboration between the Poles and British in these early years was exemplary. As the British learned from the Poles, they created their Coastal Watch Flotilla. With time they began to prevent the Poles from carrying out many purely Polish missions. Kadulski, who had made tentative plans to pick up Poles in Spain, was categorically forbidden because the British Foreign Office did not wish to offend General Franco. Also with time, the most desirable locations in southern France were restricted for SOE pick up exclusively. The British were clearly playing the "great game" of getting their agents in and out of France and, of working to persuade Vichy French officials to change sides.

It is story stranger than fiction. In a distant sea, the Poles developed a buccaneer operation before the British and French, who had centuries of experience of these waters. The names of the Polish feluccas were *Seawolf* and *Dogfish*. Before going back "home" to Britain, two of the Polish officers (Kpt. mar Marian Kadulski and por.mar Jan Buchowski), received the high British decorations: the Distinguished Service Order and Por. mar. Maciej Michalkiewicz was the recipient of the Distinguished Service Cross. Nearly five hundred Polish personnel were smuggled out to Gibraltar and then moved to Britain.

THE ORP *SOKOL*

In late 1940, after the loss of *Orzel* the Polish Navy only had one submarine in service, the *Wilk,* which due to numerous mechanical problems was not operational, and was relegated to a training role, much to the despair of her CO Kdr. por. Boguslaw Krawczyk. The morale of the crew also left much to be desired. Karnicki, the second in command, writes in his memoirs, *Marynarski Worek Wspomnien,* that he made a trip to London to see the Polish Navy Commandant, Swirski, to plead the case that a request be made to the British for a small British U-class boat. Karnicki argued that there were enough trained submarine personnel to crew the *Wilk* and also provide for the complement of a U-class submarine, which only required a crew of thirty.

In fact, the celebrated *Sokol* (Falcon) whose crew was recruited mainly from the *Wilk*, had as its crest a bucolic sheep and not a raptor. This was from the old Polish expression that the *Wilk* (Wolf) would be satisfied and the sheep whole; a reflection of the unhappiness of the *Wilk's* CO Krawczyk, that many of his crew would be siphoned off to a new boat and that he would not be able to achieve any kind of operational status.

The reality probably was, as Karnicki also mentions, that the British were launching a new sub for which they lacked a crew, due to their own heavy personnel losses and ship expansion program. Polish requests were graciously granted. On January 19, 1941, therefore, the Polish flag was raised on the boat previously named HMS *Urchin,* and now renamed ORP *Sokol.* The Poles and the British both went out of their way to make this a big publicity occasion, and General Wladyslaw Sikorski, the Polish Prime Minister and Commander-in-Chief, was in attendance as well as Commandant Jerzy Swirski, who on that day was promoted to Vice-Admiral. The British were represented by the First Sea Lord, Admiral of the fleet Sir Dudley P. R. Pound. Kpt. mar. B. Karnicki took over command of this boat and was to be her skipper for the next year.

After a two-month work up done at Holy Loch with the Seventh Submarine Flotilla, and a short stint at Dundee with the Ninth, *Sokol*, was seconded to the British Fifth Submarine Flotilla in Portsmouth, whose task was to interdict German blockade runners, sailing from the neutral South American countries to the German-controlled ports of South France. The first—and far from uneventful patrol—took place on March 26, 1941, when *Sokol* was detected by the Germans, depth-charged, and suffered damage resulting in seepage into the hull which required extensive repairs. After repairs were done, *Sokol* continued these patrols, usually of twenty days in extent, varying the mission of shipping interdiction with picketing the French ports where the German battleships, the *Gneisenau* and the *Scharnhorst*, were docked but presumed to be on the point of leaving for German ports. (The history of this episode is narrated in Chapter VIII.)

In September 1941, *Sokol* was seconded to the Tenth Submarine Flotilla based in Valetta, Malta. The Royal Navy had two submarine flotillas in the Mediterranean: one based in Malta consisting of the small U-class boats and the other based in Gibraltar, utilizing the large S and T-class submarines. On its way from Gibraltar to Malta, *Sokol* was part of the large operation Halbard, whose task was to bring supplies to Malta. This operation also included the Polish destroyers, *Garland* and *Piorun*.

Sokol was now to enter her most glorious period. Operating out of Malta, its patrols took place in the vicinity of the Italian port of Naples and the west coast of southern Italy. Nine patrols were uneventful, but on her tenth, on October 28, *Sokol* sank an Italian auxiliary cruiser, *Città di Palermo*. *Sokol* then endured the inevitable punishment of a depth-charge attack, resumed her patrolling near Capri, and after a flawed torpedo attack, surfaced and sank another enemy transport by gunfire.

On November 3, 1941, after returning to home base in Malta, *Sokol* was inspected by General Wladyslaw Sikorski, who was on his way to the Soviet Union to finalize the arrangements for the formation of a Polish army in the Soviet Union. General Sikorski decorated the Polish skipper, Karnicki, with the order of Virtuti Militari, and presented the Polish submarine with a *Jolly Roger* on which the exploits of the boat would from now on be proclaimed.

After his brief visit with the Polish sailors, General Sikorski flew into beleaguered Tobruk and visited the Polish Carpathian

Brigade, which was earning fame, together with the Australian "diggers," as the "rats of Tobruk."

Sokol's eleventh patrol was thus described in the official report by Captain (S) Tenth Submarine Flotilla. This report is given in detail, since it is a firsthand and objective account by a British senior officer and also describes the manner in which the submarines operated in this region:

ORP *Sokol*, Patrol Report No. 5. 13th–27th November, 1941.

1. The attached patrol report No. 5 *Sokol*, Lt. Cdr. B. Karnicki, together with my remarks is forwarded herewith.

2. *Sokol* sailed from Malta on 13 November for the south eastern billet in a line of four submarines disposed south westward of Cephalonia and after experiencing dirty weather, arrived in position on the evening of the 15th. An attempt to communicate by SS/T with *Urge*, next in line failed.

3. At 0300 hours of 17th Captain S 1731B/16 was received ordering *Sokol* to 36 01 N and 13 E. and the submarine was in position by 0800 hours that day, but the position was counterdemanded at 1600 hours on 18th when *Sokol* received orders to proceed to Navarino, arriving off that port at dawn on the 19th.

4. Captain (S) 1113B/18 had informed *Sokol* that three important supply ships and possibly their escorts were taking refuge in Navarino and that so far as was known, no mines, or obstruction had been laid; he should therefore use his discretion with regard to attack, having complete liberty of action. Lt. Cdr. Karnicki decided to endeavor to force the entrance and with forethought that he had shown on previous occasions, prepared everything for rapid re-loading, hoping to sink the escort first and the convoy before they could get under way.

5. At 0820/19 when three-quarter miles and 220 degrees from the south point of Pylos, *Sokol* hit bottom when at 35 feet, but a few minutes later was under control, and steady at 43 feet. At 0820 periscope fixes were taken, but two minutes later when at 40 feet *Sokol* encountered and was held by a strong indicator net which immediately fired a charge. The incident is fully reported in the narrative. The explosive charge called two motor boats to the spot and *Sokol* was in this nerve racking predicament for about eight minutes before extricating herself by going astern. Lt. Cdr. Karnicki remarked to me on return to harbour, 'it is a bad thing for any submarine to be caught in any net, but it is a pity for a Polish submarine to be caught in an Italian net before Poland had declared war on Italy'.

6. At 0043 *Sokol* having been clear three or four minutes, came to periscope depth and established that nothing was close and withdrew to the north westward. The defects were: a flooded bi-focal periscope, and inability to receive wireless messages on the main aerial.

7. At 2030 that evening a situation report was made to Captain (S) One. (The reason for this seeming inconsistency is that *Sokol* was operating in the region of Greece, an area primarily—assigned to the British First Submarine Flotilla based in Alexandria.) Throughout the 20th, patrol was maintained to the south and west of the entrances and reconnaissance showed two destroyers, one *Avieri* and one *Spica* class at anchor north of Pylos. It was observed that the larger destroyer was open to attack from the main entrance, and at 1540 three torpedoes were fired, securing two hits on the *Avieri*. The third torpedo had a dangerous gyro failure, circling *Sokol* and was observed to pass across the submarine forward of the periscope, the torpedo engine being clearly heard in the control room. The A.B. gyro relay valves of all *Sokol*'s torpedoes were carefully inspected and cleaned on the 9th November. It therefore appears

that verdigris and coppering of theses valves is not the only cause of gyro failures.

8. At 1543 *Sokol* retired, hearing minor explosions and noises as of a ships sinking and withdrew to the westward reloading. The intention had been to fire torpedoes set very shallow at the Spica class which was open to attack if the torpedoes were fired to pass between Sphakteria and Pylos. However, the offensive or possibly self preservation instinct of the smaller destroyer on seeing its consort blow up at anchor did not allow this. Between 1600 and 1610 seventeen depth charges were dropped apparently inside the harbour and at 1637 this vessel came out of the harbour and during the next hour dropped a further fifty-five charges promiscuously and ineffectively.

9. Since the supply ships were evidently anchored behind land, *Sokol* withdrew to the south west and at 2030 reported his attack and the fact that the main aerial had not been repaired allowing W/T reception. At 2315 that evening, when ten miles and 270 degrees from Cape Sapienza, one destroyer and three merchant vessels were sighted at a range of about 4000 yards steering south westward. The night was dark, and clouds and squalls made visibility variable. Since the opportunity for immediate attack had not occurred, *Sokol* gave chase on a parallel but was slowly losing ground. However, at 2335 a zig by the enemy to the south westward gave *Sokol* an opportunity for a long shot on a broad track. At 2338 three torpedoes were fired, range 6,500 yards, trackangle 125. *Sokol* dived two minutes later to reload. At 2345, seven minutes from the time of firing, two loud explosions occurred at three second intervals followed by other noises lasting two minutes. The torpedoes had been fired at twenty second intervals but it seems that one definite or possible two hits were secured. The depth of water where the attack took place exceeds 1500 fathoms. The running time of seven minutes for a range somewhat in excess of 8000 yards.

10. At 0001/22 *Sokol* surfaced having completed reloading and reported the situation to Captain (S). Visibility closed down and nothing was seen in position of attack but H.E. was heard approaching and *Sokol* dived at 0130 surfacing later to return to patrol off Navarino. The convoy that had been attacked was undoubtedly the remaining destroyer and three supply ships originally at anchor in Navarino Bay. No further incident occurred and with weather continuing rough, *Sokol* returned to Malta arriving at 0800 on the 27th November.

11. This patrol again proved the efficiency and fearless determination with which Lt. Crd. Karnicki commands *Sokol*, and resulted in the certain sinking of a large medium sized supply ship bound for Benghazi. *Sokol* had proved to be a unit of the Tenth Flotilla with an experienced and efficient crew and an outstanding able commander.

Recommendations for Awards are being forwarded under separate cover.

        signed C.M.G. Simpson
        Captain (S)
        Tenth Submarine Flotilla.

Sokol kept adding further battle trophies to its Jolly Roger. Photos of the crew of the Polish boat often show them holding their trophy with the record of gun fights, successful boardings, torpedo attacks, and encounters with anti-submarine nets. Karnicki received the British Distinguished Service Order while his second in command, Kpt. mar. Jerzy Koziolkowski and Por. mar. A. Klopotowski both were awarded the Distinguished Service Cross.

MALTA CLOSE TO COLLAPSE; ALLIED WARSHIPS LEAVE VALLETTA

In the early part of 1942, Malta experienced severe bombing by enemy air forces. Various ruses were attempted to protect the *Sokol* such as placing the boat between old barges, and flooding the tanks so that only the conning tower was above water line. But the air raids continued and the damage accumulated while the local civilian shipyard workers refused to work, claiming mortal danger, and undoubtedly they were correct. The Polish crew attempted to make emergency repairs, but the damage list included the battery packs, one of the two screws, the generators, steering mechanism, and over two hundred fifty hull perforations from shrapnel. It was decided by the British that Valletta was untenable and all ships were to be moved out. On April 17, 1942, *Sokol* left Malta, being one of the last two Allied warships to leave the island, the other being the Royal Navy cruiser, HMS *Penelope,* which was so extensively holed that with typical British humor, she was known as *"Pepperpot".*

Convoys from Alexandria were pushed by the now promoted Admiral Philip Vian, but British losses in destroyers and merchant ships were appalling, and supplies were not getting through.

The British were on the proverbial ropes in the Mediterranean. The British battleship, HMS *Barham*, was torpedoed and sunk by the German *U-331* off Crete in November 1941, and in December 1941 the two remaining battleships (HMS *Warspite* had been sent to North America for major repairs), HMS *Valiant* and HMS *Queen Elizabeth*, were sunk at their moorings by Italian-manned torpedoes, commonly called chariots. The fighter defenses on the island were also depleted. Land-based Spitfires were flown off the decks of British ships, as well as the American carrier USN *Wasp*, to reinforce the fighter defenses. It seemed that Malta was ready to be invaded by the Germans and Italians and that there was nothing to stop them. But the British held out and continued to be a thorn in the enemy's side, and the island was reinforced by a major British task force that ran the gauntlet of enemy air and surface attacks.

On June 4, 1942, the British convoy W.S.-19, consisting of six troop ships and ammunition, left Greenock, bound for Malta. It was escorted by the battleship HMS *Malaya*, two fleet carriers, four cruisers, thirteen destroyers (including ORP *Kujawiak)* and two corvettes. After replenishing oil in Gibraltar, the convoy entered the Med and was immediately attacked by German Ju-88s.

On June 14, at 1112 hours a total of sixty German planes carried out attacks, and one ship was sunk while the cruiser HMS *Liverpool* was damaged. More air attacks followed and the report was received that the Italian surface fleet was on its way. During the first stage of the battle, *Kujawiak* was credited with the shooting down of a number of enemy planes. The destroyer screen attempted to ward off the Italian surface ships but had to retire under a smokescreen. An artillery duel between the two opposing sides now developed as an Allied tanker went up in flames from air attacks. At one point the small escort class *Kujawiak* engaged an Italian cruiser at a range of 13,500 yards. While the British lost three of their warships, the Italian surface ships withdrew. The convoy endured five more air attacks but on June 16, at 0041 entered Valetta, where tragically the Polish destroyer *Kujawiak* hit a mine, exploded, and sunk. Two Royal Navy ships also hit mines and were damaged.

ORP *SOKOL* LEAVES THE MEDITERRANEAN

While Karnicki was on leave, and all Allied warships were leaving Malta, the CO of the *Sokol* was Kpt. mar. J. Koziolkowski. The Polish boat was badly damaged with particular damage to the integrity of the hull. On his way to Gibraltar the CO took the risk of sailing through the minefields on the surface, even though the recommended practice was to traverse a minefield at great depth, because of the hull's vulnerability sustained by enemy bombing.

The distance to Gibraltar of one thousand miles was covered in eleven days. The facilities in Gibraltar were insufficient for the extensive damage that had been sustained and *Sokol* left for the Clyde, arriving on July 9, 1942. In Gibraltar, Karnicki had resumed command and was present for the inspection by General Wladyslaw Anders who was on his way to London for a conference of senior Polish generals, convened by the commander-in-chief, General Sikorski.

Karnicki was not only a brave submariner but also a character of a style that the British appreciated. While most of the Polish Navy officers were highly professional, coming from solid, if not stolid, middle-class backgrounds, Karnicki's family enjoyed higher social status and his father was a general in the Polish Army. Karnicki describes one of these idiosyncratic acts which easily could have been a cause for bad feelings. Bringing his command into the port of Gibraltar, Karnicki was annoyed that the Royal Marines band on the battleship *Malaya* played "God Save the King," but not the Polish national anthem—even though the *Sokol* was a mere hundred meters away and its Polish ensign easily recognized. In addition, the arrival of *Sokol* from Malta, after gallant traversing of enemy minefields was known and appreciated in Gibraltar. Karnicki decided to make a point. While moving his command to make room for a British submarine at the pier, he came within thirty meters of *Malaya* without giving the senior ship and the senior commanding officer any salutation. Karnicki wrote, that from the Polish boat, they could observe that duty officers, etc., were all alert on *Malaya* to reciprocate a salute. But nothing happened. *Malaya* as a senior captained warship would obviously not be the first to salute. Later in the day, at a party for all officers on board the *Malaya*, a senior British officer approached Karnicki and commented that it was a custom in the British Navy for a "junior" warship to first salute the senior ship in port. Karnicki replied that this was also the Polish custom. The Royal Navy officer then enquired politely why in the circumstances, *Sokol* failed to salute the Admiral's flag on *Malaya*? Karnicki replied that the reason was that he was quite sure that he was not seen from the decks of *Malaya*. How was that possible, replied the Royal Navy officer, when you were so close to us? Well, said Karnicki, had you seen us, you would have played the Polish national anthem. There was silence and some consternation among the British officers. Apologies were made and on the following morning at flag raising, the Polish national anthem, Dabrowski's mazurka, *"Jeszcze Polska nie zginela, poki my zyjemy,"* reverberated over Gibraltar's basins.

On arrival in British waters, the Polish submarine was met by the Polish destroyer *Krakowiak* and also by the Wellingtons of the Polish Coastal Command (304) Squadron.

NOTES

1. Michael Howard, *The Mediterranean Strategy in the Second World War,* London, 1968.
2. Andrew B. Cunningham, *A Sailor's Odyssey,* London, 1961.
3. Christopher Shores and Brian Cull, *Malta: The Hurricane Years, 1940–1941,* London, 1994; and Charles Jellison, *Besieged: The World War II Ordeal of Malta, 1940–1942,* Hanover, NH, 1984.
4. Thomas P. Lowry and John W.G. Wellham, *The Attack on Taranto: Blueprint for Pearl Harbor,* New York, 1995.
5. The history of the different clandestine operations carried out by the British SOE in German-occupied Europe is confused by a variety of names often accorded identical operations. This had a purpose during the war, to limit the knowledge to the smallest number of individuals and to confuse the enemy. It now confuses the historian. Much of this work was done in limited collaboration with such various allied services as the Poles, Norwegians, and French. It is probably true to say that only the Poles worked with the British outside of their own national home. Many operations were carried out by the Poles in France and were code named *Angelica, Adjudicate* and *Monica.* SOE files in the British PRO are HS4/136, /217, /221, /222, /226, /230, /236, /237, /238, /298, /315. Also see M.R.D. Foot, *SOE: The Special Operations Executive, 1940–1946,* op. cit. Foot describes the Polish Section EU/P on p. 39.
6. Rygor Slowikowski, *In the Secret Service: The Lightning of the Torch,* London, 1988. This is a play on the word "torch" which was the code name for the Allied invasion of North Africa, to which Slowikowski contributed extensively.
7. Brooks Richards, *Secret Flotillas: Clandestine Sea Lines to France and French North Africa, 1940–1944.* HMSO, London, 1996. Also, Polish Institute M.A.R. A.V. 10/1–10/9.

CHAPTER VIII

ATLANTIC AND ARCTIC OPERATIONS, 1942–1943

POLISH WARSHIPS IN ARCTIC OPERATIONS

The Battle of the Atlantic continued, and in March 1942 alone, the Germans sank 834,169 tons of Allied shipping for the loss of only six of their own vessels. This carnage persisted throughout the year. But a new struggle was about to take place: the Murmansk bound convoys, a term which even in the average person elicits a feeling of anxiety. Unable to accede to Stalin's imperative demands for a second front, the Allies did their best to ease the pressure on their hard pressed ally. Supplying the Soviet Union was certainly one of the steps which could be and which had to be implemented to keep the Soviets fighting.

The focus of active air, surface, and unending underwater struggle moved into the Arctic Sea. The Allies strove to push the supply convoys through Soviet Murmansk, while the Germans deployed in northern Norway challenged them with their long-range planes and major battleships.

Polish warships were now to venture again into northern waters. On December 17, 1941, after being outfitted with Arctic gear, *Krakowiak* (commanded by Kdr. ppor. T. Gorazdowski) sailed to Scapa Flow to join the Royal Navy's Home Fleet (under Commanding Admiral Dalrymple-Hamilton).

Both the Germans and the British needed accurate meteorological information. The task for J Group was to interdict German operations around the Lofoten Islands. It consisted of one cruiser, four Royal Navy Tribal class fleet destroyers, and five Hunt class escort destroyers (two of them Polish) with a supporting group of minesweepers, tankers, and landing craft carrying Commando Group 12 plus a Norwegian contingent. The task force arrived at West Fjord on December 26, and landed troops at Reine and Skofjord.

At this latitude in December there is no daylight, but the whole operation was expeditiously carried out, departing for home on December 28. A number of Germans, who had operated the meteorological weather stations there, were brought back as prisoners. Supplies were left for the Norwegian islanders, but some opted to come with the Allies to the British Isles and join the Free Norwegian Forces.

POLAND AND LEND-LEASE

The American Lend-Lease Act of 1940 enabled Britain and other Allies to purchase war matériel that was manufactured in the United States, which became known as the arsenal of democracy. This act undoubtedly allowed the Allies to win the Second World War. The United Kingdom, which received close to half the total of fifty billion dollars made available by the act, could not have survived without this injection of matériel, and without Britain, the United States could not have beaten Germany.

The Soviet share of ten billion dollars was never acknowledged by the Soviets, nor was sufficient effort made by the Western Allies to force them to live up to the agreement nor to the letter of the Atlantic Charter. But not even the great sacrifice of the Soviet people and the bravery of its soldiers could have allowed the Soviets to go on the offensive without Western material aid; and without the Soviet offensives, the Western Allies could not have successfully invaded Normandy.

The Free French got over three billion dollars. The Poles received a minor allotment of the British share. At war's end, the cost (and thus the Polish debt) of all matériel used by the Polish forces in the west came to seventy-five million pounds sterling, which was written off as part of Lend-Lease.[1]

In 1941, the United States offered the Royal Navy some old S-class submarines. A decision was made that in view of the condition of the *Wilk*, the Poles would receive one of these American boats. Thus, on November 4, 1941, the old *S-25* was named, ORP *Jastrzab* ("Hawk"), and the Polish ensign was hoisted in New London, Connecticut, home of the United States Atlantic Submarine Fleet, then, as it is now, fifty years later. The commanding officer was Kpt. mar. B. Romanowski and the "godparents" were Rear Admiral R. S. Edwards USN, and the daughter of the Polish consul in New York, Miss Helena Strakacz.

After departure from New London, *Jastrzab*, bearing the identification number P-551, arrived in St. John's, Newfoundland, and the crew spent more time working up the boat. While departing New London, *Jastrzab* met the Free French submarine *Surcouf*, the largest submarine of its day, which saluted the Poles with "Bon Voyage." Very soon after that, the French submarine was lost with all its crew to friendly fire, a fate also to be experienced shortly by the Poles. The Poles were followed across the Atlantic by their British-manned sister boat *R-33*.

The feeling among the crew was that the old *Wilk* was in better shape than this "new" addition, which in fact antedated the launching of the *Wilk*. The Atlantic crossing in the winter months was hellish. The powerful and high Atlantic swell, coming from the stern, tossed the boat and covered the conning tower. Romanowski writes in his memoirs, *Torpeda w Celu*, that on the first night's watch he put on a life jacket, and then abandoned the practice, realizing that if swept overboard, there would be no way that he could ever be picked up. Even when submerged, a depth of ninety feet had to be attained before the boat stopped reeling.

On December 1, 1941, *Jastrzab* reached Holy Loch, and was shortly visited by the President of Poland and the Commandant of the Polish Navy. But there was no news of the British boat (*R-33*), and only on December 5 was the British-manned submarine found wrecked on the rocky shore of the Orkneys, having totally missed the Scottish islands on its eastward trip.

The British decided to upgrade the boat which took some weeks, so that the Christmas of 1941, a holiday always so dear to the Poles, was spent in port. But at the wish of Romanowski, *Jastrzab* was moved next to the *Wilk*, now at Campbelltown, relegated to training duties.

After the holidays, *Jastrzab* was ordered to proceed with a Dutch submarine, *O-14*, from the west coast of Scotland to Rosyth on the east, that is on the North Sea. The two submarines were initially part of a convoy which had to traverse a mine-swept channel. The ships ran into a heavy mist, and the whole convoy became disorganized. Finally, after the mist cleared, *Jastrzab* found itself in charge of six merchant ships and proceeded to deliver them to port.

POLISH GENERAL STAFF PLANNING CONFERENCE

In April 1942, General Sikorski called a meeting of the senior Polish generals to London. The agenda was the future structure and disposition of the Polish armed forces which at that time were distributed among the United Kingdom, the Middle East and a major land forces concentration still in Russia. This last group was recruited from the victims of Soviet persecution who had been released.

The most important senior officers were Lt. General Wladyslaw Anders, (GOC of the Polish Army in the Soviet Union), who flew in from the Soviet Union; Lt. General Jozef Zajac (GOC of the Polish Forces, Middle East); Lt. General Marian Kukiel (GOC of the First Polish Army Corps in Scotland); Major General Tadeusz Klimecki (Chief of Staff); Major General Stanislaw Ujejski (Inspector General of the Air Force); and of course, Admiral Jerzy Swirski (Commandant of the Polish Navy). In addition, a number of other senior generals also attended, including Major General Stanislaw Sosabowski (GOC of the Polish Parachute Brigade based in Scotland), and Major General Stanislaw Kopanski (GOC of the Polish Carpathian Division.)

The actual conference took two days and was punctuated by a meeting of Sikorski with Churchill and his advisors. General Anders was outspoken in advancing his conviction that all Polish armed forces, including the air force, should be moved to the Middle East. He sincerely believed that this gave the best chance of playing a significant role in assuring Polish sovereignty. After the experiences of his soldiers in the Soviet Union between 1939 and 1941, Anders also wanted to leave that land. Furthermore, he doubted whether the Soviets would be able to resist the next German summer offensive. On the opposite side were General Kukiel and the Polish Chief of Staff who both argued that all Polish troops should be concentrated in the United Kingdom.

General Ujejski strongly argued the need for more replacements for his bloodied squadrons and concurred that the United Kingdom offered the best location for training them.

Sikorski was still, in principle, committed to having a Polish military presence in the Soviet Union. On May 1, 1942, Sikorski articulated Polish military goals in his instructions to Lt. General Wladyslaw Anders. The most significant excerpt is as follows:

> Our war effort, carried on unceasingly and with increased intensity, has but one aim: Poland, which might be sounder, safer and stronger than the Poland which so resolutely started to fight against the barbarian aggression of our secular enemy.
>
> Which is the shortest way to Poland? From Russia, the Middle East or Great Britain? Nobody can answer this now.[2]

The allocation of fifteen hundred extra personnel to the Air Force and of a thousand to the Navy was pitifully small and inadequate keep the Polish squadrons at strength; or to allow Admiral Swirski to commission two new fleet destroyers that the British had offered. Polish plans were thwarted by both the continued lack of available manpower, by British unwillingness or inability to provide shipping to move Poles from the Middle East, as well as compounded by the reality that, in the spring of 1942, the British had to return the Australian troops from the Middle East, to protect the Australian Commonwealth from the advancing Japanese. The fundamental fact which dictated the ultimate Polish dispositions was British shortage of military personnel in the Middle East.[3]

To help the Poles on their way, the Soviets began to cut down on food rations for the Poles limiting it to about 44,000 portions. This meant in concrete facts that the Polish Army was limited to that number of men. Since in addition to soldiers, there were thousands of women and children who depended on the Polish Army for their survival, the Poles faced starvation.

At the same time, Churchill wrote to Stalin on July 17, 1942:

I am sure it would be in our common interest, Pre-
mier Stalin, to have the three divisions of Poles you so
kindly offered join their compatriots in Palestine.

Churchill went on to conclude:

If we do not get the Poles, we should have to fill
their places by drawing on the preparations now going
forward on a vast scale for the Anglo-American invasion of the continent.[4]

Thus the Polish military plans were decided without any
Polish participation, a precedent for much more serious agreements between the Western powers and Stalin in the future.
The British thus managed to effect a significant increase in
military forces in their own strategic area, while Soviets were
rid of the troublesome Poles and scored propaganda points by
bruiting the odious lie that the Poles did not want to fight the
Germans. This found a very receptive audience among many
Western liberals. Stalin could now work toward forming his
own so-called Polish Army with Russian officers and totally
subservient to his policies.

MURMANSK CONVOY DUTY; ORP *JASTRZAB* VICTIM OF FRIENDLY FIRE

On April 22, 1942, *Jastrzab* left on a mission to protect a Mur-
mansk-bound convoy, PQ-15. The first stop was in the barren
Shetlands; then came the job of covering the southern flank
of the Russian-bound convoy. The mission assigned to Allied
submarines was to act as a screen from German warships
based in occupied Norway. On reaching its assigned sector,
Romanowski admitted that he had considerable problems with
navigation since dead reckoning is difficult at best after days at
sea, but problems were compounded by bad weather, squalls,
and cloud cover which precluded astral bearing or fix and thus
a correction of position.

Diesel motors could only be run on the surface and electric
ones were limited by the endurance of the batteries, which was

about twelve hours. To recharge the batteries required coming to the surface, and this was tantamount with terrible punishment from the heavy swells. On May 2, the watch officer reported a sonar (called Asdic by the British) contact, and a periscope observation showed an old American four-stack destroyer and a small trawler. It appeared they were in search mode, bearing directly toward the submerged Polish boat at full speed. This was a sight to terrify even the bravest. It was inevitable that a depth-charge attack from the friendly ships would ensue. Romanowski describes the noise like a train rolling over the submerged boat, then the explosions of the depth charges and instantaneous popping of rivets, breaking of pipes, and jets of water pouring through the hull. The Polish commanding officer decided to stay submerged until the second ship dropped its charges, and then ordered the boat to surface before the first ship turned around to continue the attack.

Meanwhile, the Polish CO ordered full speed to avoid the expected attack, and the first part of the plan worked since the depth charges exploded far away. Immediately, the order to surface was given and the signaller with his aldis lamp was to be the first on deck. As soon as the boat surfaced, the signaller opened the hatch and as he got on the bridge fell dead from friendly machine-gun fire. The commanding officer was also hit but remained alert and saw the Polish submarine surrounded on two sides by Allied warships firing their light anti-aircraft artillery at close range. Romanowski also realized that the aim of the destroyer was to ram his boat, and gave an order for all his crew to abandon ship. Recognition flares were lit, and attempts made to communicate by aldis. The Polish crew began to appear on deck using all available hatches, and the Polish flag was displayed. The firing ceased and a silence ensued except for the groans of the wounded sailors. The destroyer crept closer to the *Jastrzab* and a voice hailed the Poles, "Are you German?"

"I am a Polish submarine, you bloody fool, can't you see P-551?"

"What can we do to help?"

"Send a doctor and engineers."

But it was too late; the inside of the boat was full of chlorine gas, and the crew could not go back. A launch from one of the Allied warships brought an engineer who decided that *Jastrzab* could not be saved. The crew abandoned the boat and were taken aboard the trawler HMS *Seagull* and the Norwegian-manned, *St Albans*. Five Polish officers and sailors were killed, and a number were seriously wounded, including the commanding officer.

The two Allied warships were a part of the escort of Convoy PQ-15 that had strayed south. The rescued Poles sailed with them to Murmansk where they boarded *Garland* and reinforced its depleted crew. It should be noted that *Seagull* was sunk on the return trip.

In his memoirs, Romanowski describes his first days after the tragedy and how he agonized over whether there had been a chance of saving his boat and the lives that had been entrusted to him. Military men who write their memoirs, usually many years after the events, seem to describe a war that has been sterilized, and where brave men win laurels or occasionally die bravely. Romanowski deserves great praise for baring his feelings and describing the other side of war: the side of death, of pain, of fear, of the smell of gangrene and of the horrible sight of burns and disfigurement, so often permanent and crippling.

Romanowski witnessed all of this after being placed in the infirmary of the small trawler, *Seagull*. His intrusive thoughts agonizing over the loss were coupled with fear since the small warship was under constant German air attack as well as engaged in continuous depth-charge attacks—hopefully this time—against enemy submarines.

Then Romanowski was joined by a small group of rescued merchant sailors, frozen and petrified. We now know the psychological symptoms of post traumatic stress disorder, and the lay descriptions of the behavior of these sailors is classic. One of them became so frightened at the sounds of the constant explosions that he wanted to jump overboard, and had to be tied down to his bunk.

Romanowski's description of the hospital in Murmansk, filled with hundreds of sailors, both naval and merchant marine, of many nationalities, some dying, some facing the loss of limbs, of loss of sight, brings a different and horrible perspective to the glamour of war.

S.1 or also called *Chart*; the first of the ten Polish motor-torpedo boats (*Scigacze*) which served under the Polish ensign during the war.

General Wladyslaw Sikorski, the prime minister of the Polish coalition government in exile (London) and also the Commander-in-Chief of the Polish Armed Forces visits the Polish destroyer, *ORP Piorun*. The Polish Navy's commandant, Admiral Jerzy Swirski is behind and to the left.

(Above) On July 4, 1943, General Wladyslaw Sikorski and all his entourage were killed in a plane accident at Gibraltar. During the funeral ceremonies, held at Westminster Cathedral in London, the Polish Navy was represented by an honor guard. To their right is a detachment of the Polish Parachute Brigade, which General Sikorski nourished for action in Poland.

(Left) One of the command bunkers of the pre-war Hel peninsula fortifications.

Recent photographs of the bunkers erected prior to the war in the Hel peninsula.

A very historic photo from Puck in the mid-twenties. The author's godfather, senior navy chaplain Wladyslaw Miegon (in navy uniform) and parents stand on the bow of one of the small Polish torpedo boats. The Very Reverend Komandor Miegon, murdered at Dachau is in the process of being beatified. Por. obs. Alfred Peszke, of the Polish Aviation Corps was at that time assigned to the Naval Air Wing, *Morski Dyon Lotniczy*.

O.R.P. Orzel.

Kapitan Jan Grudzinski. He commanded the Polish submarine, *O.R.P. Orzel*, in its heroic break out of the Baltic, and subsequently in a number of successful operations out of British waters. The first navy officer to be decorated with Poland's most prestigious order, *Virtuti Militari*. Also the first Polish officer to be decorated with the British Distinquished Service Order. Did not return from his patrol in May, 1940.

O.R.P. Blyskawica and *O.R.P. Grom* in British waters. Most likely at Harwich shortly before the Norwegian operations, where *Grom* was lost.

The Polish liner, *M.V. Chrobry* was lost in 1940 during Norwegian operations, while carrying British troops.

The Polish liner, *M.V. Batory* sailed with Allied troops throughout the war and returned to Poland after the end of hostilities. Its sister ship, *M.V. Pilsudski*, was lost early in the war.

O.R.P. Garland

O.R.P. Slazak

O.R.P. Piorun

The Polish Mercantile Marine Officer Training School continued in the United Kingdom, being based in Southampton. Photo shows the mustering of the color guard.

King George VI, accompanied by Komandor W. Kodrebski inspects the Polish Naval Cadets (midshipmen) in the United Kingdom.

After the commissioning ceremonies. The new crop of Polish naval officers, 1941.

During the war, the Polish government in London, issued stamps which were used routinely for letters posted on Polish warships and merchant ships. These stamps generated some income for the Polish government and were also useful from the point of view of public relations. This letter was addressed to the author.

O.R.P. Orkan

The Polish submarine, *O.R.P. Sokol*, returns to the Clyde after its successful operations in the Mediterranean.

A Wellington of the Polish 304 Squadron, assigned to Royal Air Force's Coastal Command.

The crew of the Polish submarine, *O.R.P. Sokol*, proudly displaying their captured German ensign and their Jolly Roger, given them by General W. Sikorski.

A Polish motor-torpedo-gunboat (S-7) at full speed in the Channel.

A Polish motor-torpedo-gunboat (S-7) on patrol. Combat stations, with all hands on deck and alert.

The three Polish submarines at the end of the war. *Wilk*, *Dzik* and *Sokol* tied up the "mother" ship, the retired and war weary *Burza*.

O.R.P. Conrad

The end of the war. Polish sailors board a German U-Boat at Weymouth.

Admiral Jerzy Swirski.

ORP *GARLAND* AND CONVOY PQ 16

The story of *Garland*'s Murmansk convoy was heroic. Kdr. por. H. Eibel in command, *Garland* departed on May 16, 1942 for Iceland, as the convoy's senior escort officer. A Polish war correspondent, Bohdan Pawlowicz, (author of *ORP Garland: In Convoy to Russia*), and an official photographer, Pawel Plonka were aboard. This was part of the Polish government's attempt to counter the growing anti-Polish and left-wing propaganda that the Poles were closet fascists and not doing their part in the war.

Garland was part of the escort for a large transport, *Stephen Castle* on its way to Reykjavik, Iceland. *Garland* then sailed to Seydisfjord in eastern Iceland and replenished its bunker oil. On May 23, the task force departed Seydisfjord. The escort fleet grew like a snowball. First, *Garland* joined up with eight other destroyers, then the destroyer squadron joined up with the Tenth Cruiser Squadron, consisting of HMS *Kent, Norfolk, Liverpool,* and the flag ship, *Nigeria.* During the night of May 24, Asdic contact was established with the enemy and a depth-charge attack was carried out by *Garland.* Oil slicks were seen, but by this stage of the war, every sailor knew the trick and postwar records contain no proof of U-boat being damaged at this location or date. During the daylight hours of May 25, the destroyers replenished their bunkers while under way, a practice brought to near perfection by the Americans in the Pacific, but relatively new for the Royal Navy, especially under such difficult climatic conditions. At 0700 the task force, now further reinforced by five corvettes, three trawlers, and two submarines, met Convoy PQ 16, consisting of thirty-five transports that had departed from Reykjavik. From the first days, the Germans reconnoitered the Allied convoy by their large four-engined Focke-Wulf Condor planes, that circled the Allied ships, always outside of artillery range.

At 0800 on May 25, east of Jan Mayen Island, the battle was joined. Since at that latitude in late May there is no night, the convoy could not even change direction to mislead the enemy. German planes flying from Norwegian bases pressed home their attacks without respite. On that first day there were three major air attacks by dive and torpedo bombers. The convoy

commodore's ship carried a Hurricane fighter which was catapulted off to intercept the enemy air attacks. Three enemy
planes were destroyed, two by the fighter plane, which was then
shot down by friendly fire. The pilot escaped by parachute and
was rescued from the icy waters. But the catapulted Hurricane
was a one-shot venture. The following day the Luftwaffe carried
out three more attacks, concentrated on the freighters.

On May 27, the convoy was south of Bear Island and at its
closest to the German air bases in northern Norway, a mere
forty-minutes flying time away. Thirteen air attacks were experienced by the now weary crews, who were beginning to run
short of ammunition. Crews bunked down fully clothed. On
May 26, the four cruisers, escorted by three destroyers,
departed from the convoy, significantly curtailing the artillery
defense. In addition, German U-boats made their appearance.

On May 27, at 1355 hours, *Garland* was attacked by seven
Ju-88s and while no bombs hit the ship directly, they did
explode in such close proximity that considerable damage was
sustained and there were casualties among the crew. Six fires
erupted and some guns were put out of action. The damage
also included the central fire control and the guns had to be
now aimed and fired individually.

There were many heroes in that convoy and many on the
Garland, but one who deserves special mention was the ship's
surgeon, por. lek. W. Zabron, who worked for thirty hours by
himself, with only the assistance of the corpsmen, tending the
many wounded and dying, while the destroyer was under constant battle stations under enemy air attack. Eight more air
attacks were repelled by the Polish warship, before the crew
could stand down at 2300. *Garland's* skipper requested help
and at 2300 HMS *Achates* loaned her own surgeon, Lt. Surgeon Lloyd Armstrong, to assist the Poles. But even two sur-
geons could not cope with the number of casualties and the
severity of injury, and permission was asked and given for the
Polish destroyer to depart at its now reduced best speed of
twenty-three knots for hospital facilities in Murmansk. At 0230
hours *Garland* spotted a German U-boat on the surface and
attempted to give chase, but its own reduced speed and the
fact that its chase track would bring it closer to enemy bases
dissuaded the captain from continuing the proverbial long-
stern chase.

On May 29, *Garland* reached Murmansk. The forty wounded were taken ashore to a Soviet hospital, which was doing its best in difficult circumstances to cope with the avalanche of wounded sailors from the Convoy PQ 15, (which included some crew from *Jastrzab*), as well as from the front lines, a mere fifty miles away.

The twenty-five dead seamen were buried at sea. One of the ironies of the situation was the serious injuries suffered by Kpt. mar. Tadeusz Kaminski, who had only recently been released from the Soviet Gulags and had now lost his leg on a mission to aid the country that had imprisoned and maltreated him for two years. Emergency repairs, in which Royal Navy engineers participated, were carried out to enable the Polish destroyer to sail for the British home ports.

Most of those of *Jastrzab*'s crew that had been rescued left Murmansk aboard the *Garland,* which had lost fifty of its crew, and the fit Polish submariners were a badly needed infusion to complement the crew of the Polish destroyer.

Polish and British awards were given to the crew of the *Garland.* Five of the crew received the highest Polish award for bravery, the Virtuti Militari: the commanding officer Kdr. por. H. Eibel; the artillery officer, por. J. Bartosik; the surgeon, por. lek. W. Zabron; and two petty officers: W. Duch and B. Bomba. Three other officers and a number of enlisted men were decorated with the Krzyz Walecznych. The British awards included one Distinguished Service Order for the Commanding Officer and a Distinguished Service Cross for Bartosik, plus Medals for a number of sailors.

While the crew of the *Garland* received their highly deserved decorations for gallantry, a Royal Navy Board convened on the matter of the loss of the *Jastrzab*. It was determined that while the Polish submarine was outside of her sector due to navigational error, and the Allied warships may have been justified in carrying out a depth-charge attack after an Asdic sounding, the attacking warships were negligent in ignoring the recognition flares. This tragic fratricidal action, not all that rare in the heat of battle, can be better appreciated if the conditions and background are kept in mind. The crews of all the warships were obviously exhausted, in a state of constant battle tension, compounded by harsh climatic conditions. The Allied escorts were small ships, tossed by the Arctic Sea gales and their navigation subject to significant error. All Allied warships were in fact ordered to depth charge any Asdic contact unless proven friendly, and to shoot at all planes if the approach appeared threatening. Finally the silhouette of the American-built submarine was not well-known to the Allied sailors.

CHANNEL OPERATIONS

That body of water which separates the Island Kingdom from Continental Europe, and which for many years of the war was the demarcation between freedom and oppression, is barely twenty-fives miles at its most narrow, between Calais and Dover. It has since been called Churchill's moat.[5]

Yet not only was this a strategic and contested area on the sea and in the air, but it was also a very dangerous and unpredictable body of water, subject to squalls, storms, and gales originating both in the Atlantic and the North Sea in addition to extreme tidal currents. Numerous shoals made navigation hazardous at low tide. This body of water, also known as La Manche by the French and the Poles, was the focus of much of the Royal Navy's coastal operations.

It was here that the small number of Polish motor-gunboats were based and operated.

The evolution of these small combat coastal craft is fascinating. Initially very small motorboats, armed only with torpedoes, they evolved and progressed to ever more tasks, increasing their armament, which eventually included even mines and depth charges. With time, the artillery armament became heavier, and in the last months of the war the boats were called motor-torpedo-gunboats.[6]

The combat activity of the MG boats resembled aerial operations. The small boats went out on relatively short excursions: by night, to attack the enemy; by day or night to escort the British convoys wending their way through the waters of the Channel. The crews spent more time in their bases ashore than at sea. This was very much the "silent service." But there was one specific action which won acclaim and led to mention in despatches. On the night of June 22, 1944, *S.2* commanded by Por. E. Wcislicki, engaged six German torpedo boats *(schnellboot)* also commonly called E-boats by the Allies. In a daring night engagement the Polish boat broke up the German formation and prevented a German attack on a British convoy. Wcislicki received the Polish Virtuti Militari and the British Distinguished Service Cross.

During the war, ten such boats served under Polish colors, but never more than three at a time. The Polish coastal craft were based in many southern English ports like Dover, Ramsgate, Margate, Portland, and even as far west as Fowey and Dartmouth, in Devon.

During this period, the Poles suffered only one mortal casualty, namely Por. mar. Janusz Justyn Sokolowski, when as commanding officer of *S.1* (Chart), he fought a fire in the engine room. Having ordered his crew to abandon ship, he entered the engine room and extinguished the fire, but was overwhelmed by the fumes.

In late spring 1944, the Poles received a number of Vosper-designed Motor-Torpedo-Gunboats, numbered *S.4* through *S.10* (British designation MTBs 424–429). These were, in fact, small battleships compared with the first motorboats of the war. Carrying a 57-millimeter gun on the foredeck, and with a 20-millimeter Oerlikon on the stern with numerous machine guns for defense, they had two torpedo tubes for offensive purposes.

These boats formed a Polish division based initially at Ramsgate under the command of Por. mar. Witold Szuster, who was awarded the British Distinguished Service Cross, and followed by the now promoted Por. mar. Andrzej Jaraczewski. The Polish motor-torpedo-gunboats were commanded by junior officers, who rotated frequently and often commanded more than one boat. The following officers held command at various times until the end of the war:

S.1 was commanded by Por. J. Sokolowski Por. T. Dabrowski Por. E. Wcislicki, and finally Ppor. J. Dobrodzicki.

S.2 was commanded by Por.E. Wcislicki, Por. M. Bochenski, Por. W. Szuster, and finally by Por. J. Krasucki.

S.3. was commanded by Por. A. Jaraczewski and Por. M. Bochenski.

S.4 was commanded by Por. L. Antoszewicz.

S.5 was commanded by Kpt. mar. W. Szuster and Por.
   M. Bochenski.
S.6 was commanded by Por. J. Dobrodzicki.
S.7 was commanded by Kpt. mar. A. Jaraszewski
S.8 was commanded by Por. S. Kopecki
S.9 was commanded by Por. K. Goralczyk
S.10 was commanded by Ppor. J. Schreiber and Por.
   R. Dulla

After Ramsgate, the division was moved to Felixstown,
near Harwich, and in January 1945, to Cowes and finally at
war's end to Portland.

THE CHANNEL DASH

As a result of the armistice terms agreed to by the French in
June 1940, all the French Atlantic ports were occupied and utilized by the Germans. As early as March 1941, the Germans
based two of their battleships, *Gneisenau* and *Scharnhorst* in
Brest. Their presence caused considerable anxiety to the
British who feared that they could break out into the Atlantic
and disrupt Allied convoys. In June 1941, the potential danger
to the allied convoys increased when the heavy cruiser, *Prinz
Eugene*, which had parted from *Bismarck* before its sinking,
arrived in Brest.

The British paid great attention to this threat, with intense
intelligence gathering by the RAF reconnaissance planes, submarines off the coast (including *Sokol* for a time), and active
and passive agents. The Brest docks and the German warships
were also primary targets for the RAF Bomber Command which
carried out a number of fruitless attacks on these warships.

In February 1942, the Germans sailed their fleet though
the English Channel to German ports. The Germans named this
operation *Cerberus* and it included major Luftwaffe fighter protection, intense minesweeping ahead of the ships and, most
important, the element of surprise. The British were caught
flat-footed, in their own backyard and were badly embar-
rassed. In British naval history this operation became known
as the Channel Dash.[7]

One of the interventions carried out by the Royal Navy in
the narrow waters off Dover was a torpedo attack by three

motor-torpedo boats escorted by two Polish motor-gunboats, *S.2 (Wilczur)* and *S.3 (Wyzel)* commanded by Ppor. Mar. Euge-niusz Wcislicki and Ppor. Mar. Andrzej Jaraczewski, respec-tively. The Polish escorts were caught in the fire of heavy artillery emanating from the two German battleships. The Poles returned to port along with the three Royal Navy boats, undamaged and with no casualties.

The British torpedo attack was unsuccessful, as was the suicidal torpedo attack pressed by the Swordfish planes of the Fleet Air Arm from land bases (all planes having been lost). No German ships were sunk. But *Gneisena*u was in fact badly damaged and was never again a threat.

DIEPPE

In addition to the small torpedo boats, bigger Polish warships also operated in the Channel, prominent being, *Krakowiak,* (CO Kpt. mar. J. Tchorznicki) and ORP *Slaza*k, (CO Kdr. ppor. N. Tyminski).

On August 17, 1942, *Slazak* took part in the ill-fated Allied Dieppe landings. Its artillery was used to support the Canadian troops who bore the brunt of the operation and of the losses. The Polish destroyer shot down four German planes, and in turn suffered damage and casualties from enemy air activity. Tyminski received the British Distinguished Service Cross for his leadership and later in the war, the Polish Virtuti Militari.

It was over Dieppe that the Polish Air Force won its second great aerial victory. The five Polish fighter squadrons flew 224 sorties and destroyed eighteen percent of all German planes shot down by the RAF Fighter Command.[8]

In October 1942, *Krakowiak* accompanied by the Royal Navy destroyer HMS *Fernie* and two motor-torpedo boats car-ried out a sweep off Cape Hague and sank a number of German transports. On November 1, 1942, accompanied by HMS *Tynedale, Krakow*iak successfully attacked a German convoy off Normandy. Then these operations were joined by *Slaza*k, CO Kpt. mar. B. Wronski, and the two Polish Hunt-class escort destroyers worked together. On November 30, both war-ships escorted a convoy that was bound for Gibraltar; resuming convoy duty between Gibraltar, the Clyde, and Mil-ford Haven.

RESCUE OPERATIONS

Not all the events were a matter of mere brute aggression and survival. Sometimes, the crews were able to experience the joy of rescue. Wronski in his memoirs, *Wspomienia Plyna Jak Okrety*, recounts one of these events.

The Polish destroyer, *Slazak*, as escort leader was convoying the typical collection of freighters, sailing at the fastest speed of the slowest ship, which would be about seven knots. The weather was, as the author describes, typical convoy weather: stormy, overcast, with periods of drizzle. The slow speed and constant buffeting of the waves was tiresome, but fortunately the bad weather kept the German planes grounded, and their motor-torpedo-boats, the famous E-boats, in harbor.

At about 2000 hours a radio message was received to proceed to a point X to pick up a number of downed airmen. The break in the monotony was welcome, the command of the convoy was delegated to the skipper of an armed trawler, while *Slaza*k departed for the reported position. The course allowed the destroyer to enjoy a following wind and the ship increased speed. Extra lookouts were posted and the whole crew became aware that it was a rescue mission. This was sufficiently unusual that the off-duty watch stayed to witness the event. There was also a lot of empathy for the poor airmen, bobbing around in the dark, vast ocean in a small rubber dinghy. At 2200 hours, position X was reached and the grid search began. Visibility was next to nil. The navigator calculated the presumed drift of the dinghy. Nothing was observed. The Poles now shot off a couple of flares to illuminate the area, but nothing was seen. Suddenly one of the watch reported a light off the starboard bow. Nobody else could confirm this. The commanding officer ordered the powerful searchlights to illuminate the area in question. Some of the officers were troubled, since to use the lights was to identify their own position to enemy submarines. The commanding officer responded to the unasked question: It's a matter of lives.

The starboard watch now reported a light and, in fact, a small light could be seen in the light of the ship's reflector. But it was only the remnants of the warship's phosphorous flare floating on the water. Still no sign of the downed airmen. At midnight, an order was received that if the airmen had not been picked up, *Slazak* was to rejoin the convoy. With heavy hearts—and after one more sweep—*Slazak* sailed to rejoin the convoy and entered port in the morning hours.

At noon, refueling was completed and the crew stood down, only to receive an order to depart base immediately to pick up downed airmen. *Slazak* departed at night, at full speed, heading for the reported position. Again a cloud covered a dark November night, but the sea was calm. The following short November day was spent searching for the dinghy. A RAF flying boat, a Sunderland, made its appearance and identified itself by aldis lamp. They reported negative sightings but the Sunderland flew off to the projected point, after overflying the warship to get the right bearing. Half an hour later, the Sunderland returned and reported by aldis that there were no survivors in the area searched, and finished with the typical British "Good Luck."

The commanding officer and navigator huddled. There seemed no point in going ahead, since the Sunderland, a slow flying boat, had checked out the area. What could be done? The captain could imagine the cold, wet, and lonely airmen on the dinghy. A new course was plotted. The destroyer heeled and went west. The thought kept coming back that perhaps they should have stayed the course, perhaps the Sunderland did not see the small raft. It was known to happen. By 2000 hours doubts were pervasive when no dinghy had yet been seen.

The CO decided to zigzag one half hour more in the general area and then zigzag back. Exactly at the moment that the return course was being plotted, the watch reported a light off the starboard bow. Indeed, there were two rubber rafts. *Slazak* proceeded slowly to pick up the airmen. The base received the report within minutes that six British airmen had been picked up, and that all were well after fifty hours at sea. The captain wondered why he had decided on the course he had and extended the time of the search.

As *Slazak* reported its mission accomplished and plotted a course for home, a radio message was received to proceed to point Y to pick up downed airmen. The new plot indicated estimated time of arrival in the morning at daybreak. The sea was calm. At 0800 position Y was reached but there was no sight of a dinghy, only porpoises performing for the crew.

The commanding officer decided to follow the drift of the wind. Suddenly an alarm for action stations was sounded when four unidentified planes were observed "in the sun," always a threatening position that was usually adopted in preparation for an air attack. They turned out to be RAF Coastal Command Hudsons, however. Morse communication by means of Aldis lamp did not go well but the Poles requested assistance in the search. The Hudsons responded but nobody aboard could understand their Morse communication. While the Poles were getting more irritated at the plane's crew incompetence in the use of Morse, one of the Hudsons kept circling and acting like a dog that tries to show its master a course. The Poles decided to take the course which they thought the Hudson was trying to indicate. The Hudson then flew off and was lost to sight for less than half an hour, then observed to be circling. All's well that ends well. The Hudson was circling over a dinghy, and *Slazak* picked up four more airmen who had been at sea for seventy-two hours. They turned out to have been the airmen for whom *Slaza*k was searching originally. The airmen reported that they had seen the flares at a distance but had no rockets with which to respond.

The commanding officer ordered the following signal sent to base:

"Four airmen picked up. Condition satisfactory."

After a minute he added,

"Next Please."

Response came back;

"Well done. Next in Base."

*Slaza*k became know as the shepherd of the dinghies.

But how many died of exposure and wounds while praying desperately to be picked up by ships and planes that they could see, but did not see *them*? How many parents and wives and lovers were left with the tragic words: "MISSING IN ACTION, PRESUMED DEAD."

THE BATTLE OF THE ATLANTIC REACHES ITS CLIMAX

The bloody war on the Atlantic went on, as thousands of sailors, on both sides, as well as neutrals, died in horrible circumstances.

It was in 1942 that the Germans reached their apogee of destruction. From the shores of the United States, where Coast Guard patrols on the Outer Banks would find bodies washed shore each morning; to the middle of the Atlantic and all the way to the balmy and humid southern Atlantic, as well as into the frigid waters and relentless cold of the Arctic Sea, the German U-boats operated with relative impunity, leaving a trail of Allied dead. Losses included not only the ships, which were hard to replace, but also foodstuffs, and war material of which the most vital was oil and gasoline.

By this time Doenitz's wolf packs were effective, while Goering's long-range Kondors had achieved a reasonable level of coordination with the German navy. These planes, based in southern France, flew into the Atlantic, reconnoitered the slowly moving Allied convoys, and radioed the course and position of the ships. The wolf packs, strung like a net over hundreds of miles of the Atlantic, could engulf the incoming convoys like a Tartar horde. It needs telling again that during the Second World War most submarines operated primarily on the surface, and most attacks were carried out at night and on the surface. Before the advent of airborne radar, this was safe for the attacking submarines which only submerged to avoid enemy attacks. While the U-boats were slower by ten knots than the surface warships of the Allies, the speed of the convoy was the proverbial speed of the slowest merchant ship, usually under ten knots.

Both sides made advances in the technology of killing each other. To protect their U-boats from allied air attacks, huge U-boat pens, marvels of construction, were built by German slave labor mostly in French-occupied territory. These defied not only the heaviest bombs that the British could drop, but even after the war have withstood the ravages of time and stand as permanent tributes to the madness of war.

Since the most dangerous time for German U-boats was close to their own U-boat pens, where the Allies had air superiority and could concentrate their own submarines and surface warships, the Germans developed a system to supply their U-boats at sea. A class of milch U-boats was developed which would rendezvous with U-boats in the middle of the Atlantic and supplied them with oil, torpedoes, and food, taking off wounded or sick and also bringing mail.

On the Allied side, merchantmen were armed with artillery pieces and naval personnel assigned as gunners. Some Polish naval gunners were seconded to Polish merchant ships. While Allied fortunes improved after March 1943, the losses of the merchantmen were still serious, and on any given day there were seven hundred merchant ships at sea, carrying cargo that was essential to sustain the civilian population and vital for the continued war effort. As the Polish naval historian, Wronski, wrote, *"they were the real heroes of the Battle of the Atlantic."* (Figures for merchant navy personnel killed are not reliable but the best estimate is that just over thirty thousand men were lost on British registered ships alone!)

A number of large and relatively fast merchantmen were converted into auxiliary cruisers. Some were even equipped with catapults, and carried one Hurricane to discourage the German long-range patrol planes. After shooting down the big four-engined Kondors, or at least chasing them off, the pilot was expected to land on the sea, or parachute.[9] With time, some of these large merchantmen were converted into small carriers, where the pilot had a much better chance of landing successfully. The auxiliary carriers operated as nuclei of small task forces, accompanied by a small group of corvettes. These very small warships were slowly replaced by the larger frigates, and these in turn were equipped with "hedgehogs" and "squids," which were more sophisticated dispensers of deadly depth charges. Rather than the old, primitive method of merely dropping the depth charge astern, the new system also allowed for projecting the charges ahead and to the side.

In 1942, a total of 1,664 Allied merchant ships of a combined tonnage of seven million seven hundred tons were sunk and the Germans lost eighty-seven U-boats. The pace accelerated in early 1943 and reached a critical point when, in March 1943, one hundred twenty Allied ships of 693,389 tons were sunk for the price of fifteen U-boats.

But this was the turning point in the Battle of the Atlantic. Allied planes continued to increase their patrolling range and were now equipped with radar, which forced the German U-boats to spend more time submerged. To counter this the Germans developed the schnorkels, which allowed boats to run on diesels while submerged and thus were no longer hostage to batteries, which required charging every twelve hours.

One of the most crucial successes in the war against the U-boats was the Allied acquisition of air bases in the Azores. This closed the last—but huge—sector of the Atlantic where German submarines had been safe from Allied air activity and where they had been resupplied by their milch boats.

The Allied diplomatic success was simply a function of the neutral country always paying heed to the local power. Allied victories in North Africa and the clearly progressively defensive posture of Germany had now persuaded the Portuguese dictator, Antonio Salazar, to accommodate Allied pleas and to make the Azores available for Allied operations. The Swedes and the Swiss were also beginning to play a more genuinely neutral role instead of their formerly very marked pro-German posture.

For many decades, few were aware of the vital role played by Bletchley Park in England, the secret intelligence-gathering and code-breaking center, in the Battle of the Atlantic. It was here that the British built on the pre–1939 seminal work of the Poles breaking the German codes by developing a *bombe* or early mechanical computer. This work went into history as Ultra. But the German naval codes defied the British the longest.

The Polish destroyers continued in this unending battle, where the damage was more likely to be from the sea, and the enemy was usually unseen. Storms and gales damaged ships and swept men overboard. Epidemics of tuberculosis were common, because of the poor food, close quarters, poor hygiene, cold, and damp.

Blyskawica spent most of 1942 either in convoy duties or licking her wounds from the Atlantic gales. On November 5, 1942, commanded by Kdr.ppor. L. Lichodziejewski, she participated in the North African invasion as Escort Command for a task force of fast liners carrying nearly thirty-two thousand troops, and also comprising three cruisers, one carrier, and a screen of five destroyers. The landings at Bougie were unopposed, but enemy planes carried out numerous attacks against the Allied flotilla. As a result *Blyskawica* sustained some damage and had to repair to Gibraltar's yards for a month for a refit. For his leadership Lichodziejewski was awarded the British Distinguished Service Order and the Polish Virtuti Militari.

On the night of February 21, 1943, *Burza* detected a submarine on her Asdic, while escorting an eastbound convoy close to Newfoundland. Since there were no intelligence reports of Allied submarines in the vicinity, three depth-charge attacks were delivered and the German U-boat surfaced, to be raked by fire from the 40-millimeter AA guns. The coup de grace was delivered by the United States Coast Guard cutter, *Campbell*, which intentionally rammed the U-boat, but was badly damaged by the U-boat's hydroplanes, which ripped a hole in the hull of the cutter. As a result the American crew had to be transferred to the Polish *Burza*, but the American CO Lt. Cdr. Hirshfield, stayed on his ship, which was protected by the Poles, until a tug arrived and towed the *Campbell* to port. The German submarine that had been sunk was the *U-606*.[10]

In late spring 1943, the British naval authorities thus summarized the Polish naval contribution:

> It has been said by a British officer who has had Polish and other allied ships under his command: They share our sorrows and rejoice in our victories in a manner which makes them seem closest of all our allies. They have the gift of being sympathetic rather than critical and enthusiastic instead of envious.

> The Destroyers have been working with zeal and efficiency on escort and it is suggested that some be employed where there is greater opportunity for action. (WO 193/33 80751)

And indeed the assignment of Polish destroyers began to change. Both *Piorun*, (commanding officer Kdr. ppor. T. Gorazdowski), and the brand new *Orkan*, (CO Kdr.por. S. Hryniewiecki) were assigned to the Royal Navy's base at Scapa Flow. *Orkan* took part in some of the convoys to Murmansk, while *Piorun* was part of the destroyer screen for the British battleships that gave indirect protection to the convoys. On March 16, 1943, *Orkan* was part of the escort for the official visit of King George VI to Scapa Flow, while *Piorun*, under the command of Kdr. por. S. Dzienisiewicz, sailed as escort for the battleships *Nelson* and *Rodney*, and the carrier *Indomitable* bound for Gibraltar. *Piorun* then took part in the landings at Salerno while *Blyskawica* departed for the Mediterranean in the summer of 1943.

Burza, CO Kpt. mar. F. Pitulko, and *Garland*, CO Kpt. mar. B. Biskupski, spent the early months of 1943 convoying between the Clyde and Newfoundland.

It would be tedious and boring to enumerate each operation and each departure from the home port. Suffice it to say that the warships sailed and usually returned, their crews went on leave or rest, the ships were refitted and modernized, and crews after rest sailed for the essential shakedown exercises. This was usually done away from prying eyes, at Scapa Flow, the base of the Royal Navy's Home Fleet, which continued to keep an eye on the potential danger to British convoys bound for Russia from the remaining German battleships *Tirpitz*, *Scharnhorst*, and *Gneisenau*.

In such a short period of time, this very small number of Polish warships had participated intensively in surface and underwater operations in the North Sea, North Atlantic, Western Approaches, the Bay of Biscay, the English Channel, and the Mediterranean.

POLISH BOUNDARIES ARE THREATENED

As the Soviet Union survived the second winter of its war against the Germans, its confidence grew and its demands became progressively more vocal. Tragically for the Poles, these demands were echoed in the West by many Soviet sympathizers. The United States ambassador to Moscow, Joseph E. Davies, wrote as follows in a well publicized article in *Life:* "The Soviet Government is not a predatory power like Germany and Japan's." He then argued, "It would be natural for them to demand what any other people would, under similar circumstances. First they would naturally want back that which had previously been taken away from them by force after the last war [*i.e.*, the Polish-Russian war of 1920]."

The editors of *Life* went on to compare Lavrenty P. Beria's NKVD to the United States FBI. The editors furthermore compared the Soviet Union favorably with American democracy: "like the USA, the USSR is a huge melting pot, only in a different way. It contains 175 nationalities speaking 150 languages and dialects. They don't mix as much as our ethnic groups do; yet the system by which all these people are held together runs parallel to ours in that it is a federation."[11]

In such pro-Soviet atmosphere, all Polish efforts to argue their case where met with impatience at best, and, too often, with responses that were offensive and derogatory.

KATYN

The German discovery in Katyn, in German-occupied Soviet territory, in the spring of 1943, of the mummified bodies of Polish officers who had been missing since 1940, led the Polish government to turn to the International Red Cross for an impartial investigation. The Soviets professed themselves insulted and broke the barely two year restored diplomatic relationships with the Polish government in London, accusing the Poles of tacit collaboration with Germany.[12]

ADDITIONAL WARSHIPS JOIN THE POLISH NAVY

On January 15, 1943, the Poles added an old British D-class cruiser, HMS *Dragon*, to their establishment. This was a reflection of the policies of the Polish Naval Commandant that in the future, Poland would be a major Baltic sea power. This was also very much in line with the rather grandiose and exaggerated big navy concepts which preoccupied Admiral Swirski. His negotiations with the Polish Air Force Inspectorate for an independent naval aviation were in line with such a strategic principle of an autonomous naval force.[13] Admiral Swirski had in fact requested the loan of one of the brand-new small British built *Dido*-class cruisers. Had this been achieved, the commitment of so many Polish personnel and resources might have been worthwhile, but the old cruiser was merely a floating artillery battery.

There was an additional and unnecessary political note to this commissioning. By the end of 1942, the Poles were already faced with implacable and insistent demands from Moscow that all territories that had been taken from the Poles in 1939 remain under Soviet control. There was a distinct sense that the British were yielding to Soviet pressure at Poland's expense.

Hoping to make a point, the Poles stated they would name their new cruiser ORP *Lwow*, after Poland's major eastern city, and one of the major bones of contention between the Poles and the Soviets. The British Government made it clear that this was unacceptable, and that if the Poles persisted in this, the warship would not be released for service under the Polish ensign.[14]

About eleven months later, at the infamous Tehran Conference in December 1943, the Western Allies accepted the principle that the Polish-Soviet boundary would run along the Molotov-Ribbentrop demarcation of September 1939 and thus acceded to Soviet wishes. The Polish city of Lwow was lost.

Not wishing to lose the cruiser and not wishing to change their posture, however, the Poles accepted the British cruiser under its original British name as ORP *Dragon*.

On April 30, the Polish Navy was strengthened by the addition of a brand new fleet-class destroyer of the Milne-class which was christened the ORP *Orka*n. This was a fine addition to the Polish Navy. Brand new, it represented the best in British naval design for a fleet destroyer.

THE COMMANDER-IN-CHIEF IS KILLED

On July 4, 1943, after visiting the Polish 2 Army Corps in the Middle East, the troops that had been evacuated from the Soviet Union in the middle of 1942, the Polish commander-in-chief and prime minister, General W. Sikorski was killed in a plane crash at Gibraltar. The general's daughter, who acted as his personal secretary, as well as General Klimecki, the Chief of Staff of the Polish forces and also Sikorski's adjutant were killed. Among the dead was also the British member of Parliament and strong friend of Poland, Victor Cazalet. Polish political fortunes were badly affected at this juncture, and the controversy whether this was an accident or willful sabotage endures to this day.

The position of commander-in-chief was given to General W. Sosnkowski, and the leader of the Polish Peasant Party,

Mr. Stanislaw Mikolajczyk, assumed the premiership of the Polish coalition government in exile.

The body of the dead Polish commander-in-chief was transported from Gibraltar to the United Kingdom aboard the *Orkan* and was interred in Newark, England, at the Polish Air Force cemetery. This small English town has the largest single Polish military cemetery in the United Kingdom, where over four hundred Polish airmen are buried. These crews were either killed in routine or training flights, or died in combat operations as their flak-damaged Wellingtons and Lancasters failed them in the last minutes over the British Isles. (In 1993 Sikorski's body was moved with great pomp and circumstances and interred at Wawel Castle next to Kosciuszko and Prince Poniatowski.)

Churchill gave a magnificent eulogy at Sikorski's funeral service in Westminster Cathedral, of which significant parts follow:

> I mourn with you the loss of your Prime Minister and Commander-in-Chief, General Sikorski. I knew him well. He was a true statesman, a true soldier, a true comrade, a true ally, and above all a true Pole.

Churchill finished with a very touching but pointed comment on the reality of the war:

> Soldiers must die. But by their deaths they nourish the nation which gave them birth. Be worthy of his example. Prepare yourselves to die for Poland—for many of you to whom I speak must die, as many of us must die, as he died, for his country and the common cause. In the farewell to your dear leader let us mingle renewed loyalties. We shall not forget him. I shall not forget you. My own thoughts are with you and will be with you always.[15]

This certainly uplifted the hearts of the Polish ally, in the midst of increasing anti-Polish propaganda coming from the left.

The war continued and, as Churchill said, many were still to die, including most of the crew of the *Orkan* which brought Sikorski's body to Britain from Gibraltar.

NOTES

1. Warren Kimball, *"Lend-Lease"* in I.C.B. Dear and M.R.D. Foot, eds. *The Oxford Companion to World War II*, Oxford University Press, 1995, pp. 677–683.
2. *Documents on Polish–Soviet Relations: 1939–1945*, in two volumes, London, 1961 and 1967, Vol.1 pp. 344–347.
3. Polish Institute, London, A. XII. 1/129. Also, Winston S. Churchill, *Hinge of Fate*, p. 496. *"The Levant-Caspian front is almost bare . . . the four Polish divisions when trained would play a strong part in delaying a German southward advance."*
4. Winston S. Churchill, *Hinge of Fate*, op.cit. p. 269.
5. Robert Jackson, *Churchill's Moat: The English Channel in World War II*, London, 1995.
6. Harald Fock, *Fast Fighting Boats, 1870–1945: Their Design, Construction and Use*, Naval Institute Press, Annapolis, MD, 1978.
7. Terence Robertson, *Channel Dash: The Fantastic Story of the German Battle Fleet's Escape Through the English Channel in Broad Daylight*, New York, 1958; Richard Garrett, *Scharnhorst and Gneisenau: The Elusive Sisters*, Newton Abbot, 1978.
8. Norman Franks, *The Greatest Air Battle: Dieppe, 19th August 1942*, London. 1992.
9. Ralph Baker, *The Hurricats*, London, 1978.
10. Navy Department, Office of the Chief of Naval Operations Washington, Serial No. 10. *Report on the Interrogation of Survivor from U-606 Sunk on February 22, 1943*. U.S. Gov. Printing Office, Washington, 1943. Also National Archives R 26. Log page for the period from US Coast Guard Cutter *Campbell.*
11. Jospeh E. Davies, *Mission to Moscow,* New York, 1941. Article in *Life* is from March 29, 1943.
12. Janusz Zawodny, *Death in the Forest: The Story of the Katyn Forest Massacre,* University of Notre Dame Press, IN 1962.
13. Also see Appendix D, Naval Aviation.
14. It is an interesting commentary on the change in British Governmental attitudes that on March 23, 1941, the (British) Air Ministry News Service carried the following communiqué: *"At dawn to-day yet another Polish squadron took to the air ready to defend Britain, manned by young and tremendously keen pilots and ground staff. Vilna (Wilno) is to be the name of the squadron. The Polish leader and several of the other pilots hope to return to their homes there one day."* Wilno was another city which was contested. But March 1941 antedated the change of the Soviets' status, from Germany's ally to an eagerly embraced member of

the United Nations coalition. This change of policy and the nearly sycophantic deference to Soviet wishes is well illustrated in the events of 1944, when the Royal Air Force heraldry office querried whether it was appropriate and politically correct to officially sanction the crest of the Polish 303 fighter squadron. This squadron derived its traditions from, and its crest was close to identical to that, which had fought the Russians in 1919–1920. While the Foreign Office gave an official reassurance to the herald's office (PRO FO 371/39519), the fact is that in the magnificent Westminster Abbey stained-glass window commemorating the Battle of Britain, the two Polish squadrons are represented, not by their crests, which were on their cowlings, but by stylized white crowned eagles. The crest and the story of the Polish squadron which so concerned the British heraldry office had to do with the American volunteers to Poland in 1919–1921. Robert F. Karolevitz & Ross S. Fenn, *Flight of Eagles,* Sioux Falls, SD, 1974, and Kenneth Malcom Murray. *Wings over Poland*, New York, 1932. The Americans symbolically adapted the Kosciuszko peasant cap, the crossed scythes of his troops, and the stars of the thirteen colonies that Kosciuszko fought to liberate. The tradition of the American flyers was continued in the interwar period and then in exile by the Polish Military Aviation, renamed in 1940 the Polish Air Force. After a historical hiatus, on May 19, 1993 the Polish Minister of Defense issued an order that the 1st Polish Fighter Regiment based in Minsk Mazowiecki (near Warsaw) was based on the traditions of the 7th Fighter (Kosciuszko) Squadron of 1918–1921; the 111 and 113 (Kosciuszko) squadrons of the First Aviation Regiment in Warsaw; and finally of the 303 (Kosciuszko) and 316 (Warsaw) squadrons of the Polish Air Force in the United Kingdom.

15. This magnificent speech is not to be found in Churchill's World War Two history, nor is there any reference to his accident or death. Given the fact that Sikorski was the only Allied prime minister or commander-in-chief to die in the line of duty it is at best paradoxical!

I found the draft of this speech in the British Public Record Office (FO 371/7683), and it was printed by the *Daily Telegraph*, July 15, 1943.

CHAPTER IX

1943
THE FIRST YEAR OF ALLIED VICTORIES
THE BATTLE OF THE ATLANTIC IS WON
POLISH POLITICAL UNCERTAINTIES

ORP *DZIK* AND *SOKOL*

The crew of the sunk *Jastrzab* were seconded in late 1942 to take over a brand new U-class submarine, which was launched on October 11, 1942, at Barrow, England. The commanding officer became Kpt. Romanowski. The new submarine, a sister boat of *Sokol*, was named ORP *Dzik*. The crew completed their work up at Holy Loch and were then assigned to the Royal Navy's Seventh Submarine Flotilla based in Dundee.

Now both *Sokol* and *Dzik* were operating together in the Arctic waters and off Norway. *Sokol* undertook a number of combat patrols from Dundee to the Arctic Sea. The mission of the patrols as it had been before its Mediterranean duty, was to act as a screen against the *Scharnhorst*. This German battleship had been badly damaged during the Channel Dash but was now back in service, based in northern Norway, and again a threat to the Allied convoys to Murmansk. It was to be finally engaged and destroyed by the British Home Fleet later in the year, after *Sokol* had departed to join *Dzik* in Malta as part of the Tenth Submarine Flotilla in the spring of 1943.

For Kpt. mar. Koziolowski, the commanding officer of *Sokol,* this was a return to the Mediterranean, but for Romanowski, the CO of *Dzik,* it was his first venture and a challenge to emulate *Sokol* which he met with great success.

Much had happened in the region between the time *Sokol* left the Mediterranean and she and her sister boat came back.

In October 1942, the British Eight Army routed the German and Italian forces at El Alamein. The Axis forces were rolled all the way back to Tunisia. In November, the Allies carried out their largest amphibious operation to date, *Torch*, in which American and British armies landed in French Vichy territory in Algeria and Morocco. French naval units initially staged a vigorous opposition, but the land forces quickly accommodated to the new power structure and joined de Gaull's Free French.

The Allies learned many valuable lessons in carrying out these relatively unopposed amphibious operations which were invaluable in future operations, both against the Italian mainland in September 1943 and in Normandy in June, 1944.

By May 1943 North Africa was completely cleared of German and Italian forces, and the siege of Malta was to all intents and purposes ended.

While based in Malta the Polish submarines undertook patrols off Calabria and north to the region of Bari on the Adriatic Sea. But the naval war was moving east, to the Aegean Sea. Both boats were moved to Beirut and worked with the First Submarine Flotilla, their assignment to interdict German coastal shipping between the Greek occupied islands of Dodecanese. During that period the command of ORP *Dzik* was for a time assumed by Kpt. mar. Klopotowski.

Sokol returned to Devonport on March 31, 1944, after carrying out a total of thirty-two patrols, and having sunk 23,460 tons of enemy shipping. *Dzik* returned to Plymouth on April 8 after twelve patrols, having sunk 45,080 tons of enemy shipping. Some of these successes were achieved by torpedoes, many by gunfire, and in some instances enemy ships were boarded and sunk by explosives.

After returning to the United Kingdom, both underwent refits, and *Sokol* was assigned to the Ninth Flotilla based in Dundee. She undertook four patrols off Norway and then joined the *Dzik* as a training ship. The boats were too small for the Royal Navy's Pacific operations, and the European war was finished as far as Allied submarines were concerned.

Koziolowski received a bar to his Distinguished Service Cross, and Klopotowski and Romanowski were so honored for the first time.

POLISH SURFACE SHIPS IN THE MEDITERRANEAN

In the summer of 1943, the two Polish escort destroyers, *Slazak*, (commanding officer Kdr. ppor. W. Fara), and *Krakowiak*, (CO Kpt. mar. W. Maracewicz), after operating in the English Channel with occasional escorts to Gibraltar, were seconded to the Mediterranean and began their escort duties between Gibraltar, Algiers, and Tripoli. Then both warships participated in the invasion of Sicily (Operation *Husky*) where they had to fend off the sporadic attacks of the German Luftwaffe.

There was enough concern about German U-boats penetration into the Mediterranean, however, that the British formed the Forty-Eight Escort Group, consisting of the two Polish warships, one Royal Navy destroyer, and five corvettes. *Slazak* was appointed to be the leader. During one of these convoys, when the Allied group was accompanied by two Royal Navy submarines, there was another tragic instance of *"friendly fire."* In this instance, the American freighter, *Yankee Arrow*, opened fire on the British submarine, HMS *Unison*, which suffered a number of dead before the Polish destroyer could intervene and stop the tragedy. Paul Kemp in his original study documented one hundred fifty such naval tragedies during the Second World War.[1]

A month later, in August 1943, the escort group was dissolved and the Polish destroyers assigned to Task Force V under Rear Admiral Vian of *Bismarck* and *Altmark* fame. This was a large task force, consisting of five carriers and three cruisers escorted by ten Hunt-class destroyers, including the two Poles. *Slazak,* now commanded by Kdr. ppor. T. Tyminski, was Destroyer Leader. On September 8, 1943, Task Force V supported the Salerno landings. After that, the warships operated independently, with *Krakowiak* resuming escort duties, while *Slazak* protected the two British battleships, *Warspite* and *Valiant*, which were shelling German positions at Salerno.

As the Allies were bogged down in their Italian Campaign, more troops had to be brought in, and that required more convoys. In November 1943, *Slazak* was once again leader of a destroyer escort consisting of three British, four American, and one Greek destroyer.

The Germans now introduced their famous glider bombs and *Warspite* was damaged, while one troopship was sunk.

In turn, *Krakowiak* sailed with a British force into the Aegean and took part in the invasion of Leros, which was supported by the warship's artillery.[2]

At the end of the year, the two Polish ships took part in convoying between North Africa, Egypt, and Italy. Both warships took part in the escort of the troopships carrying the Polish 2 Army Corps from Egypt to Italy. This sixty-thousand-strong corps, consisting of two infantry divisions and an armored brigade, comprised some of the over one hundred thousand Poles released by the Soviets in 1941 from their Gulags. They had slowly made their way through the British Levant, for a time reinforced the British PAIFORC (official British acronym for British Forces in Persia and Iraq), had been retrained and given modern equipment, and were about to enter combat.

But disease and British demands for adherence to the British Army establishment reduced the number of potential Polish divisions for operations in Italy. Now they were on their way into a fierce campaign, like heroes out of Sienkiewicz's novel, looking for battle to forget the ever growing taste of impending defeat and loss.

CRYPTOLOGY AIDS NAVAL OPERATIONS

In 1943, the British won their cryptological battle with the German Naval codes.[3] This allowed the British to send their small auxiliary carriers to those points where the Germans were concentrating or being resupplied from their milch U-boats. This also allowed the Allies to steer their convoys away from German wolf-pack concentrations. By May, the critical losses in Allied shipping had been reduced to the point that the Germans lost forty-one U-boats and sank a mere fifty-eight ships, totaling 299,428 tons. Admiral Doenitz ordered all U-boats to the South Atlantic and the waters off the Azores in order to regroup.

Allied shipping losses were now below 200,000 tons per month and the Germans were consistently losing over twenty boats per month. In August, 1943, the loss of a further thirty-six

U-boats was a crisis for the Germans and augured victory for the Allies.[4]

The Polish warships were fully committed to this final outcome. In the summer of 1943, *Burza* was assigned, as Flag Officer-in-Charge, to West Africa and now convoyed between Freetown and Lagos, and on July 12, 1943, crossed the equator. During this time there were no contacts with the enemy, but the fact that *Burza* was not tropicalized and the crew not acclimatized to such heat made for very difficult conditions and led to many medical problems, primarily dermatological conditions and frequent heat exhaustion. On the trip back to the Clyde, *Burza* repulsed an attack by a German long-range four-engined Kondor.

In October 1943, both *Burza* and *Garland* escorted carriers to the Azores, and were part of the anti-submarine task force. In December 1943, *Burza* sailed for Gibraltar and continued convoying until March 1944. Requiring a major refit, she was placed in reserve and the crew taken off. By this time the Allies had a sufficient number of modern escort warships.

Garland, being better equipped for work in the tropics, now sailed out of Freetown as its home port.

ORP *ORKAN* IS SUNK

Shortly after carrying the body of Poland's commander-in-chief from Gibraltar to the United Kingdom, the Polish destroyer *Orkan* resumed patrolling in the Bay of Biscay as part of Force W with two Canadian destroyers, HMCS *Athabascan* and *Iroquois* of the British Tribal-class. The primary aim was to blockade the German-controlled ports of France so that the infamous blockade runners, which often used Spanish neutral waters, would not bring badly needed foreign supplies to reinforce the German war machine. It also interdicted the German U-boats using these ports and often meant stopping and searching Spanish trawlers suspected of aiding the German submarines. During this stint, the most memorable event was the rescue of four German naval officers and thirty-seven sailors from a U-boat *(U 459)* that had been sunk by a RAF Coastal Command plane.

After a short overhaul in Hull, *Orkan* was again seconded back to Scapa Flow and rejoined the Home Fleet. This was shortly followed by an assignment to Londonderry, as part of the Escort Support Group. Accompanied by the HMS *Musketeer, Orkan* sailed in the dangerous waters off Iceland in active support of Convoys ONS 19 and then 204.

The next convoy sailing from Canada, SC 143, became the focus of a very determined German attack, and the Allied destroyers were sent to support the convoy, based on radio decryption from Bletchley.

This was one of the bloodiest battles between the Germans submarines, using all their new technology and improved tactics, and the Royal Navy, utilizing their electronic wonder, the H/FD/F or "Huff Duff." British electronic surveillance was now able to pick up, and even track, the radio conversation between the attacking German U-boats.

As the battle unfolded, an ever growing number of enemy submarines were identified; in the night battle, with the Allies using star shells indiscriminately to discourage the enemy from surfacing, intense depth-charge attacks were carried out. The Germans in turn, for the first time, used acoustic torpedoes. The German attack, as in most of the so-called wolf-pack attacks. was carried out on the surface, as the Germans only submerged when under attack. The Allied tactic was to hold out through the night, forcing the Germans to submerge and thus to lose their best opportunity to attack the Allied convoy.

Daylight hours were relatively safe, since the Allied aircraft were able to keep the Germans submerged, where they were barely able to keep up with the convoy.

At approximately 0603 hours of October 8, 1943, *Orkan* sustained a torpedo hit, which resulted in two major explosions and the near instantaneous sinking of the warship. Only one officer and a small number of seamen survived what was in Kondracki's words, a scene straight out of Dante's inferno. The Polish destroyer became engulfed in flames and sank within minutes of the two explosions. The few survivors were haunted by the screams of the men burning alive inside the sinking ship. At 0610 *Orkan* sank to the terrible dirge of the burning sailors. The survivors, floating in freezing oil-covered water, heard the final underwater detonation as the depth-charges exploded, putting an end to the terrible anguish and agony of the trapped sailors of the doomed ship.

Nine officers and one hundred sixty-six sailors were lost. Many died in the freezing waters awaiting daylight for rescue. The Allied ships were still fighting a death-and-life battle with the U-boats, and it was not until 0730 that Commander Cubrey of the *Musketeer* was able to pick up the few Polish survivors. A number of British sailors jumped overboard to help the exhausted Poles climb the lines to safety.

After rescuing the Poles, *Musketeer* rejoined the convoy and the battle continued. But daylight brought reinforcements in the form of Iceland-based Liberators, which destroyed two German U-boats (*U-419* and *U-643*) and a Sunderland, which sank the *U-610*. The German U-boat (*U-378*) which had sunk *Orkan,* escaped the air attack but a mere two weeks later was sunk by American planes from the escort carrier *USS Core*, off the Azores, where Doenitz had moved his battered fleet to escape the Allied onslaught.

The grievous loss of a smart and modern ship like the *Okran* and—even more important—of a brave and well-trained crew was hard to replace in the unique circumstances under which the Poles operated in exile. It seemed to confirm the old maritime superstition, that women and dead men aboard, bring bad luck to ships.

After four years of strife, the Allies had won complete air superiority, had overcome the German U-boat menace, and had completely checkmated the ever smaller German surface fleet. On December 26, 1943, the Royal Navy had managed to pounce on the German battleship *Scharnhorst* as it attempted to interdict a Russia-bound convoy, and in the ensuing classicly old-fashioned artillery exchange, the British sank the enemy. Only thirty six German sailors were rescued.

STRATEGIC PLANNING OR WISHFUL THINKING?

From the first months of the reconstitution of the Polish military headquarters and armed forces in the West, the Poles worked at developing a clandestine force in occupied Poland. In the first months, while still in France, these plans were focused on couriers and radio communications between Poland and headquarters in exile.

Following the defeat of France, in the United Kingdom, the Poles formed a special branch of the headquarters staff, Bureau VI, for all matters pertaining to communication with and supply of the clandestine forces, which in a matter of time became known as the *Armia Krajowa* (*AK*), or Home Army.

The opening of the SOE files in the British Public Record Office, Kew Garden, pertaining to Poland (HS4) to general research brought out one surprise, namely, that the first plans for an insurrection in Poland, with air support from the United Kingdom, were in fact drawn up by British staff: "Characteristics of a Modern Insurrectional Movement: Description of a Descent Region and its Work during Descent." (PRO HS4/155)

These plans were eagerly embraced by the Poles, who were assumed by many, including the author, to have been the originators of these strategic concepts, rather than eager disciples. After the involuntary entry of the Soviet Union into the war, these plans no longer fitted British policies and the Poles were repeatedly urged to confine their clandestine operations to intelligence-gathering and sabotage.[5] The final negative— and from the Polish view tragic—decision regarding the integration of the Polish Home Army into Western plans was made by the Combined Chiefs of Staff in Washington on September 23, 1943: "The Combined Chiefs of Staff are unable at the present time to see their way to the allocation of the equipment required for the Polish Secret Army."[6]

Even this flat and nonnegotiable statement, based on the realities of the United States foreign policy towards the Soviet Union, did not stop the Poles from planning for a future positive change in the strategic situation. But as the British in their cold realism stated, "Tell Tabor [the Polish senior liaison officer with the Polish underground] he is living in a fool's paradise." (PRO HS4/147)

THE TEHRAN CONFERENCE

The meeting of the leaders of the three major military powers fighting the Germans took place in the capital city of Iran (Persia) in November 1943.

It is accepted by all historians that at this conference, or the first summit meeting, the Western Powers accepted Soviet hegemony over Eastern Europe and conceded Soviet claims to territories occupied in 1939–40 in collusion with Germany. The Polish government now knew that the historic *kresy* (the eastern marshlands of Poland), including the cities of Lwow, Wilno, Grodno, and the oil district of Boryslaw were lost. The Poles in exile became divided into two camps. One, led by Polish Prime Minister Stanislaw Mikolajczyk, planned to salvage what was possible by working closely with Churchill. Mikolajczyk offered the Soviets a de facto control over disputed territories, pending some future, to be determined arbitration. This was rejected, because clearly the Soviets only wanted complete submission from their satellites. The other camp, led by the commander-in-chief, General Kazimierz Sosnkowski came to the conclusion that nothing would be salvaged, and that collaboration in appeasement could lead to only one result: Polish accession to the territorial losses. The Polish underground leadership, naively convinced of the good will of the West, also adamantly refused to approve any plans by the government in exile to concede Polish territories.

A schism now divided the Polish leadership with a growing possibility of a break up of the constitutional Government. The danger of Sosnkowski flying to Poland and revoking allegiance to the Polish government was a nightmare. Facing the alternatives in early 1944, it is most likely that the Polish armed forces in exile and the Polish underground would have stood by him solidly. It needs to be pointed out that, according to the Polish constitution, the commander-in-chief had major prerogatives and was accountable only to the president, not to the prime minister and the cabinet. Therefore the ultimate issue was: Where does the president stand?

President Wladyslaw Raczkiewicz did compromise, whenever he could do so, but never accepted any decision which would have entailed the Polish government's assent to loss of territory.

NOTES

1. Paul Kemp, *Friend or Foe: Friendly Fire at Sea, 1939–1945,* Barnsley, 1995.
2. Lew Lind, *Battle of the Wine Dark Sea: The Aegean Campaign, 1940–1945,* Kenthurst, Australia, 1994.
3. David Kahn, *Seizing the Enigma: The Race to Break the German U-Boat Codes, 1939–1943,* Boston, 1991.
4. David Syrett, *The Defeat of the German U-Boats,* University of South Carolina Press, 1994.
5. Michael Alfred Peszke, *Battle for Warsaw, 1939–1944,* Boulder, CO, 1995, pp. 78–175.
6. National Archives, Washington CCS 334 218.

CHAPTER X

1944
VICTORY IN THE WEST,
TRAGEDY IN WARSAW—
HARBINGER OF POLAND'S FUTURE

POLISH NAVY'S PLANS FOR THE FUTURE

The main plans for moving the Polish forces to Poland were made *for* the Polish Army and Air Force. In the official British directive regarding the Polish forces, written and made available to the Polish commander-in-chief on July 4, 1943 (i.e., after General Sikorski's death), it was stated that, "The ultimate aim will be to concentrate the Polish Force in Poland." The Directive also acknowledged that; "The Polish Parachute Brigade will be reserved for direct action in Poland, but the moment and method of this employment must be governed by availability of aircraft." (PRO WO193/41 80751)

But the Naval Commandant in January 1942, stated that after the war—Germany's defeat already being taken for granted—the Soviet Union would become a paramount naval power in the Baltic, regardless of its economic devastation, and would not be confined to its pre-1939 access to the sea. It was assumed that the Soviet Union would have far-reaching demands and the sovereignty of the Baltic Republics was regarded as dubious. It was opined that in the long run, complete domination of the Baltic by the Soviets, would not be welcomed by the British because of their traditional policy of balance of power. It was therefore hoped that the British would see in Poland and its ports a counterbalance to the Soviet Union. Polish naval experts concluded that the current high degree of collaboration between the Polish Navy and the Royal Navy gave good ground for optimism and that it would be to Poland that the British would look to Poland for building a British economic and naval presence in the Baltic. The document then elaborated the steps which needed to be taken by the Polish commander-in-chief and staffs in London to ensure that the Polish Navy and the Polish coastline would be in a position to play a role in such hoped for developments.

These internal strategic goals found their expression in the articulated open policy statements during the *Polish Maritime Exhibition* in London, opened by the First Lord of the Admiralty, Alexander, on February 10, 1944.

Poland's "Sea Exhibition" (as the Poles called it), was divided into a historical section dealing with pre–1939 peacetime development; the current war effort, and future goals. It was that third that struck some of the British officials as controversial.

In that third section the Poles made the following declaration:

(a) The Baltic Sea must be an open sea, and German control of the Baltic has to cease. This is indispensable for a lasting World Peace. The Baltic in the hands of one power is a permanent menace to such a Peace.

(b) It is highly desirable to increase the tonnage of the British Mercantile Marine in the Baltic. It played a very small part before the War. For instance, in 1937 it represented only 6.8 per cent of the tonnage that passed through the Kiel Canal.

(c) A larger access to the sea will enable Poland and the Central Eastern European States to be independent of the German transport system.

According to British internal Foreign Office documents, the exhibition was originally planned in 1943, and Lord Alexander had accepted the invitation to open it officially. A year later the whole policy dynamic had changed, and in the words of the confidential memo of January 28, 1944, from the Admiralty to the Foreign Office:

On receiving from the Polish Minister of Information a short description of the exhibits and aim of the Exhibition, the First Lord is a little shaken.

The advice which has been given to him is that since it is no part of the policy of H.M. Government to ostracise the Poles, there is no reason why he should not fulfil the engagement so long as he keeps his speech to an objective tribute to the part which the Polish Navy and Merchant Marine have played in this war. The First Lord would be grateful to know at the earliest possible moment whether the Foreign Office concur with this view.

Roberts of the Foreign Office indeed concurred with this advice and stated that the Polish aims were, in general, in line with British policy:

which is directed to giving Poland a good Baltic coastline at the expense of Germany and as compensation for loses to Russia. In view of the considerable service of the Polish Navy and Merchant Marine (including the convoying of supplies to Russia) I can see no reason why the First Lord should not accept this invitation. (PRO FO 371/39506)

THE LAND WAR CONTINUES

On land the Germans were still a colossus, even though they had suffered overwhelming losses at the Eastern Front. But as the old soldier's saying goes, "You haven't been to war, until you've fought the Germans." There were still many more bloody land battles to be fought since the Germans still had a lot of fight left and much inventiveness, all committed to destructive pursuit.

It was in 1944 that the Germans began to rain their V-1 and V-2 flying bombs and rockets onto London and the southern English counties, and it was in late 1944 that the first operational jets in the world were used by the Luftwaffe against Allied formations.

But it was no longer a question as to whether the Allies would win, merely when; and with the changed dynamics of the alliance and the position of strength enjoyed by the Soviets, the question for the Polish government was whether anything would be salvaged from Soviet Communist imperialism. The Tehran Conference of December 1943 boded ill for the Poles. But discouraged as the Poles were, and apprehensive about the continued erosion of their political and diplomatic support in the United Kingdom, there was no question of not continuing the war against the primary enemy, Germany.

THE FINAL BATTLES

In the northern waters the presence of the sole remaining operational German battleship, *Tirpitz*, based in Norwegian fjords, still posed a potential danger to Allied convoys. The Home Fleet had to stalemate any German surface attack, and the possibility of a near suicidal one-way departure to attack the huge convoys with American troops coming to the United Kingdom had to be considered.

After a thorough refit, the Polish destroyers, *Piorun* and *Blyskawica*, participated in the Royal Navy's attempt both to thwart if not destroy the potential menace of the *Tirpitz*, lurking in the northern fjords of occupied Norway, but also to mislead the Germans that the invasion would be directed at regaining Norway, and not France.

The Home Fleet still had to screen the continued Allied convoys, carrying endless supplies to the Soviet Union, without which that country could not have survived or become a postwar power to be feared and courted.

The Royal Navy's Home Fleet was powerful indeed. It consisted of the brand-new battleships HMS *Anson* and HMS *Duke of York* (the vanquisher of the *Scharnhorst*), the fleet carriers *Victorious* and *Furious,* six small escort carriers, carrying planes for anti-submarine operations, and numerous cruisers and destroyers.

Piorun took part in one of these attempts to engage the enemy surface fleet, code named, Tungsten. These attacks were harbingers of the future, namely air attacks carried out by the Royal Navy's Fleet Air Arm dive-bombers from the carriers. The operations were successful so far as the convoys were concerned and, certainly, also succeeded in bottling up the German surface warships, but did not succeed in sinking the *Tirpitz,* which was however damaged. These operations were repeated but either weather conditions or simple bad luck denied the Allies complete success. In addition, the Royal Navy used midget submarines in an attempt to sink the German battleship. *Tirpitz* was finally knocked out, but not in a classic surface engagement as had sunk the *Scharnhorst,* nor in a carrier attack, as had finally destroyed the *Bismarck,* but by the "Tall Boys" bombs of the RAF's Lancasters on November 12, 1944.

While the Royal Navy had to protect the convoys, it also had to prepare for the impending invasion. Both Polish destroyers returned to Plymouth in May 1944, for the final preparations for the impending invasion of the Continent.

OPERATION OVERLORD

The invasion of German-occupied France, directed at the region of Normandy, code named Overlord, was carried out by Allied forces on June 6, 1944, under the overall command of the American General, Dwight D. Eisenhower; while the naval part of the operation was code named Neptune and was commanded by the Royal Navy's Admiral Sir Bertram Ramsay.

The Poles did not participate in the first wave that stormed the beaches. However, all but one of the fourteen Polish air squadrons based in the United Kingdom took part, the only exception being the 304th which was part of the RAF Coastal Command and involved indirectly. While most of the Polish squadrons took part in the air battle over Normandy, only two Polish wings were specifically dedicated to the 2nd Tactical Air Force and were organized as the 18th Fighter Group under a Polish senior officer, Colonel Gabszewicz.

The 18th Fighter Group consisted of three Allied wings, totalling nine fighter squadrons of which five were Polish, namely the 302nd, 306th, 308th, 315th and 317th; while two were RAF, one Belgian, and one Royal New Zealand Air Force. These two Polish wings had an actual establishment of 230 officers, 618 noncommissioned officers, and 1,525 airmen, which represented close to thirty percent of the whole strength of the Polish Air Force in mid-1944. The third Polish fighter wing, consisting of 303rd, 316th and 307th remained in the United

Kingdom as part of the Royal Air Force's new command, Air Defence of Great Britain. But these squadrons also flew operations on behalf of the invading forces from bases in southern England.

On June 6, 1944—D-Day—the pilots of 18th Fighter Group flew four missions each and the entire group scored thirty victories, more than the pilots of any group. By June 11, the squadrons were operating out of field bases in Normandy.

On July 9, one of the Polish wings returned back to the United Kingdom to reinforce defenses against the German flying bomb attacks.[1] The German flying bomb (V-1) offensive had taken the British public by surprise. Coming at a time of victories, when many assumed the war would be over by the end of the year, the new horror seemed unfair and unthinkable. The British threw all their energies into combating this terrible new weapon. The V-1 launchers were bombed, batteries of anti-aircraft artillery placed in Southern England, and fast fighter squadrons placed on standing patrols to intercept V-1s over the sea. The speed of the flying bombs did not allow for the standard radar interception and fighter squadron scramble. The Polish squadrons which took part in this operation scored a total of 190 successes, which was ten percent of the total number shot down. Again the friendly *Illustrated London News* carried a sympathetic story on August 5, 1944 captioned "Exit Two Robots. Polish Fighter Pilots in Action over the Channel." The illustration showed one of the Polish-flown Mustangs tipping the wing of the flying bomb to send it out of control into the sea.

OPERATION NEPTUNE

All but one of the Polish surface warships, namely *Garland,* also took part in the invasion. The Polish medium cruiser *Dragon* (commanding officer Kmdr. por. Stanislaw Dzienisiewicz) was part of Task Force D and gave the Canadians artillery support, while the two small destroyers, *Slazak* (CO Kmdr. ppor. Romuald Tyminski) and *Krakowiak,* (CO Kmdr. ppor. Wszechwlad Maracewicz), were deployed on the eastern wing of British landings near Ouistreham to cover Allied minesweepers and landing craft. The danger here was from the

German torpedo boats, their famous E-boats, which had already shown their effectiveness at Slapton Sands.

But it was the two fleet destroyers, the *Blyskawica* (CO Kmdr. por. Konrad Namiesniowski) and *Piorun* (CO Kmdr. ppor. Tadeusz Gorazdowski), that were involved in the most dramatic sea battle of the *Neptune* Operation. Both Polish warships were part of the Tenth Destroyer Flotilla, based at Plymouth, which consisted of two divisions: 19th and the 20th of which *Blyskawica* was the leader.

On the night of June 5 to June 6, 1944, the eve of D-Day, elements of the Tenth Destroyer Flotilla, including *Blyskawica*, swept the shores of northern France from the region of Calais south to Dieppe, Le Havre, Cherbourg, and St. Malo. The purpose was to assure the Allied command that there were no enemy surface ships or convoys in the region where the landings would take place. No enemy ships were sighted and all but two of the Allied destroyers returned to Plymouth in the morning, as the crucial battle began. Before turning back north, the crews observed and heard the thousands of Allied planes heading for Normandy. HMS *Tartar* and *Blyskawica* remained at sea, patrolling between Eddystone Rocks Lighthouse and the shores of Brittany.

The *Kriegsmarine* interventions were limited to E-boat attacks against the heavy Allied shipping.[2] The Germans shortly began to lack torpedoes and with land routes paralyzed by Allied aircraft, decided to deliver the torpedoes from Brest to Cherbourg by sea. This fact only became known after the war. This was the background to the nighttime action of June 8. The German destroyer division commander was Kapitanzur-See Baron von Bechtolsheim, and his flag was on a brandnew destroyer, the *Z-32*. Other German warships were *Z-24*, *ZH-1*, (all three *Z* destroyers were the new and heavily armed *Narvik class) and T-24* (*Elbing* class), which had sunk the Canadian destroyer *Athabascan* by torpedoes in a night action on April 28, 1944. These four German warships departed Brest, initially taking a southward course, to mislead Allied reconnaissance, and then turned north heading for Cherbourg. But Canadian patrol planes identified them and notified Allied Naval Headquarters. The Tenth Destroyer Flotilla departed Plymouth at speed, joining up with *Tartar* and *Blyskawica* on patrol. This led to a major encounter off Ushant in which the

Allied navies, totally destroyed the German naval ability to interdict the Allied landings.

The two divisions consisted of:

19th—HMS *Tartar*, (flotilla leader—Captain B. Jones), HMS *Ashanti*, *HMCS Huron* and HMCS *Haida*.
20th—ORP *Blyskawica*, ORP *Piorun*, HMS *Javelin* and HMS *Eskimo*.

In weather described as overcast, with intermittent rain, a light southwesterly wind, calm sea, and visibility of one to three miles, the Allied force sailed south from Plymouth. At midnight the Allied warships were about fifty miles from the shores of Brittany. The distance between the divisions was four thousand yards.

At 0116 hours on June 9, *Tartar* got a radar bearing on a German force at a range of ten nautical miles. The direction was given as 251 degrees. The position when contact was established was 49.03N & 04.11W. Very shortly the other Allied warships also established radar contact. All crews were at their full alert and with heightened nerves, since it was common knowledge that the German practice was to initiate a torpedo attack at a distance of less than nine thousand meters.

The Allies now had a brand new radio interception system called "headache" which picked up internal enemy transmissions. Its limitation was the need to have fluent German speakers aboard the Allied warships. Headache was aboard one British destroyer *Eskimo* and the *Piorun*. At 0128 *Eskimo*, using this new intercept system, reported that enemy destroyers had fired torpedoes. At the same time, Allied warships opened artillery fire on the enemy ships. The Allies used illuminating shells. *Blyskawica* achieved covering fire on the lead ship in her second salvo and managed to get in twelve salvos altogether, with the result that the lead German Destroyer, *Narvik*, was on fire.

The German warships with their 150-millimeter caliber artillery, however, outgunned the Allied warships, equipped only with 120-millimeter guns. There is some dispute whether *Blyskawica* changed course because she was heavily engaged or as a result of the German torpedo attack. It is likely that both reasons played a part. Normally, one would turn into the torpedoes to "comb" them but, straddled by enemy shells as well, it would make sense to turn away. None of the German torpedoes hit their targets.

While *Blyskawica* lost contact with the enemy, *Piorun* did not. *Tartar* in the best tradition of the Royal Navy turned to the enemy and received punishing artillery fire. A number of British officers and other rank were killed and *Tartar* was in bad straits, but saved by *Ashanti*, which carried out a torpedo attack on the lead German destroyer. Hit by a British torpedo, and carrying an extra supply of torpedoes for its E-boats, the German flag ship exploded.

Tartar, because of damage withdrew, and the battle was carried on by the Canadians. *Piorun*, which had not turned with *Blyskawica*, continued its artillery fire and found itself between the two divisions of Allied warships.

It should be remembered that the action was taking place at night, and took about ten minutes to complete. Decisions were made as in a fighter plane, on impulse, without thinking and certainly not on the basis of a planned strategy. *Blyskawica* rejoined the Canadians, after coming perilously close to being attacked by them. This was prevented only by the Polish commander lighting up his ship. Since *Piorun* was missing from the ranks of the 20th division, there was a short-lived fear that the explosion (*i.e.*, of the German destroyer) was the *Piorun* being hit.

The Allied warships now embarked on the search for the remaining German warships. *Blyskawica* was now leading the Allied contingent, and at 0449, at a bearing of 195 degrees, the enemy was sighted and attacked. The Germans sought the protection of their own land-based artillery, but Allied superiority was overwhelming, and another German destroyer was beached and exploded.

One irony was that the search and chase for the Germans was confounded by an Allied minefield, QZX.1330, which had been placed to hinder Germans from interdicting Allied convoys. Since the Allied officers knew about this minefield, they were forced to sail around it, while the Germans oblivious to their danger sailed directly through and two escaped.

At 0537 the action was called off. The Allied warships had sailed close to the German-occupied shores of France, looking for the two damaged German destroyers, to no avail. The German action named *(Torpeden)* was a fiasco.

The Allied command issued the following report:

> This action, one of the very few which had been
> fought between large and modern destroyers at night
> during this war, effected the destruction of half the
> enemy's force and inflicted damage on at least one of
> the two who escaped. It was thus a not inconsiderable
> success and a useful contribution to the safety of our
> convoys. (PRO ADM 199/1944 80751)

POLISH WARSHIPS IN ACTION

After expending all its ammunition in support of the Canadian
ground forces, the Polish cruiser *Dragon* returned to Plymouth
to replenish supplies. On sailing back to the coast of Normandy
to continue its artillery support of Allied troops, it was hit by a
German one man submarine and suffered extensive damage. A
number of Polish sailors were killed in the ensuing explosion
and fire. The cruiser had to be beached, and the British Admiralty urged the Poles to allow the ship to become part of the
breakwater. This was agreed to, but since the majority of the
crew were saved, the Polish Navy wished to replace the cruiser
as soon as possible. There is an interesting comment on this in
the Foreign Office minutes, authored by Roberts. (PRO FO
371/39506):

> Admiralty (i.e. British) told me that the Poles had
> put in a request for another cruiser to replace the
> Dragon which has been beached and became a total
> loss. They naturally wanted a modern cruiser, and
> indeed after the performance of the Polish Navy, they
> well deserved one. There is little likelihood of any fur-
> ther use of modern cruisers except in the war against
> Japan in which the Polish Navy would probably not
> take part.

Nevertheless, the Poles were loaned a sister ship the HMS
Danae and renamed the O.R.P. *Conrad.* This seemed like a
prophetic choice, naming the last Polish warship to be commissioned in the war after the *nom de plume* of the Polish-born

writer, Joseph Korzeniowski, who became a self-imposed exile from his country and found his genre in the psychological studies and writings about the human spirit, while working as a merchant marine officer in British employment.

Allied naval operations in the English Channel continued. The Allies had complete air and naval superiority between the southern English ports and the beachheads in Normandy, but the two ends of the Channel were still being contested since the Germans still held most of French Brittany and the ports of Brest, Lorient, and Bayonne. They also still occupied the regions of France opposite Dover and the entire Belgian and Dutch coast.

German naval forays were made from both ends to disrupt the transport of war matériel to the Allied forces in France, and it was in these areas that all naval combat took place over the next six months. There were also functioning German U-boat bases in southern France and, until the end of 1944, these ports received German blockade runners from South America.

The Allied naval effort was thus diverted to choking off both points, and the Royal Navy's home ports for these operations became Harwich for the northeast and Plymouth for the southwest.

The two Polish fleet destroyers continued to operate based out of Plymouth and progressively moving their operations into the Bay of Biscay.

On June 13, 1944, *Piorun* (CO Kdr. ppor. Tadeusz Gorazdowski) and *Ashanti* (CO Lt. Cdr. Crawford) sailed to the vicinity of St. Malo. At 0025 hours on June 14, *Piorun* got a radar contact of four blips. Both Allied warships proceeded on an intercept course, and twelve minutes later star shells illuminated enemy warships (minesweepers) of the 600-ton M-class. At a range of 2,300 yards, artillery fire was opened on visual sighting of the star shells.

Within minutes, one of the enemy warships was on fire, however, it now became obvious that there were seven enemy warships, and that their returning fire was both vigorous and, as always with the Germans, accurate. While the Germans, ship for ship, were smaller and slower, they had among them fourteen 105-millimeter guns. A number of hits were registered on *Piorun,* causing some casualties and a fire erupted which was contained. At 0048 *Piorun* decided to fire a torpedo salvo, and, as a result, a second enemy minesweeper blew up. But *Ashanti* had not been idle either, and two other German warships were now burning. The remaining enemy ships now attempted to break away. The Allied destroyers took a course to prevent the Germans from seeking the protection of their shore artillery, in which they were unsuccessful, as the Allied warships came under heavy and accurate shore fire from German shore artillery based on occupied Jersey. This did not save the German warships which continued to receive heavy and accurate Allied fire but the Germans gallantly returned fire, which again scored hits on *Piorun*. At this time, the star shells had been expended and Allied ship artillery fire was radar controlled. Another German ship received damage, and again German batteries on Jersey came into play. At this point, with three enemy ships sunk and one presumed, the two Allied warships broke off the engagement and returned to Plymouth.

On the following day *Blyskawica*, as leader and accompanied by *Eskimo* and the *Piorun,* sailed on patrol to the other of the German-occupied Channel Islands, Guernsey. There was no contact with the enemy on sea, though all three destroyers came under fire from the shore artillery.

On June 26, 1944, *Blyskawica* boarded the Polish commander.-in-chief, General Kazimierz Sosnkowski, and transported him to the Allied beachhead in Normandy for a personal inspection.

The two Polish fleet destroyers enjoyed a short break from the Neptune operations on July 1, when both went to meet and escort HMS *Prince Robert* headed for Plymouth. On July 7 and 8, both Polish destroyers again sailed on patrol to the vicinity of Jersey with no contacts with the enemy.

On July 14, *Tartar* (as leader), *Haida,* and *Blyskawica* sailed for a patrol off the French port of Lorient. A small enemy convoy was intercepted and destroyed.

Between July 22 and 25, 1944, *Blyskawica* (leader) and *Haida* carried out two patrols in the vicinity of Ile de Bas off the Brittany coast. Both patrols were uneventful.

On July 30, the Royal Navy dispatched a major task force (Force 26) to the Bay of Biscay to attack enemy shipping which consisted of two Royal Navy cruisers, HMS *Diadem* and *Bellona,* the carrier *HMS Striker*, six destroyers of the Tenth

Flotilla, including *Piorun* and *Blyskawica,* and three destroyers of the Eleventh Flotilla.

The task force split the following day: *Blyskawica* accompanied *Diadem,* while *Piorun* went with *Bellona.* After all-night patrolling and no contact with the enemy, the two groups joined up and *Blyskawica* refueled from the carrier *Striker.* The Task Force returned back to Plymouth on August 3.

Between August 3 and 6, 1944, the two Polish destroyers again patrolled near Ile de Bas with no enemy contact. During subsequent patrols, the Polish warships occasionally came under fire from coastal batteries, made contact at times with U-boats, and frequently came across French trawlers from which French agents were boarded.

On August 11, *Piorun* went on patrol with *Diadem* near La Rochelle. A radar contact was established and the ship was identified as a German blockade runner (though some other sources identify it as a German auxiliary cruiser) and shelled by *Piorun.* The German ship (*Sperrbrecher 7*) was on fire when the Poles received a message from *Diadem:* CLOSE AND FINISH HIM OFF. Two torpedoes were fired; one hit the German ship, which broke up and sunk. The German ship was approximately eight thousand tons.

These operations lasted until the German capitulation in May, 1945, since many of the French Atlantic ports were held by the Germans to the bitter end. At times the Polish destroyers were diverted to escort troopships from the United States.

The following troopships and warships were escorted during the last months of 1944. On September 30, MS *Mauretania;* on October 3, *SS Aquitania;* on October 9, the carrier HMS *Indefatigable;* on October 29, *Queen Elizabeth* and *Dominion Monarch;* on November 16, MS *Pasteur* and *Ile de France;* and on December 14, MS *Sobieski.* All these converted liners were carrying additional American troops for the Continent. In many cases, however, because of the continued German occupation of the French Atlantic ports, the ships sailed to England, where the troops disembarked and were transported to the continent on smaller craft.

Gorazdowski, commander of *Piorun,* received a bar to his Distinguished Service Cross.

Polish warships and Polish motor-torpedo-gunboats (MTGs) also operated in the northeast part of the Channel. The Poles operated with Royal Navy, Royal Canadian Navy, and Dutch MTGs in primarily defensive operations against German E-boats. This was also the mission of the two Polish escort destroyers, *Krakowiak* and *Slazak,* which were assigned to the Royal Navy's Sixteenth Flotilla and based in Harwich. Their operations consisted of interdicting German convoys to German-held Atlantic ports like Dunkirk and Calais and also preventing German attacks against shipping supplying the Allied armies.

On October 15, 1944, *Slazak* acted as escort to *HMS Garth,* which carried King George VI on an inspection of Allied forces.

POLISH LAND FORCES IN THE WEST

The late summer and autumn of 1944 were momentous months indeed. Poles played a part in the mostly victorious battles in the West, but suffered diplomatic defeats that sealed the fate of Poland for a fifty-year period.

In August 1944, the Polish Armored Division became operational and took part in the Allied victory of the Falaise pocket.[3] On September 21, the Polish Parachute Brigade, was dropped into the flawed Arnhem operation.[4]

THE WARSAW UPRISING

On August 1, 1944, the Warsaw Uprising broke out and lasted for two months. The political and military failure of the uprising finalized Poland's subjugation to the Soviets.[5] The paradox of the Polish parachute brigade being destroyed in a badly executed operation, while its primary goal, Warsaw, was being destroyed, bereft of Allied help, was a bitter and discouraging episode for the Polish forces in the West.

ORP *GARLAND*'S LAST HURRAH

In early 1944, ORP *Garland* (commanding officer Kdr. ppor. B. Biskupski) after convoying between Freetown, Takoradi, and

Gibraltar, sailed into the Mediterranean and began convoy work between North African ports, Naples, and Malta. Between May 14 and May 16, as leader of twelve Allied destroyers, British, American, and Greek, she carried out an antisubmarine sweep in the region of Sardinia and Sicily. Most of the summer was spent in these activities, with some time out for refitting in Alexandria and Valetta. On September 9, *Garland* was assigned to Force A, composed of one cruiser, four auxiliary carriers and ten destroyers, which sailed for Crete. She then provided support during the invasion of Kythera and took part in the blockade of Santorini.

While at sea, the *Garland*'s lookout spotted smoke coming from the water. This was quickly identified as diesel exhausts from a schnorkel and the position marked with phosphorous flares before depth-charge attack was initiated. A total of three such attacks were delivered, at 1645, 1722, and the final one, at 1728 hours. While carrying out the attack, *Garland* reported her contact and requested additional help. At 1800 a British destroyer joined the pursuit and also depth-charged the suspected area of the U-boat. In the early hours of the following day (*i.e.*, September 19), the U-boat surfaced in close proximity to *Garland,* which opened fire with all her artillery. After a few minutes, the firing was stopped and the U-boat was sunk by depth charges. The boat was the *U-407.*[6]

In late 1944, a civil war broke out in Greece and the British took very strong and prompt action to support the Royalists and anticommunists, by landing British troops at Piraeus. *Garland* participated indirectly by escorting carriers involved in these operations. The landing of British troops in Greece, the transfer of all French divisions from Italy to take part in the invasion of southern France, and of the transport of all remaining Canadians to northwest Europe depleted the Allied armies in Italy, and made the Polish 2 Army Corps an essential element in that campaign.

After a short refit in Alexandria, *Garland* was back in action, escorting the HMS *Black Prince* in a sweep off Kos and Stampalia. In October, *Garland* sailed as far north as Salonika and shelled German positions and installations in Kassandra.

On November 20, 1944, *Garland* departed from the Mediterranean, closing a long and improbable chapter in the history of the Polish Navy. Who, in the early days of the war, would have thought that so much action would be seen by Polish warships in that sea, so far from Poland?

NOTES

1. Christopher F. Shores, *2nd Tactical Air Force,* Reading, England, 1970; and *Destiny Can Wait: The Polish Air Force in the Second World War,* London, 1949.
2. James Foster Tent, *E-Boat Alert: Defending the Normandy Invasion Fleet,* Naval Institute, Annapolis, MD, 1996.
3. John Keegan, *Six Armies in Normandy,* NY, 1982.
4. George Cholewczynski, *Poles Apart: The Polish Airborne at the Battle of Arnhem,* New York, 1993; and Martin Middlebrook, *Arnhem, 1944,* Boulder, CO, 1994.
5. Jan M. Ciechanowski, *The Warsaw Rising of 1944,* Cambridge University Press, 1974. Janusz K. Zawodny, *Nothing But Honour: The Story of the Warsaw Uprising, 1944*, Hoover Institute Press, 1978.
6. Lew Lind, *The Battle of the Wine Dark Sea: The Aegean Campaign, 1940–1945,* Kenthurst, Australia, 1994.

CHAPTER XI

1945
VICTORY OF THE ALLIED COALITION AND
DEMISE OF THE
SECOND POLISH REPUBLIC

THE YALTA CONFERENCE AND ITS CONSEQUENCES

The Conference of the three leaders of the Allied Coalition, Stalin, Roosevelt, and Churchill took place in February 1945, in the small resort town of Yalta in Soviet Crimea. It capped the Soviet's efforts to impose their political system and their boundaries, not only on Poland, but also on the whole of Eastern Europe. But unfair as this imposed system was on everyone, it was particularly egregious for Poland. It was the only one of these eastern European states that had actively opposed and then fought the Germans, even at a time when the Soviets and the Germans were collaborating. Yet, territorial loss and an alien political and economic system was dictated to the Poles in the same fashion as those countries that had been willing or passive German client states. That this was a goal of Soviet policy was understandable to the Poles, who had lived next to that imperious giant—that the western democracies seemed tacitly to endorse it was heart breaking.

Poles had already sensed this impending doom in late 1943, after the Tehran Conference. Russian inaction during the Warsaw Uprising was the final proof. All Polish efforts to present their viewpoint to the Western democracies came to naught. The British Foreign Office commented on this mass-media antagonism

> Any intelligent Russian reader of the British Press would, I fear, draw the conclusion that Stalin could do almost anything he liked with Mr. Mikolajczyk (The

163

Polish Prime Minister) and the Poles without arousing any unfortunate reactions in this country.

The following is also minuted, from early August 1944, at the time of the Warsaw Uprising

I am sure nothing we can say to the press would persuade them to give direct support at the present juncture to the Polish Government. But I should have thought we might have pressed them to publicise the gallant fight which the Polish Army is putting up, especially in Warsaw. At present they are playing this down almost ostentatiously. (PRO FO 371/39408)

It took Churchill considerably longer to articulate his concern, when, in March 1945, he wrote to President Roosevelt seeking a unified approach to the Soviets: "At Yalta we agreed to take the Russian view of the frontier line. Poland has lost her frontier. Is she now to lose her freedom ?"[1]

It was too much of a coincidence for all Polish warships to be in port being refitted, when the nefarious Yalta Conference, that decided Poland's postwar fate, was taking place. The British must have been concerned about some form of strong protest from the Poles. But professional discipline held; although in the 2 Army Corps in Italy, whose soldiers were primarily from the regions of Poland given away to the Russians, there was vocalized discontent. The crews of the Polish bomber squadron, sent on a mission to assist the Russians by bombing targets in eastern Germany, also expressed their unhappiness, but carried out the mission.

Even though every Polish soldier, sailor, and airman knew that the cause of Poland had been despicably abandoned by the Western powers, there was no breakdown in discipline in any of the three Polish services. The 2 Army Corps went on to capture Bologna, the First Armored Division to the capture of Wilhemshaven, and the Polish squadrons continued to fly operational missions. With the depletion of Allied forces from Italy, the Polish 2 Army Corps was crucial to Allied operations.

Wronski writes in his memoirs, *Wspomnienia Plyna jak Okrety,* that in February 1945, his command, ORP *Slazak* went for a refit in London. He was invited by Admiral Dunbar-Nasmith for lunch, who before sitting down to eat asked Wronski, as a naval officer and gentleman, whether Lwow was a Polish city. Wronski replied that Lwow had never been part of Russia, not even during the hundred-year-long partitions, and that in Lwow there were three Catholic cathedrals of the Latin, Uniate, and Armenian rites, testifying to Polish tolerance. Furthermore Lwow had the third-oldest Polish university, Jana Kazimierza, founded by the Polish king in the seventeenth-century, in addition to one of Poland's two major polytechnic (science) academies and the magnificent Ossolineum Library.

The British admiral, after listening in silence, said "*I am sorry.*" Poles wished that more Englishmen had the civil courage and the grace to utter such words, which in the long run cost nothing![2]

THE FINAL DAYS

After the refits, necessary or not, the Polish warships resumed operations. *Piorun,* under the command of Kdr. ppor. J. Tchorznicki left Milford Haven and sailed to, where else? Scapa Flow. *Piorun* took part in one more major operation, escorting carriers in the North Sea. *Garland,* commanded by Kpt. mar. K. Hess, left the dockyard at Plymouth, also for Scapa Flow, and then returned to Plymouth for patrols off the Channel Islands which were still held by the Germans.

Blyskawica was refitted at Cowes, where she had been built, and departed under the command of Kdr. ppor. L. Lichodziejewski for Rosyth, and later took part in Operation Deadlight, which was the massed scuttling of surrendered German U-boats, the weapon that nearly delivered the war to Germany. *Blyskawica* had fought longer than any other Allied warship.

Poland's new cruiser, *Conrad,* a replacement for the *Dragon,* saw no action, but under the command of Kdr. por. R. Tyminski, had the pleasant duty of being the first Allied warship to sail into Wilhemshaven, the cradle of the German Navy, which was occupied by the units of the Polish First Armored Division.

The fighting in Europe came to an end May 8, 1945, and the Polish Navy was now busy delivering food to the various liberated countries of Western Europe. But Polish ports and the hunger of the Polish civilian population was beyond its reach. The Baltic was out of bounds. The warships that had been loaned from the British were returned. The warships that belonged to the Polish government were ultimately returned and every visitor to Gdynia may see the destroyer, *Blyskawica,* in its berth as a museum ship.

With the war in Europe finished, many strange and paradoxical things were about to happen. Germany was beaten and occupied, but in Britain's general elections, the Conservatives lost badly and the chief architect of the British victory, Churchill, lost his premiership (though he retained his parliamentary seat). On July 4, the British Government, now led by Mr. Clement Attlee of the Labour Party, notified the Polish government in exile that London no longer recognized it as the government of Poland. This was the government that had been recognized by the British throughout the war, and to which the Polish Armed Forces owed allegiance. In turn, the Polish forces also entered a strange limbo since they were an armed force of a country with an externally imposed government that was recognized by their host country.

THE FATE OF THOSE WHO RETURNED

Some of the Poles, particularly those who came from western Poland, and those who had been recruited from among the Polish migration living in France, and who had families, chose quick demobilization and returned to their homes.

Of the two hundred Polish naval personnel interned in Sweden, only one officer and less than thirty other rank returned with the three submarines back to Poland.

The majority of the Poles who fought in the West did not return to Poland to live under the hated Communism and Soviet rule. Some did, motivated by the desire to rejoin their families, by patriotism, and a wish to rebuild the country, and in some cases by bitterness at their treatment by their British ally. Occasionally opportunism also played a part. For most who returned and attempted to play a civic or professional role in the rebuilding of their homeland, the communist dictatorship was ruthless. Probably, at least half of the prewar officer cadre of the Polish Navy and of Polish Army who had been taken prisoner of war in 1939 returned to Poland after their liberation by the Allies. Many initially resumed their prewar military rank and function. But whether returnees from the West, or liberated prisoners of war, all were suspect and became victims of Stalinism.

As the "iron curtain" descended on the old and proud but devastated state, so did the brutal repression of any citizen who showed a tendency to independent thinking, of any citizen who displayed pride in the prewar accomplishments of the Polish Republic, of any citizen who did not display complete subservience in thought or action to the new political reality and allegiance to the Soviet Union.[3]

The senior officer corps of the Polish People's Republic became suspect, in particular those who had earned their commissions before the war, those who had fought in the West, and those who failed to show a correct attitude of admiration for Communism and the Soviet Union. Polish military symbolism was modified to resemble the Soviets' and Soviet officers were transferred to Polish service. The crown was removed from the eagle, and the naval uniform became a typical Soviet light blue.

Arrests, protracted and terrible interrogations, and in some cases state-sanctioned murder were the rule, not the exception. Those who survived write that they were often imprisoned in the same cells as captured German Gestapo officers, to humiliate as much as possible. In the Polish Navy, Komandors Stanislaw Mieszkowski, Zbigniew Przybyszewski (the gallant commander of the artillery at Hel in 1939), and Jerzy Staniewicz were executed, to be rehabilitated in 1956. Kontr-Admiral Adam Mohuczy, who commanded the Polish Submarine Squadron in 1939 and went into German captivity, died as a result of brutal treatment at the hands of his Communist inquisitors—after surviving five years in a German prisoner of war camp.

The war against the Polish people was waged at all levels; the most successful was the insidious propaganda directed at all that was honorable and Polish. It would have brought a smile of approval from Goebbels. As the Soviet charge directed at the Germans for the Katyn atrocity was being laughed out of court at Nuremberg, the Communists organized an anti-Jewish pogrom in Kielce. On February 16, 1989, Moscow admitted that the Katyn murders were organized by the NKVD but the Jewish tragedy of Kielce is still blamed on the Poles in many Western circles.[4]

After 1956, the Soviet General Rokossovsky was sent back to the Soviet Union and all of the victims were judicially rehabilitated, but a veil of deceit and prevarication still prevailed over many aspects of the Second World War. These blank spots were particularly blatant in any aspect of the role played by the Soviet Union in its collaboration with Germany, the murder of Polish officers at Katyn and many other camps by the Soviets, the deceitful and treacherous role played by the Soviets during the Warsaw Uprising, and finally the arrest and murder of Polish Underground Army officers after the war during the Soviet occupation.

It was only in the Catholic churches that memorials could and did begin to be unveiled to the victims of Communism, and to the achievements of the Polish Home Army and the Polish armed forces, who fought in the West, libelled as "capitalist lackeys." The most prominent houses of worship where such plaques were placed were the Cathedral of Saint John in Warsaw and the Basilica of Jasna Gora in Czestochowa. The pantheon for the Polish Navy became the twelfth-century Church of Saint Michael, the Archangel, in Oksywie. For the Polish Navy veterans, this little church on the hill of Oksywie, overlooking the naval port, was the place where Polish naval heroes and Polish warships were honored by appropriate plaques.

THE POLISH FORCES IN EXILE

Even though this is a history of the Polish Navy, a word should be said about the overall strength of the Polish armed forces loyal to the constitutional government of Poland, in London, at the end of the Second World War.

Total ground forces were 171,220 officers and other ranks, composed of the First Armored Corps in Scotland and the

2 Army Corps in Italy, three infantry divisions, two armored brigades, and one parachute brigade. This does not reflect the establishment of the Polish Underground Army *(Armia Krajowa)*, which was dissolved by the Polish president in early 1945 after most of Poland had been occupied by the Soviets. According to British estimates, the Polish Home Army in late August, 1944, consisted of close to 750,000 men (PRO HS 4/318). Total Air Force personnel strength was 19,400 officers and other ranks, comprising fourteen squadrons.

On October 1, 1939, after the majority of the Polish naval personnel had gone into German captivity, the total establishment of the Polish Navy was 813 officers and other rank. This number was primarily comprised of the crews of the three destroyers, two submarines, and two training ships with their trainees which were already in Western waters or had broken out of the Baltic during the September campaign. This group represented the most worthwhile cadre and, by war's end, even the seamen had advanced to noncommissioned officer rank.

The Naval Service recruited actively from among the Polish emmigrants living in Western Europe and North America. With the release of the Polish captives from the Soviet Gulags in 1941, the number of officers and other rank reached 3,545 by November 1944. By war's end, that number had grown to 4,043. This number does not include the air and ground crews of the Polish Coastal Command Squadron, nor of course, of the crews of the Polish merchant ships.

THE ROLE OF THE POLISH ARMED FORCES IN THE WAR

The role of the Polish military in exile in the West was three-fold: Firstly, to play as strong a part as possible in the western anti-German military coalition; Secondly, to support the Polish Underground and ensure that the Polish government would establish control of Polish territories after the Germans were driven out or defeated; and Thirdly, to guarantee that the Polish government in London, beset by a hostile left wing and Communist propaganda, would be accorded the rights of a sovereign and constitutional government.

The Polish Navy certainly did its share in the Allied coalition and was rivalled, in confronting anti-Polish propaganda, only by the fame won by the Polish air wings.

There is no evidence, anecdotal or archival, that would suggest that the Polish Navy planned any clandestine operations in the Baltic on behalf of the Polish Home Army.

The Polish Armed Forces managed to keep the constitutional Government recognized as long as war was waged. In that sense, the Polish Navy played a very modest role compared to the Polish 2 Army Corps in Italy. To document this point, Churchill's letter in late 1944 to Stalin needs to be noted. Churchill again extended his unconditional support for Russian policy but was pragmatic enough to be concerned about the Polish forces who owed no loyalty to the Russian sponsored Lublin Committee,

> The desire of His Majesty's Government for the reconstitution of a strong and independent Poland, friendly to Russia, remains unalterable. We have practical matters to handle with the Polish Government, and more especially the control of the considerable Polish Armed Forces, over 88,000 excellent fighting men, under our operational command. These are now making an appreciable contribution to the United Nations' war effort in Italy, Holland and elsewhere. Our attitude towards any new Polish Government (i.e. in London) must therefore be correct, though it will certainly be cold.[5]

Given its small size (even by the standards of the Polish armed forces in exile) the navy did more than its share. But was there a need to attempt to become a big ship navy?

Given the available manpower, the commitment of a large body of men to crew an old and outdated cruiser, like the *Dragon*, was questionable. Two fleet-class destroyers could have been commissioned for the same expenditure of resources. The seeming lack of interest on the part of the Polish Navy in obtaining expertise in minesweeping is also puzzling. Were the Poles to return to Baltic waters, as was hoped until the Yalta conference, there would have been a great need for such vessels.

THE 1946 VICTORY PARADE IN LONDON

The actual end of the Second World War came only in August 1945, when Japan surrendered unconditionally. The Allied victory was celebrated by the British Empire in June, 1946, approximately a year later.

The Polish forces, of whom the majority were still in the West, were not invited to participate in the formal victory parade in London. A few outspoken members of the British Parliament, pointed out this absurdity, in a letter to the *Daily Telegraph*:

> Poles fought at Tobruk, Falaise and Arnhem. Units of the Polish Navy took part in most of the major actions at sea from September 1939 to VE Day; Polish fighter pilots shot down 772 German planes between July 1940 and VE Day, at the Victory Parade on June 8, 1946,—Ethiopians will be there; Mexicans will be there; the Fiji Medical Corps, the Labuan Police, and the Seychelles Pioneer Corps will be there—and rightly too. But the Poles will not be there.

The letter concluded rhetorically,

> Have we lost not only our sense of perspective, but our sense of gratitude as well? We fear so.[6]

In its official victory parade held in Plymouth, however, the Royal Navy had the grace to invite the Poles.

SUMMARY OF THE POLISH EFFORT

The Polish Navy sailed a total of 1,213,000 miles, the record setter being *Piorun* with 218,000, followed by *Garland* with 217,000 and *Blyskawica* with 146,000 miles. A total of 787 convoys were escorted and 1,162 combat patrols carried out. Total losses were twenty-three officers, eight officer cadets, 137 noncommissioned officers, and 263 sailors.

In the text of this history, I have frequently mentioned recipients of high Polish and British decorations. But I was not able to mention every name. Fifty-one officers and other rank of the Polish Navy were awarded the Virtuti Militari, close to a thousand the Krzyz Walecznych (Cross of Valor), two the Gold Cross of Merit, seventeen the Silver Cross of Merit and more than fifty the Bronze Cross of Merit.

In addition to Admiral Swirski's award of the Most Honourable Order of the Bath, Knight Commander, or as the British say, a KCB, two senior Polish naval officers (Kmdr. Karol Korytowski and Kmdr. Stanislaw Rymszewicz), received the Most Excellent Order of the British Empire, Commander of the Order (CBE), and seven the officer ranks, (OBE and MBE). Eleven were awarded the Distinguished Service Order, twenty-two received the Distinguished Service Cross, while Koziolkowski and Gorazdowski received bars to their initial awards. Twenty-four noncommissioned officers received the British Distinguished Service Medal. Finally, four Polish naval officers received the French Legion d'Honneur, and eight the croix de guerre.

FIFTY YEARS LATER

In 1980, the system of corruption, deceit, and lies that controlled and dehumanized the people of Eastern Europe began to crack under a number of internal and some external pressures. The pathetic modern-day "Potemkin Village" staged during the Moscow Olympics of 1980 strained the limited resources of the Soviet system beyond the breaking point. The restive satellites, plundered by the Soviets to impress the tourists, went one step further toward their own economic disaster.

The Soviet failure in Afghanistan demoralized the system, which in spite of complete control over the mass could not keep the disaster secret. The election of a Pole, the Cardinal from Cracow, to the Holy See inspired the Polish nation. Solidarity *(Solidarnosc)* was formed in Gdansk, and civil strife led to the inevitable defeat of Communism. The system no longer had the heart to indulge in mass murder and that is what it would have taken to repress the Poles.[7]

For close to forty years the West practiced a policy of containment. There is some evidence that with the growing influence of the Catholic Church in Poland, electrified by the Polish

Pope, the policy of the United States underwent a change and the Solidarity Movement was supported by clandestine American funds.

By 1990, the Soviets were on their out way of Poland. In May 1995, the Polish nation voted in a referendum to accept a new democratic constitution which pays tribute to past accomplishments.

At the time of writing, the Poles, having got rid of their Eastern imposed communistic tyranny, are close to, but not quite yet, in concert with the European Community of Nations. The same forces which aided and justified the Stalinist Soviet terror attempted to thwart Poland's entry into the North Atlantic Treaty Organization (NATO), which is seen by the majority of Poles as essential to future security.[8]

The symbolic aspects of sovereignty have returned. The Polish Eagle again has a crown, the navy uniform is the prewar dark blue. Polish surface ships again have names like *Orkan, Piorun, Grom*; the submarines, *Orzel, Dzik, Wilk*.[9]

Poland's Navy brings to its NATO partners the dowry of a well trained cadre, a good support system in the numerous ports of the south Baltic, from Swinoujscie (at the mouth of the Oder, to the prewar ports of Gdynia, Oksywie, Gdansk and Hel). The fleet is well balanced, with predominance of small, rocket carrying (surface to surface and surface to air) patrol ships, anti-submarine chasers and minesweepers.

It appears that the horrible suffering of the past generation is now to be requited. Only history will tell.

NOTES

1. Warren Kimball ed. *Churchill and Roosevelt: The Complete Correspondence, Vol. III, Alliance Declining,* Princeton University Press, 1984, p. 565.
2. Bohdan Wronski, *Wspomnienia Plyna jak Okrety,* London, 1981, pp. 185–186.
3. Krystyna Kersten, *The Establishment of Communist Rule in Poland, 1943–1948,* University of California Press, 1984. Edward J. Rozek, *Allied Wartime Diplomacy: A Pattern in Poland,* New York, 1958; Jan Ciechanowski (Polish ambassador to the United States during the war years), *Defeat in Victory,* London, 1948. The

President of the World Federation of Polish Jews, living in New York, however, was enthused by the changes in Polish leadership; Joseph Tenenbaum, *In Search of a People: The Old and the New Poland,* New York, 1948, pp. 209–229.

4. Arthur Bliss Lane, *I saw Poland Betrayed: An American Ambassador Reports to the American People,* New York, 1948, pp. 240–254.

5. Sir Llewellyn Woodward, *British Foreign Policy in the Second World War,* Vol. III London, 1971, p. 239.

6. *Daily Telegraph,* London, June 5, 1946.

7. George Weigel, *The Final Revolution: The Resistance Church and the Collapse of Communism,* Oxford University Press, 1992.

8. In the months, preceding the United States debate on enlarging the North Atlantic Organization (NATO), arguments were advanced, which seemed like a replay of 1944 and 1945. *New York Times* on March 11, 1998 expressed grave concern about "tinkering" with Europe. The editorial postulated that expanding NATO would harm the prospects of democracy in Russia. Apparently no thought given to the fact Hitler was democratically elected. Mr. Thomas L. Friedman on the pages of the *New York Times* saw a direct consequence of Russian mischief in Iran and NATO expansion. Obviously, the thesis being that if Russia got what it wanted, then it would be such a good partner in United States strategic policies. Mr.Patrick Buchanan strenuously objected to the expansion because American soldiers might be asked to die for Bialystok. Mr Michael Mandelbaum on the page of *Newsweek,* December 23, 1996 argued that expansion was harmful to American interests in the Middle East. Mr. Jim Hoagland, *Washington Post,* May 3, 1998, praised the nineteen US senators who voted against expansion and thus in his opinion showed courage and intellectual honesty, and forecast a deterioration of United States and Russian collaboration. But the most outlandish argument against expansion was made by one of those senators, who were praised by Hoagland, John W. Warner of Virginia, who on the floor of the United Senate, expressed fear of antagonizing Russia by erecting a ring around it.

9. Jaroslaw Cislak, *Polska Marynarka Wojenna, 1995,* Warsaw, 1996.

APPENDIX A

TEXT OF THE POLISH-BRITISH AGREEMENT

(With Protocols)
London, August 25, 1939

The Government of the United Kingdom of Great Britain and Northern Ireland and the Polish Government:

Desiring to place on a permanent basis the collaboration between their respective countries resulting from the assurances of mutual assistance of a defensive character which they have already exchanged:

Have resolved to conclude an Agreement for that purpose and have agreed on the following provisions:

Article 1.

Should one of the Contracting Parties become engaged in hostilities with a European Power in consequence of aggression by the latter against that Contracting Power, the other Contracting Power will at once give the Contracting Power engaged in hostilities all the support and assistance in its power.

Article 2.

i. The provisions of Article 1. will also apply in the event of any action by a European Power which clearly threatened directly or indirectly, the independence of one of the Contracting Powers, and was of such a nature that the Party in question considered it vital to resist with its armed forces.

ii. Should one of the Contracting Powers become engaged in hostilities with a European Power in consequence of action by that Power which threatened the independence or neutrality of another European State in such a way as to constitute a clear menace to the security of that Contracting Party, the Provisions of Article 1. will apply, without prejudice, however, to the right of the other European State concerned.

Article 3.

Should a European Power attempt to undermine the independence of one of the Contracting Powers by a process of economic penetration or in any other way, the Contracting Powers will support each other in resistance to such attempts. Should the European Power concerned thereupon embark on hostilities against one of the Contracting Parties, the provisions of Article 1. will apply.

Article 4.

The methods of applying the undertakings of mutual assistance provided for by the present Agreement are established between competent naval, military and air authorities of the Contracting Parties.

Article 5.

Without prejudice to the foregoing undertakings of the Contracting Parties to give each other mutual support and assistance immediately on the outbreak of hostilities, they will exchange complete and speedy information concerning any development which might threaten their independence and, in particular, concerning any development which threatened to call the said undertakings into operations.

Article 6.

i. The Contracting Parties will communicate to each other the terms of any undertaking of assistance against aggression which they have already given or may in future give to other States.

ii. Should either of the Contracting Parties intend to give such an undertaking after the coming into force of the present Agreement, the other Contracting Party shall, in order to ensure the proper function of the Agreement, be informed thereof.

iii. Any new undertaking which the Contracting Parties may enter into in future shall neither limit their obligations under the present Agreement nor indirectly create new obligations between the Contracting Party not participating in these undertakings and the third State concerned.

Article 7.

Should the Contracting Parties be engaged in hostilities in consequence of the application of the present Agreement, they will not conclude an armistice or treaty of peace except by mutual agreement.

Article 8.

i. The present Agreement shall remain in force for a period of five years,

ii. Unless denounced six months before the expiry of this period it shall continue in force, each Contracting Party having the Right to denounce it at any time by giving six months notice to that effect.

iii. The present Agreement shall come into force on signature.

> Halifax
> Raczynski

PROTOCOL

The Polish Government and the Government of the United Kingdom of Great Britain and Northern Ireland are agreed upon the following interpretation of the Agreement of Mutual Assistance signed this day as alone authentic and binding:

1. (a) By the expression of "a European Power" employed in the Agreement is to be understood Germany.

   (b) In the event of action within the meaning of Article 1 or 2 of the Agreement by a European Power other than Germany, the Contracting Parties will consult together on the measures to be taken in common.

2. (a) The two Governments will from time to time determine the hypothetical cases of action by Germany coming within the ambit of Article 2 of the Agreement.

   (b) Until such time as the two Governments have agreed to modify the following provisions of this paragraph, they will consider: that the case contemplated by paragraph (1) of Article 2 of the Agreement is that of the Free City of Danzig; and that the cases contemplated by paragraph (2) of Article 2 are Belgium, Holland, Lithuania.

(c) Latvia and Estonia shall be regarded by the two Governments as included in the list of countries contemplated by paragraph (2) of Article 2 from the moment that an undertaking of mutual assistance between the United Kingdom and a third State covering those two countries enters into force.

(d) As regards Roumania, the Government of the United Kingdom refers to the guarantee which it had given to that country; and the Polish Government refers to the reciprocal undertakings of the Roumania-Polish alliance which Poland has never regarded as incompatible with her traditional friendship for Hungary.

3. The Undertakings mentioned in Article 6 of the Agreement, should they be entered into by one of the Contracting Parties with a third State, would of necessity be so framed that their execution should at no time prejudice either the sovereignty or territorial inviolability of the other Contracting Party.

4. The present protocol constitutes an integral part of the Agreement signed this day, the scope of which it does not exceed.

Halifax
Raczynski

(One of the original English language copies of this Treaty is in the Polish Institute and General Sikorski Museum, London. A.II. 76/1. and A.II. 76/2. Both are graced with the respective family seals of the signers.)

APPENDIX B

Text of the Polish-British Naval Agreement

Signed in London on November 18, 1939

The Government of the Polish Republic and the Government of the United Kingdom of Great Britain and Northern Ireland desiring to make provisions for the cooperation of certain units of the Polish Naval forces with those of the United Kingdom, have agreed as follows:

Article 1.

A detachment of the Polish Navy shall be attached to the British Navy for the duration of the hostilities and so long as may be mutually agreed.

Article 2.

The units or groups of the Polish Naval Detachment under the Polish flag and under the command of Polish officers and manned by Polish crews, shall cooperate with the British Fleet and shall constitute a part of the Allied Naval Forces.

Article 3.

The Polish Naval Detachment shall include the following units:
  a) vessels which are already attached to the British Navy,
  b) other vessels which it may be possible to incorporate in the Polish Naval Detachment during the period of hostilities.

Article 4.

The personnel of the Polish Naval Detachment to be recruited shall be Polish nationals of the following categories:
  a) men now on service in units operating as well as those detached to supervise the units under construction,

b) officers and men of the Naval Reserve who are available on the territory of Allied Powers and in neutral countries and who will be called up for active service on the strength of the mobilization decree issued by the President of the Polish Republic,

c) officers and men of the Polish Mercantile Marine who do not belong to the Naval Reserve, but who may be called up for active service in the Navy in case of increased demand,

d) skilled men who may volunteer to serve in the Navy in case of increased demand.

Article 5.

For the purpose of:

a) concentrating personnel of the categories mentioned in Article 4 (b), (c), (d),

b) the formation of reserves for the units operating,

c) training in special branches which may require strengthening, a suitable naval depot will be established at a place allotted by the British authorities, which shall be under the command of Polish officers and staffed by Polish petty-officers and instructors.

Article 6.

Any costs incurred by the British naval authorities in connection with the operation of this agreement shall, on demand, be reimbursed by the Polish Government to the Government of the United Kingdom.

Article 7.

The ways and means of enlarging the Polish Naval Detachment as well as recruiting, concentrating and supplementing personnel, the organization of command, training of officers and men, etc., shall be dealt with by separate agreements between the contracting governments.

In faith whereof the undersigned, duly authorized thereto by their respective Governments have signed present agreement.

Raczynski
Cadogan

The focus of this work does not allow the reproduction of the other military agreements signed by the Polish government during the war. But for the record, it needs to be stated that agreements were signed by the Poles with the French on January 4, 1940, regarding the Polish ground forces and military aviation; with the British on August 5, 1940, regarding the Polish ground forces and the Polish air force that were based in the United Kingdom; with the Soviets on July 14, 1941, regarding the formation of the Polish Army in the Soviet Union. That last was a short-lived agreement. The final one was signed on April 6, 1944, between the Polish Government and the Government of the United Kingdom and restored full control of the Polish authorities over the Polish Air Force, as had been the case for the Polish Navy and the Polish Army.

APPENDIX C

LIST OF MAJOR POLISH NAVAL UNITS

This list of Polish warships does not include the numerous smaller ships, such as torpedo boats, minesweepers, trawlers, submarine chasers, motor-torpedo-gunboats, and other auxiliary and training ships.

The Poles had the following convention for naming their warships. Fleet destroyers were named after climatic phenomena such as thunder, gale, etc.; torpedo and escort destroyers after denizens of Polish provinces; submarines after rapacious birds and animals. Smaller craft were named after birds.

The numbers below the names of the warships are the identification numbers that were used in operations conducted with the Royal Navy and were only used after the September Campaign.

Wicher, Burza
H 73
(Gale, Storm)

Destroyers. French built, similar to the *Simoun*-class, 1929.

Wicher sunk by enemy air action in September, 1939 off Hel.
Burza on active combat to April 1944. Combat operations: Home Fleet, Convoy, Western Approaches, then training ship. After WW II, *Burza* became a museum ship in Gdynia.

Rys, Zbik, Wilk
N 63
(Lynx, Bobcat, Wolf)

French-built submarines in 1929–1930. *Wilk* broke out to the United Kingdom in September 1939.

Zbik and *Rys* sustained damage from enemy action while on patrol in Baltic and sought internment in neutral Sweden. Both returned to Poland after the War. Combat operations for *Wilk*: North Sea.

Gryf
(Griffin)

French-built minelayer and training ship. Ordered 1934, launched 1936, but commissioned in 1938. Damaged by enemy air action September 1939. Beached, guns removed for land defense, which are still on exhibit in the Military Museum in Warsaw.

Blyskawica, Grom
H 34 H 71
(Lightning, Thunder)

Polish-designed and British-built destoyers with many unique features. Fast, (39 knots) and equipped for minelaying. Commissioned 1938. Combat operations for *Grom*: Nore Command, 1st Destroyer Flotilla, Harwich, Norway; sunk off Narvik, May 1940.
Combat operations for *Blyskawica*: Nore Command, 1st Destroyer Flotilla, Harwich, Norway, Convoy escorts in Western Approaches, Mediterranean

Fleet, Home Fleet, Channel
operations.

Orzel, Sep
A 85
(Eagle, Vulture)

Dutch-built and designed
oceangoing submarines. Commissioned just before the
war, 1939. *Sep* sustained
damage and was ineterned in
Sweden. *Orzel* broke out to
the United Kingdom and lost
on patrol, May 1940. Combat
operations for *Orzel:* Baltic,
North Sea.

Ouragan (ex-French *Ouragan)*
H 16

French destroyer of the
Simoun-class.
Details as for *Burza.* After the
capitulation of France, taken
over by Royal Navy and
August 1940 transferred to
the Polish Navy. Returned to
the Free French on April
1941. Combat operations:
Western Approaches.

Garland (ex–HMS *Garland)*
H 37

British *G*-class destroyer
transferred to the Polish
Navy in May 1940. Built
1934. Returned to the Royal
Navy after World War II, then
transferred to the Royal
Dutch Navy as *Marnix.*
Combat operations: Mediterranean, Western Approaches,
convoys to Murmansk, Home
Fleet.

Piorun (ex–HMS *Nerissa)*
G 65
(Thunderbolt)

British *Javelin*-class destroyer
built 1939, transferred to the
Polish Navy in September
1940. Returned to the Royal

Navy after World War II and renamed *Noble*. Combat operations: Convoy duties in Western Approaches, Mediterranean Fleet, Home Fleet, Channel.

Krakowiak (ex–HMS *Silverton)*
L 115

Kujawiak (ex–HMS *Oakley)*
L 72

Slazak (ex–HMS *Bedale*)
L 26

British-built *Hunt*-class destroyer escorts. The first two transferred to the Polish in April and June 1941. *Slazak* in April 1942. *Kujawiak* sunk off Malta 1942. *Krakowiak* and *Slazak* both returned to Royal Navy and served under original names. Combat operations for *Kujawiak*: Channel operations, Mediterranean, Lost off Malta. Combat operations for *Krakowiak*: Home Waters in the Channel, Mediterranean Fleet and Escorts, Neptune operations. Combat operations for *Slazak*: Home Fleet at Scapa Flow, Channel operations including Dieppe landings, Mediterranean Fleet, Neptune, Home Fleet.

Sokol (ex–HMS *Urchin*)
U-97
(Falcon)

Dzik
P 52
(Wild Boar)

British-built, 1939 and submarines of the small U-class. Transferred to the Polish Navy in January 1941 and October 1942 respectively. After the war, both returned to the Royal Navy. Combat operations for *Sokol:* Bay of Biscay, Mediterranean, Home Fleet. Combat operations for

Dzik: Home Fleet, Mediterranean.

Jastrzab (ex–USS *S-25*)
P 511
(Hawk)

United States-built submarine of the *S*-Class, (Hawk) transferred to the Polish Navy on November 1941. Combat operations: Home Fleet. Lost on 2/5/1942.

Orkan (ex-HMS *Myrmidon*)
G 90
(Monsoon)

British-built *Milne*-class fleet destroyer launched March 1942 and transferred to the Polish Navy in November 1942. Combat operations: Home Fleet at Scapa Flow, Western Approaches. Hit by an acoustical mine fired by U-378 on 8/X/1943 with loss of 178 crew.

Dragon (ex–HMS *Dragon*)

Conrad (ex–HMS *Danae*)

British light cruisers built 1916–1918. *Dragon* transferred to the Polish Navy in January 1943. Combat operations for *Dragon:* Home Fleet, Convoys to Murmansk, Neptune. Lost due to enemy small submarine during the invasion of Normandy. *Conrad* loaned as replacement in October 1944, and returned to Royal in 1946. Combat operations for *Conrad*: Home Fleet.

The following English-language descriptions of Polish warships have been published: Kolesnik, Eugene, *"Thunder and Lightning: The Polish Destroyers Blyskawica and Grom,"* *Warships,* London, 1980; Twardowski, Marek, *"The Jaskolka Class*

Minesweepers," Warships, London, 1980; Budzbon, Prze-
myslaw, *"Wicher and Burza: Big Ships of a Small Navy,"* War-
ships, London, 1980; and, *"Pride of Poland: The Orzel Class
Submarines," Warships,* London, 1987.

APPENDIX D

POLISH NAVAL AVIATION

The Polish Navy and Polish Military Aviation, (the precursor of the Polish Air Force), had a difficult time coming to a real collaboration in the interwar period of 1921–39. The small naval aviation unit, based at Puck, was the epitome of a service Cinderella, with the Polish Aviation Command unwilling to nourish its resources, nor in the early years willing to give it up to the Navy. The Navy on the other hand saw the naval aviation service, the *Morski Dywizion Lotniczy* (MDL), as an extension of its naval capability but even more importantly as competition for scarce budgetary resources.

This lack of collaboration was by no means unique to the Polish services, but Poland lacked the fiscal capability to create dual services as did the United States and the United Kingdom, where the navy had its own carrier aviation and the other services also had air capability. The United States solved the problem by triplicating its organic aviation, so that the United States Navy had its own land and carrier based planes, while its Marine Corps also had its own organic aviation. In addition the United States Army had its own Air Corps, all in addition to the United States Air Force.

The British organization was more parsimonious, but the Royal Navy retained all carrier and some land-based planes in the Fleet Air Arm, while the Air Ministry (*i.e.*, RAF) was delegated the responsibility for all land-based planes and even some flying boat and seaplane squadrons. These were grouped in the Royal Air Force Coastal Command, whose mission was long-range reconnaissance and interdiction of enemy shipping. This functional division is important, since during the war years, the Polish Naval Command, often alluded to the British structure as a template for its own plans for future growth.

In 1933 the Polish Naval Wing (MDL), was finally placed under the command of the Navy which became totally responsible for all matters regarding personnel, equipment, training, doctrine, and, of course, budget. Thus the commanding officer of the Polish Military Aviation was able to wash his proverbial hands of the unit.

The naval authorities decided that all its planes were to be either flying boats or floatplanes, even though the performance of land-based planes has always been superior. Land-based planes had the necessary endurance for flights over most of the south Baltic. The Polish-built single-engined Karas *PZL-23* which became operational in 1935, had a range of 600 kilometers, which allowed it to fly as far north as Gotland; while the two-engined Los *PZL-37* had a range of a thousand kilometers.

In the last months before the onset of hostilities, the Polish Naval Command requested the command of Poland's Military Aviation to second a squadron of fighter planes and one of the *Karas* reconnaissance aircraft to the coastal region. It was too late. The resources of Poland's aviation were stretched too far anyway, and the Aviation Command was not interested in basing its few combat planes in such an exposed situation. Polish naval air doctrine was somewhat confused and far from well developed but did entail artillery spotting, reconnaissance, and in 1939, after the order for Italian torpedo seaplanes, torpedo attack capability. No thought appears to have been given to the fact that the land and dockyard facilities were in need of protection from enemy aircraft until the last days of peace. This was relegated to anti-aircraft artillery. In 1939, all the planes in the establishment were one-engined patrol float-planes. Puck, an old imperial German naval air base was barely adequate to the needs of the service, had no active anti-aircraft defense, and was completely exposed to German ground attack from the west, since it was not even on the fortified part of the Hel Peninsula.

The MDL was in fact a training unit for potential future growth and for training naval personnel in collaboration with aviation. Just prior to the outbreak of the war, the crews of the MDL flew a total of fifteen reconnaissance missions around the German ports of Stettin and Pillau, reporting on the German naval concentrations and the increased intensity of

German shipping to East Prussia, that enclave which was seen as a threat to Warsaw, being a mere one hundred kilometers distant. After the outbreak of the war, the crews flew a number of shallow reconnaissance missions, inevitably at night since the daylight hours were close to suicidal. Within a few days, the planes were all destroyed at their moorings during daylight hours, and the professional cadre of the MDL fought as infantry. On October 1, 1939, when the naval force under Kontr-Admiral K. Unrug capitulated, the aircrews and mechanics shared the fate of the naval personnel.[1]

In 1939, the Polish Naval Command purchased six Italian three-engined torpedo seaplanes of the Canti-class. Only one reached Poland before the outbreak of hostilities and was not equipped for operational use. After the September campaign, Poland's air and military attaché in Rome, Colonel Marian Romeyko, attempted to hold the Italians to their contractual obligation and have the five remaining Canti planes delivered, since Italy was not yet at war. The Italians agreed, subject to financial agreements which stipulated that payment be in Western currency. Then the Poles approached the British with this proposal and urged that the British pay for these planes out of the loan made to Poland just before the war. The Poles in turn obligated themselves to provide air and ground crews. The British were disinterested, not surprising given their aloof attitude toward Polish air personnel until after the Battle of Britain in the summer of 1940.

In 1943, the Polish Naval Command in London, began discussions with the appropriate Polish Staff and Polish Air Staff authorities to create a Polish Naval Air Arm, analogous to the Royal Fleet Air Arm and the RAF Coastal Command. But Swirski wished to go even further than the British model and proposed that all air units with naval missions should be under naval command, which certainly not the case for the RAF Coastal Command.[2]

On October 5, 1943, Swirski and his staff formally postulated the Polish Navy's plans and vision for the future, and stated as their goal the possession and control of aviation units with the following capabilities:

- torpedo squadrons
- land- and carrier-based fighter squadrons

- reconnaissance units consisting of land and flying boats
- training and reserve units

Swirski urged that the 304 Polish Coastal Command Squadron be placed under naval command, and that other air and ground personnel be transferred to the Polish Navy and trained in various aspects of air warfare, including operations from carriers.

Swirski's ambition to create a large surface navy in the Baltic after the war was seen by many as unrealistic. Swirski requested a commitment from the Polish Air Force Staff, and also obtained an endorsement of his long-term goals from the commander-in-chief. He urged that the available Air Force personnel be retrained in carrying out torpedo attacks. Elements of 304 squadron were in fact sent to Norfolk for such retraining, but the Wellington was found unsuitable for low-level flight. It has to be commented that Swirski called for Beaufighters for this role. In addition, Swirski asked for a section of three Catalina seaplanes, five pilots for training on Seafires for carrier-based operations, five pilots to be trained for catapult duties, and the assignment of three officers and eighteen other rank to train as torpedo specialists.

In November 1943, the Polish Navy formed a small headquarters for its naval planning; the first section chief was Major T. Moszakowski.

The Polish Air Staff took a very negative attitude to Swirski's arguments. It argued that in 1943 alone, the Allies had sunk 250 German and Italian submarines; achieved in the following manner:

Axis submarines sunk by	Number	Percents
land-based planes	120	48%
carrier-based planes	20	8%
Allied surface warships	80	32%
Allied submarines	12	4%
other	18	7%

The Polish Air Staff also cited German figures for the fourth quarter of 1943, in which the Germans claimed to have sunk a total of 185 Allied ships, of which sixty-five were sunk by U-boats, and sixty by the Luftwaffe. All Luftwaffe operations were from land bases, none from carriers. The remaining presumably were by German surface or were lost to mines.

Finally, the Polish Air Staff stated categorically that, even with the planes currently in establishment of the Polish squadrons in the United Kingdom, all areas of the Baltic Sea could be covered by land-based Polish air units, and that the need for carrier-based operations was not persuasive. Undoubtedly, the Polish Air Force Staff were aware of the great success of the Coastal Command's land-based strike wings which interdicted German shipping in the North Sea. The Air Staff acknowledged that an independent naval air arm should exist but confined it to catapult planes for reconnaissance and seaplanes for rescue.

Another postwar statistic illustrated the same argument: the Polish 304 Squadron assigned to the RAF Coastal Command in the summer of 1942, by the end of the war, had sunk two German U-boats, *U-441* and *U-321*, while the Polish Navy in six years of operations also destroyed two German U-boats, namely *U-606* and *U-407*.[3]

At the same time, the Polish Air Staff accepted the navy's needs for active collaboration with the air force, on an analogous basis to that existing between the British Admiralty and Air Ministry. It offered upon return to Poland after the war, to place some resources of the Air Force under the responsibility of the Polish Navy. These were to include: the 304 squadron, one of the existing fighter squadrons (with one more to be formed), and one torpedo squadron, still to be formed.

In the spirit of such cooperation, the Polish Air Force assigned a group of officers, headed by Lt. Col. Jan Buczma to the RAF Coastal Command.

These discussions which a times had a tone of recriminations between Admiral Swirski and the Polish Air Force Commander, General Mateusz Izycki, eventually died out because of the unfolding political situation in which the Polish Armed Forces found themselves in late 1944 and early 1945. The forced resignation of the Polish commander-in-chief, General Sosnkowski, in November 1944 also weakened Admiral Swirski's position. (See, Polish Institute London, Archives, LOT A.V. 1/3xv i A. XII26/49.)

POLAND'S COASTAL COMMAND SQUADRON

In 1942, one of the bloodied Polish bomber squadrons, the 304 Land of Silesia, was diverted from the Royal Air Force Bomber Command to the Coastal Command. The losses of the RAF Bomber Command had been severe, in every respect comparable to the bloodletting of young officers in the First World War in the suicidal "over the top" attacks on German positions. The bomber crews referred to themselves as "dead men on leave." By early 1942, the Poles had run out of replacements for their bomber crews. The four Polish bomber squadrons had lost close to a thousand crew members, an attrition which could not be replaced; normally establishment of each squadron had a complement of just over a hundred flyers, and the Polish squadrons were always short of that goal. Furthermore, RAF policy dictated that after thirty operational flights, the crews had to be given some form of leave and noncombat assignments. By 1942 many of the Poles, who had survived operations, were now being rotated out of combat squadrons. Therefore, one of the squadrons (301) was disbanded, and the 304 reassigned to Coastal Command where the tours of operation were longer and purportedly safer. Yet in the Coastal Command operations carried out by this squadron, flying various makes of the two engined Wellington, the Poles lost 106 crew by war's end.

The squadron's mission was antisubmarine patrolling, and the main weapon were antisubmarine depth charges. The squadron was based in various places, initially in the romantic, wild Hebrides, on the Isle of Tiree, with the RAF 224 and was part of the RAF Coastal Command Fifteenth Group. It finished the war on the lovely coast of Devon, as part of the Nineteenth Group at Davidstow Moor and Chivenor. In between, it was based in South Wales and also moved to Norfolk in March 1943, for training in torpedo attacks. Over the Atlantic, the greatest enemy was fog and the ever and unpredictable danger of icing. When flying over the Bay of Biscay the danger were the lurking long-range German two-engined fighters.

As the war progressed the antisubmarine patrols were carried out at night, when the U-boats were on surface charging their batteries and most vulnerable to aerial attack. This was a result of the Allied improvements and progress in radar technology which could pick up a blip at a distance of thirty-five miles. The Polish 304 Squadron was equipped with Wellington Mark XIVs which had this new radar plus Leigh lights. At night, the radar identified the German U-boat, and in the attack approach, the powerful lights not only illuminated the enemy but blinded their anti-aircraft crew.

The Wellingtons were designed to be night bombers and their defensive capability was limited, so that any chance meeting with a German fighter plane was very dangerous. Unless the Wellington could escape or hide in a cloud, it was tantamount to death, either from enemy bullets, the ensuing crash or the prolonged agony of bobbing on the sea in a small rubber dinghy.

In February 1943, one of the Polish crews made history. While on a patrol to the Bay of Biscay, the Poles were attacked by four Ju-88 two-engined fighters. This should have been the death knell for the Polish crew. But the pilot, Major Emil Ladro, brought the heavy machine to sea level, headed for home, and proceeded to embark on evasive tactics as he was instructed in course changes by his second pilot, a forty-eight year old senior Polish officer, Lt. Col. Jan Bialy, and veteran of the September Campaign. The rear gunner kept up defensive fire while the front gunner was seriously wounded on the first German attack. The radio operator obtained a fix from his navigator, and alerted his base to the crisis. After a few minutes one of the German planes, trailing smoke, peeled off for home, but the three remaining fighters kept up the attack for fifty-nine minutes, arguably the longest such aerial battle of the war. Having exhausted their ammunition, and probably running short of gasoline, the three Germans flew off after a chivalrous dipping of their wings. But their luck ran out as three Royal Air Force Beaufighters, alerted by the hard-pressed Poles, intercepted the Germans and shot them down.

This was the kind of news that public relations officers dreamed of, and it was made into a victory of Allied collaboration, since one of the Beaufighter pilots (White) was an American. Much was also made of the fact that Lt. Col. Jan Bialy at forty-eight was thought to be the oldest combat pilot in the Allied air forces. Both the *Daily Herald* and *Manchester Guardian* carried the story.

The squadron was very successful; it sank two U-boats, damaged five more, and won the Coastal Command's first prize for navigation in 1943.[4]

There is also a gallow's humor story associated with the Squadron. After returning from patrol, in the process of being debriefed by the RAF intelligence officers, the Poles would state that they had once again failed to locate the Atlantic Charter, but were sure it was there somewhere, since Churchill had signed it!

NOTES

1. Andrzej Olejko, *Morski Dywizion Lotniczy,* Pruszkow, 1992; and Jerzy Rozwadowski, *Morski Dywizion Lotniczy,* Albany, 1973.
2. At the beginning of the war, the RAF Coastal Command had sixteen squadrons with 183 planes and by war's end had sixty-six squadrons consisting of 1,117 planes. These squadrons were used ubiquitously, as military needs demanded. So an RAF Coastal Command squadron could be moved from patrol duties to minelaying in enemy waters, to bombing missions against land targets, such as dockyards. The priorities were decided by the RAF Coastal Command headquarters in collaboration with the Admiralty and Air Ministry.
3. Hilary St. George Saunders, *Royal Air Force, 1939–1945, Vol. 3: The Fight is Won,* London, HMSO. 1993. (Third Edition) p.404. The following figures are cited for the total number of German and Italian submarines destroyed during the Second World War in the Atlantic, Arctic, Home Waters, Mediterranean, and as far afield as the Red Sea, Black Sea, and Indian Ocean:

   Allied shore-based aircraft: 339

   Joint action by naval and shore-based aircraft: 41

   Allied naval and ship-borne aircraft: 391.

   Also see Roy Conyers Nesbit, *The Strike Wings: Special Anti-Shipping Squadrons, 1942–1945,* HMSO, London, 1995.
4. *Destiny Can Wait,* London, 1949.

APPENDIX E

THE POLISH WOMEN'S
NAVAL AUXILIARY

Polish women had always stood next to their men in the defense of their country, and had inspired their husbands, sons, and brothers with their selfless dedication and patriotism. Polish women fought in the many uprisings, they tended their wounded, exhorted them, loved them, and buried them.

In turn they were loved, cherished, and even adored. Pilsudski's last will called for his heart to be buried with his mother. They fought in uniform in the Polish-Russian war of 1919–1920, and some, like Porucznik Zulinska, were even commissioned as an officer in a cavalry regiment, the First Szwolerzer, and awarded the Virtuti Militari.

With this tradition, it is surprising how late in the war women became formally enrolled in the Polish armed forces, even though they played a heroic part in the Polish Underground and were parachuted to Poland as couriers.

On February 12, 1940, while based in Paris, the Polish Ministry of Military Affairs (later renamed the Ministry of National Defense) promulgated policies and instructions regarding the formation of a women's military service. In the early stages of the war, Polish women living in exile volunteered for service and worked in a host of roles, primarily in the Polish Red Cross. A number of them went to Norway with the Polish Podhalanska Brigade where they distinguished themselves.

Many thousands of women (and children) were among the released Gulag inmates, and this large group of civilians made essential some form of semimilitary organization to effectively provide care for the sick, feeble, and thousands of orphans. Hence the *Pomocnicza Sluzba Kobiet,* or Women's Auxiliary Service, was created in the Middle East. About a year later the next step was taken, and the Polish authorities formed the *Pomocnicza Wojskowa Sluzba Kobiet*, or Women's Military Auxiliary Service, and based it on the British model.

Based on this pattern, the *Pomocnicza Morska Sluzba Kobiet* (Women's Naval Auxiliary Service) was formed on December 12, 1942. By the middle of 1944, the service, which had been part of the overall army services, had enough women to become fully autonomous, under its first inspector, Ewa Miszewska. The Polish women were initially trained by the Royal Navy's Women's Service (Wrens), but as their experience and numbers grew, a Polish training center was started on ORP *Baltyk,* and the Polish *mewki* (gulls) began to undertake many roles which allowed the freeing of men for sea and combat operations. By the end of the war, their numbers in the Polish Navy had reached just over a hundred, but the total of Polish women in uniform in all three services was close to eight thousand.

APPENDIX F

THE POLISH MERCHANT MARINE

The Polish Ministry of Commerce and Trade's collaboration with the Polish Naval Command successfully kept the majority of Polish ships out of the Baltic on the outbreak of the war. Thus only nine percent of the mercantile marine tonnage was lost in September 1939.

There were some intended exceptions to this order, such as a number of small fishing trawlers that had been mobilized, and a number of ships which were intentionally kept in the Baltic to facilitate transportation of supplies for Poland. It was planned that freight from the west would go through Swedish and Finnish ports to the Baltic countries and then by rail to Poland. But the first months of the war in the west were problematic. In spite of the growing international losses in shipping, there were more merchant ships available for contract than available cargo. There was also a tendency for independent contractors to arrange for cargoes to be embarked on neutral ships. There were still a number of countries that proclaimed neutrality and had been spared involvement in the war, still confined to Germany, Poland, France, the United Kingdom and its Commonwealth. Cargoes carried on neutral ships were spared attack, though not always spared the annoyance of searches and inspection.

The Polish Merchant Marine had to endure some difficult days made worse by losses in their crews. Some of the unemployed (thus unpaid) seamen, from the uncontracted ships, sought work on other, non-Polish, shipping lines. There was also a patriotic move on the part of many young officers and Polish nationals to enroll in the Polish Armed Forces and especially the Polish Navy. On the liner MS *Chrobry* (sunk during the Norwegian Campaign) one hundred eleven out of 266 crew members volunteered for service in the Polish Armed Forces in November 1939. MS *Sobieski* lost twenty-seven of its crew, who then travelled to France from Dakar in October 1939 to join the Polish Forces. Steps were quickly taken by the Polish Government to discourage such transfers, and official instructions were promulgated to emphasize that service aboard Polish merchant ships was equally honorable as in the armed forces.

On October 9, 1939, the Polish Government in exile combined the Ministry of Treasury with the Ministry of Commerce and Trade, which in turn formed the Polish Transport Committee to oversee the Polish Merchant Marine. Poland became represented in the *Commission Interallieé des Transportes Maritimes*. Polish legal jurisdiction was implemented through Polish consuls. This turned out to be laborious and the Poles implemented their Sea Courts based on the British Allied Powers Maritime Court Acts of 1941.

Eleven small cargo ships were caught in the Baltic, the Danish Straits or the ports of the North Sea, in proximity to German air and naval assets. These ships, which were bottled up in Swedish ports, were civilian vessels and could not be interned by a neutral country, but if intercepted outside of neutral territorial waters were subject to German capture or even sinking. The Polish captains slowly congregated in Goteborg from where it was a night's sail to Bergen. The Royal Navy provided the escort for the Polish ships to get to the United Kingdom on the final leg. Many of the Polish ships bottled up in the Baltic in Swedish ports took aboard the Merchant Marine cadets from the training sailing ship *Dar Pomorza,* also in a Swedish port. Three ships had been deep in the Baltic and took longer to reach the United Kingdom. These were SS *Slask* (Master Mariner Zielinski), SS *Rozewie*, (Master Mariner Lehr) and SS *Poznan* (Master Mariner Deyczakowski). The last ship to leave the Baltic was *Rozewie* which had to sail all the way from Stockholm, and reached Scotland on November 18, 1939.

All four of the modern liners were safe, but the safety was relative, since Italian authorities made a legal attempt to take possession of the liner *Batory* after its arrival in New York, in lieu of the debt owed to the Italian dockyards. The abrupt departure of the liner for Halifax saved the ship and Polish authorities from protracted legal battles. These legal issues affected a number of other Polish ships, particularly of the

Gdynia-Amerika Line (GAL), and the Polish Government had to resort to a number of expediencies, such as chartering the ships to foreign companies or obtaining British financial support.

Poland's Merchant Marine Academy training ship, the *Dar Pomorza,* was one of the ships that did not make it out of the Baltic, since being a square rigged sailing ship with an auxiliary engine, she lacked sufficient speed. But her corps of cadets was evacuated to Britain and eventually proved a priceless asset to Poland's merchant marine. At the beginning of the war a small number of cadets decided to make it back to Poland through the Baltic countries and took part in the final battles of the September Campaign.

A Polish Merchant Marine Officer Cadet School was recreated in the United Kingdom. It was initially based at the Navigation Department of University College, Southampton. Over a hundred sixty young Poles trained and obtained licenses to work as deck officers in the Polish Merchant Marine. Another sixty obtained engineering training. Forty-one obtained their Master Mariner's licenses between 1939 and 1944, when such training was being phased out. Thus, thanks to some good fortune, both the naval training ship *Iskra* and the merchant academy training ship, were able to get their young trainees to the west and to provide the Polish navy and merchant marine services with a rich crop of young officers.

All Polish merchantmen became integrated into the Allied Merchant Navy Pool (British Ministry of War Transport and its executive branch, the Combined Shipping Adjustment Board), and sailed with Allied and Polish troops, and Allied cargoes all over the world.

Some Polish ships carried Poles from the Balkans to the Levant. Polish merchantmen took part in the run to Murmansk, sailed back and forth between the Americas and the United Kingdom, participated in the North African landings, the Salerno landings, and the invasion of Normandy and the subsequent invasion of Southern France. Two Polish liners carried the troops of the 2 Polish Corps to Italy in late 1943.

The history of these long, exhausting, and desperately dangerous voyages has its human side, for example, the captain of *Morska Wola*, Master Mariner Stanislaw Zelwerowicz, who was accompanied for four years by his wife; and made forty

trips together between Britain and the North American continent. Polish ships (*Pulaski, Sobieski,* and *Kosciuszko)* even took
part in the British operations against the Japanese-occupied
Malay Archipelago after the cessation of hostilities in Europe,
since Poland had joined the United Maritime Authority. This
authority had complete control over all Allied shipping.
Sobieski transported British Indian Army troops from Italy to
Bombay, and was then assigned to take part in the planned
invasion of Malaya, which was to take place in mid-September
1945. The capitulation of Japan made this moot. These Asian
operations were concluded by repatriating liberated British
prisoners captured in the 1942 Singapore campaign.

On September 20, 1945, the first ship entered the port of
Gdynia. Master Mariner Boleslaw Mikszta brought his SS
Krakow back to the home port after six years of war. There
was great elation in the port, since there was still optimism
that the defeat of Germany would mean, what was averred,
liberation.

Eleven Polish ships were lost due to enemy action, the
major losses being the three liners *Pilsudski, Chrobry,* and
Warszawa. At the end of the war the Polish Merchant Marine
consisted of 1,169 officers and sailors. This was a major reduc-
tion from the early war period and the difference was made up
by the employment of foreign sailors, who numbered 827.

The Polish Merchant Marine was augmented by a number
of American-built Liberty ships and finished the war with a
tonnage comparable to its pre–1939 statistics. The Polish Merchant Marine carried 500,000 passengers, civilian and military,
and five million tons of cargo, often of critical strategic importance, over some of the most difficult and dangerous routes.

APPENDIX G

TABLE OF EQUIVALENT NAVAL RANKS*

Polish Navy	Royal Navy	U.S. Navy
pod-chorazy	Midshipman	Midshipman
Podporucznik Marynarki (ppor. mar.)	Sub-Lieutenant	Ensign Lieutenant, JG (Junior Grade)
Porucznik Marynarki (Por. mar.)	Lieutenant	Lieutenant
Kapitan Marynarki (Kpt. mar.)	Lieutenant-Commander	Lieutenant-Commander
Komandor podporucznik (Kdr. ppor.)	Commander	Commander
Komandor Porucznik (Kdr. por.)		
Komandor (Kdr.)	Captain	Captain
no equivalent		Commodore
Kontr-Admiral (Adm.)	Rear Admiral	Rear Admiral
Wice Admiral (Adm.)	Vice Admiral	Vice Admiral

*As can be seen there is a fairly wide discrepancy in the equivalent naval ranks, quite unlike the army and air force ranks which are very straightforward.

SOURCE NOTES

This book is based on both primary archival and personal accounts, as well as comprehensive secondary sources which are listed below.

The main archival or primary material is from the Polish Institute, London, and the British Public Record Office (PRO). The pertinent Polish Institute material may be found under B-1028, B-1029, B-1031, B-1033, B-1039, B-1104, B-1045, and Mar. Av.51/1, this last being a comprehensive summary of the actions of the Polish Navy prepared for the Polish Navy Commandant at war's end. The PRO archives are under ADM 199/1187, /1178, /1180 and /1807. Citations from the PRO's archives appear with the permission of the Controller of Her Majesty's Stationery Office.

A number of memoirs were published following the war and should be acknowledged since they also provide a primary source for the history of the maritime events: Borys Karnicki, *Marynarski Worek Wspomnien* (A Sailor's Sea Bag of Memories), Warsaw, 1987, Jozef Bartosik, *Wierny Okret* (The Faithful Warship), London, 1947; Eryk Sopocko, *Orzel's Patrol, The Story of the Polish Submarine*, London, 1942; A. Domiszek, *Opowiadania Marynarskie* (Sailors' Tales), London, 1945; Stanislaw Henryk Mayak, *Dokad Idziemy?* (Where Are We Going?), London, 1947; Bohdan Pawlowicz, *ORP Garland: In Convoy to Russia*, London, 1943; and *Krew na Oceanie* (Blood on the Sea), NY, 1955; Boleslaw Romanowski, *Torpeda w Celu* (Torpedo on Target), Warsaw, 1981; Bohdan Wronski, *Wspomnienia Plyna jak Okrety*, (Reflections Float by like Warships), London, 1981; Stanislaw Biskupski, *Sokoly Siedmiu Morz* (Falcons of the Seven Seas), Warsaw, 1972; Franciszek Dabrowski, *Wsponmnienia z Obrony Westerplatte* (Reflections from the Defense of Westerplatte), Gdansk, 1957; Antoni Seroka, *32 Dni Obrony Helu* (The 32 Days of Hel's Defense), Olsztyn, 1979; Edward Jan Krutol, *Wrzesien na Oksywiu* (September in Oksywie), Warsaw, 1984.

205

The following English-language books were published by the Polish Ministry of Information in London during the war: Henryk Baginski, *Poland's Freedom of the Sea*, London, 1942; and Peter Jordan and Alexander Janta, *Seafaring Poland*, London, 1944. The following English-language monograph appeared during the war and is more of historical interest though factually correct; Arthur D. Divine, *Navies-in-Exile*, NY, 1944.

For a general background to the events of the Second World War, the war at sea, and the Polish part in the struggle against Germany, the following are suggested. Whenever possible (for obvious reasons) English-language studies are listed.

For a general account of the Second World War, pride of place has to go the six-volume account by Winston S. Churchill, *The Second World War*, Boston, 1948, 1949, 1950, 1951 and 1953 respectively. Churchill, who initially, as First Lord of Admiralty, and after June 1940, as Prime Minister and Minister of Defense of the British Government, was responsible for the conduct of the war. This superb account won the Nobel prize for literature. Since Polish political and diplomatic futures was to a large extent determined by British foreign policy, Llewellyn Woodward's, *British Foreign Policy in the Second World War*, (three volumes), London, 1970 and 1971, should be noted. (Of the forty-six chapters, four are devoted to Polish issues.) For an excellent list of chronological events during the war, see Robert Goralski, *World War II Almanac, 1931–1945: A Political and Military Record*, NY 1981. The official British history of the war at sea is Stephen Wentworth Roskill, *The War at Sea, 1939–1945*, Her Majesty's Printing Office, London, in three volumes, 1956, 1958, and 1960. For an account of the submarine war waged by the Germans, see John Terraine, *The U-Boat Wars, 1916–1945*, NY, 1989. For a superb account of the role played by *Ultra* in the Battle of the Atlantic, see David Kahn, *Seizing the Enigma: The Race to Break the German U-Boat Codes, 1939–1943*, Boston, 1991. A superb comprehensive account of the Second World War can be found in Weinberg, Gerhard L., *A World at Arms: A Global History of World War II*, Cambridge University Press, 1994.

There is a continued absence of English language general histories of the Polish military effort in World War II, but Steven Zaloga and Victor Madej's *The Polish Campaign, 1939*,

NY, 1985, stands out. For the Polish Air Force, see *Destiny Can Wait*, London, 1949. This later was produced, written and sponsored by the British Air Ministry and is heavily weighed to a British view of the war. Nonetheless, it is still inspiring and moving!

The main published sources for Polish military history are in Polish. The keystone study is the seven-volume *Polskie Sily Zbrojne w Drugiej Wojnie Swiatowej* (Polish Armed Forces in the Second World War), Polish Institute, London. The volumes relevant to the Polish Navy are: Tom 1, *Kampania Wrzesniowa, Czesc 5, Marynarka Wojenna i Obrona Polskiego Wybrzeza* (Volume 1, September Campaign, Part 5, The Polish Navy and the Defense of the Seacoast), London, 1959; *Tom 2, Polskie Sily Zbrojne, Kampania na Obczyznie*, Czesc 1 and 2. (Campaign in Exile, Parts 1 and 2), London, 1962 and 1975. Also see, Andrzej Rzepniewski, *Obrona Wybrzeza w 1939* (Defense of the Seacoast in 1939), Warsaw, 1970; W. Krzyzanowski, A. Piechowiak, and B. Wronski, eds., *Marynarka Wojenna: Dokumenty i Opracowania*, (Navy: Documents and Studies), London, 1968; Stanislaw M. Piaskowski, *Kroniki Polskiej Marynarki Wojennej, 1918–1946*, (The Chronicles of the Polish Navy, 1918–1946), Sigma Press, Albany, NY, in three volumes, 1983, 1987, and 1989 (This is easily the most comprehensive and detailed account of the Polish Navy. It includes all pertinent orders, promotions, assignment of personnel, instructions, and discussion of policies. This work, a true labor of love, is without parallel.); Miroslaw Kulakowski, *Marynarka Wojenna Polski Odrodzonej* (The Navy of Reborn Poland), Toronto, 1988; J.T. Targa, ed. *Polska na Morzu* (Poland on the Sea), Gdynia, 1936; Czeslaw Rudzki, *Polskie Okrety Podwodne, 1926–1969*, (Polish Submarines, 1926–1969), Warsaw, 1985; Jerzy Pertek, *Wielkie Dni Malej Floty* (Great Days of a Small Fleet), Poznan, 1987, and by the same author, *Dzieje ORP Orzel* (The Orzel Epic), Poznan, 1972; *ORP Burza*, Warsaw, 1992; Tadeusz Kondracki, *Niszczyciel ORP Orkan, 1942–1943* (The Destroyer Orkan, 1942–1943), Warsaw, 1994. Edmund Kosiarz, *Od Pierwszej do Ostatniej Salwy* (From the First to the Last Round), Warsaw, 1973; and *Obrona Helu w 1939* (The Defense of Hel in 1939), Warsaw, 1979; Zbigniew Flisowski, *Westerplatte*, Warsaw, 1979. A well illustrated album written and produced by the Polish Naval Self-Help Association. *Polska*

Marynarka Wojenna: Od Pierwszej do Ostatniej Salwy w Drugiej Wojnie Swiatowej, (The Polish Navy: From the First to the Last Round in World War Two), Rome, 1947. For an excellent study of the Polish Riverine Flotilla, see Jozef Wieslaw Dyskant, *Flotylla Rzeczna Marynarki Wojennej, 1919–1939* (The Riverine Navy, 1919–1939), Warsaw, 1994.

For detailed descriptions of all of the warships, including the Polish warships, mentioned in this monograph see, *Jane's Fighting Ships*, London, for the years 1939 through 1945. For specific details, with exquisite diagrams of all the Polish warships, see Stanislaw Piaskowski, *Okrety Rzeczpospolitej Polskiej, 1920–1946* (Warships of the Polish Republic, 1920–1946), Albany, NY, 1981; and reprinted, Warsaw, 1996.

For the history of the Polish navy prior to the eighteenth-century partitions, see Jozef Wojcik, *Dzieje Polski nad Baltykiem* (Polish Experiences on the Baltic), Warsaw, 1972; Marian Krwawicz, *Marynarka Wojenna i Obrona Polskiego Wybrzeza w Dawnych Czasach* (The Polish Navy and Defense of the Seacoast in Past Times), Warsaw, 1961; Eugeniusz Koczorowski, *Flota Polska w latach, 1587–1632* (The Polish Fleet in the Years, 1587–1632), Warsaw, 1973; Jozef Wieslaw Dyskant, *Oliwa, 1627*, Warsaw, 1993.

For the Polish Merchant Marine, see Jerzy Pertek, *Druga Mala Flota* (The Second Small Fleet), Poznan, 1983; and, *Krolewski Statek 'Batory'* (The Royal Ship *Batory*), Gdansk, 1975; Jan Kazimierz Sawicki and Stanislaw Andrzej Sobis, *Na Alianckich Szlakach, 1939–1946* (On Allied Courses, 1939–1946), Gdansk, 1985; Jan Kazimierz Sawicki, *Polska Marynarka Handlowa, 1939–1945* (Polish Merchant Navy, 1939–1945), Gdynia, 1991.

Last, but possibly not least, as a source of reminiscences and autobiographical history is the biannual periodical published by the Polish Naval Association in London, *Nasze Sygnaly* (Our Signals).

For a general history of Poland, see the English-language Bibliography.

In certain very unique areas, to emphasize a particular and significant point, I have cited the appropriate archive, book, or article at the end of the relevant chapter.

Poland's central European location, in what has often been called a less than desirable neighborhood of Russia and Germany has led to very fluctuating boundaries. Unless the reader is a an expert on Poland's political geography, it would be a good idea to consider glancing at a book which reviews the changing boundaries of Poland's millennium. Iwo Cyprian Pogonowski's, *Poland: A Historical Atlas*, Hippocrene Books, NY, 1987, is strongly suggested.

BIBLIOGRAPHY

This is a short English-language bibliography of Polish history during the Second World War.

Anders, Wladyslaw, *An Army in Exile*. London, 1949.

Baluk, Stefan and Michalowski, Marian. *Poland at Arms: 1939–1945*. Warsaw, 1990.

Barbarski, Krzysztof. *Polish Armour: 1939–1945*. London, 1982.

Beck, Jozef. *Final Report*. New York, 1957.

Bor-Komorowski, Tadeusz. *The Secret Army*. London, 1950.

Cambridge History of Poland, in two volumes. Original publication Cambridge University Press, 1941, and reprinted New York, 1971.

Cannistraro, Philip V., Edward D. Wynot, Jr., and Theodore P. Kovaleff. *Poland and the Coming of the Second World War: The Diplomatic Papers of A.J. Drexel Biddle Jr., United States Ambassador to Poland, 1937–1939*. Ohio State University, 1976.

Cholewczynski, George. *Poles Apart: The Polish Airborne at the Battle of Arnhem*. New York, 1993.

Ciechanowski, Jan. *Defeat in Victor.*, London, 1947.

Cienciala, Anna M. *Poland and the Western Powers: A Study in the Interdependence of Eastern and Western Europe*. University of Toronto Press, 1976.

Davies, Norman. *God's Playground: A History of Poland*. Columbia University Press, 1984.

———. *Heart of Europe. A Short History of Poland*. Clarendon Press, 1984.

———. *White Eagle—Red Star: The Polish-Soviet War 1919–1920*. London, 1972.

Destiny Can Wait: The Polish Air Force in the Second World War. London, 1949.

Documents on Polish-Soviet Relations 1939–1945. London in two volumes 1961 and 1967.

Englert, Juliusz and Krzysztof Barbarski. *General Anders.* London, 1989.

Englert, Juliusz, and Grzegorz Nowik. *Pilsudski.* London, 1991.

Filipow, Krzysztof and Zbigniew Wawer. *Passerby, Tell Poland....* Warsaw, 1991. One of the few English-language books on the Polish Armed Forces in the West, superbly illustrated.

Garlinski, Jozef. *Poland in the Second World War.* London, 1985

Henderson, Neville. *Failure of a Mission: Berlin, 1937–1939.* New York. 1940.

Iranek-Osmecki, George. *The Unseen and Silent.* London, 1954.

Jedruch, Jacek. *Constitutions, Elections and Legislatures of Poland, 1437–1977.* University Press of America, 1982.

Jedrzejewicz, Waclaw, editor. *Poland in the British Parliament, 1939–1945,* New York, in three volumes published 1946, 1959 and 1962.

————.*Jozef Lipski: Diplomat in Berlin, 1933–1939.* Columbia University Press, 1968.

————.*Julian Lukasiewicz: Diplomat in Paris.* Columbia University Press, 1970.

————. *Pilsudski: A Life for Poland.* New York, 1982.

Kacewicz, George. *Great Britain, the Soviet Union and the Polish Government in Exile, 1939–1945.* The Hague, 1979.

Karski, Jan. *The Great Powers and Poland, 1919–1945: From Versailles to Yalta.* University Press of America, 1985.

Kersten, Krystyna. *The Establishment of Communist Rule in Poland, 1943–1948.* University of California Press, 1991.

Kleczkowski, Stefan. *Poland's First Thousand.* London, 1944.

Korbel, Jozef. *Poland Between East and West: Soviet and German Diplomacy toward Poland, 1918–1933.* Princeton University Press, 1963.

Kot, Stanislaw. *Conversations with the Kremlin.* Oxford University Press, 1963.

Kozaczuk, Wladysla., *Enigma.* (Translated and edited by Wladyslaw Kasparek), University Publications of America, 1984.

Lane, Arthur Bliss. *I Saw Poland Betrayed: An American Ambassador Reports to the American People.* New York, 1948.

Lukas, Richard C. *The Strange Allies: United States and Poland, 1941–1945.* University of Tennessee, 1978.

———. *Forgotten Holocaust: The Poles under German Occupation.* University of Kentucky, 1986.

Newman, Simon. *March 1939: The British Guarantee to Poland. A Study in the Continuity of British Foreign Policy.* Oxford University Press, 1976.

Nowak, Jan. *Courier from Warsaw.* Wayne State University Press, 1982.

O'Malley, Sir Owen. *The Phantom Caravan.* London, 1954. (O'Malley was British ambassador to the Polish Government in London throughout most of the war.)

Pease, Neal. *Poland, the United States and the Stabilization of Europe, 1919–1933.* Oxford University Press, 1986.

Perlmutter, Amos. *FDR and Stalin: A Not so Grand Alliance, 1943–1945.* University of Missouri Press, 1993.

Peszke, Michael Alfred. *Battle for Warsaw, 1939–1944.* Boulder CO. 1995.

Pienkos, Donald. *For Your Freedom Through Ours: Polish American Efforts on Poland's Behalf, 1863–1991.* Boulder, CO. 1991.

Polish Ministry of Information. *Polish Troops in Norway.* London, 1943.

Polish White Book: Official Documents concerning Polish-German and Polish-Soviet Relations, 1933–1939. London, (date not given but undoubtedly between 1941–1944).

Polonsky, Anton. *The Great Powers and the Polish Question, 1941–1945.* London, 1976.

Prazmowska, Anita. *Britain, Poland and the Eastern Front, 1939.* Cambridge University Press, 1987.

Raczynski, Edward. *In Allied London.* London, 1962. (Raczynski was Polish ambassador to the Court of St. James throughout the war.)

Riekhoff, Harald von. *German-Polish Relations, 1918–1933.* Johns Hopkins University Press, 1971.

Roberts, Geoffrey. *The Unholy Alliance: Stalin's Pact with Hitler.* Indiana University Press, 1989.

Roos, Hans. *A History of Modern Poland.* New York, 1966.

Rothschild, Joseph. *Pilsudski's Coup D'Etat.* Columbia University Press, 1966.

Rozek, Edward J. *Allied Wartime Diplomacy: A Pattern in Poland.* New York, 1958.

Sword, Keith, ed. *Sikorski: Soldier and Statesman.* London, 1990.

Taylor, A.J.P. *The Origins of the Second World War.* New York, 1985.

Terry, Sarah Meiklejohn. *Poland's Place in Europe.* Princeton University Press, 1983.

Wandycz, Piotr S. *The United States and Poland.* Harvard University Press, 1980.

———. *Lands of Partitioned Poland, 1795–1918.* University of Washington Press, 1974,

———. *Soviet-Polish Relations 1917–1921.* Harvard University Press, 1969.

———. *Czechoslovak-Polish Confederation and the Great Powers, 1940–1943.* Indiana University Press, 1956.

———. *France and Her Eastern European Allies 1919–1925.* Minnessota University Press, 1961.

———. *Twilight of French Eastern Alliance, 1926–1936.* Princeton University Press, 1988.

———. *Polish Diplomacy: Aims and Achievements 1919–1945.* London, 1988.

Watt, Donald Cameron. *How War Came: The Immediate Origins of the Second World War, 1938–1939.* New York, 1989.

Weigel, George. *The Final Revolution: The Resistance Church and the Collapse of Communism.* Oxford University Press, 1992.

Weinbaum, Laurence. *A Marriage of Convenience: The New Zionist Organization and the Polish Government, 1936–1939.* New York, 1993.

Weinberg, Gerhard L. *The Foreign Policy of Hitler's Germany. Starting World War II, 1937–1939.* University of Chicago Press, 1980.

Willmott, H.P. *The Great Crusade: A new complete history of the Second World Wa.,* London, 1989.

Woodward, Llewellyn. *British Foreign Policy in the Second World Wa.,* London, 1962.

Woytak, Richard A. *On the Border of War and Peace.* Boulder, CO, 1979.

Wynot, Edward D. *Polish Politics in Transition: The Camp of National Unity and the Struggle for Power, 1935–1939.* University of Georgia Press, 1974.

Ulam, Adam B. *Expansion and Coexistence: The History of Soviet Foreign Policy 1917–1967.* New York, 1968.

Umiastowski, Roman. *Poland, Russia and Great Britain, 1941–1945.* London, 1946.

———. *Russia and the Polish Republic.* London, 1944.

Zagorski, Waclaw. *Seventy Days: A Diary of the Warsaw Insurrection 1944.* London, 1957.

Zaloga, Steven, and Victor Madej. *The Polish Campaign, 1939.* New York, 1985.

Zaloga, Steven J. *The Polish Army 1939–1945.* London, 1982.

Zamoyski, Adam. *The Polish Way: A Thousand Year History of the Poles and their Culture.* New York, 1988.

———. *The Battle for the Marchlands.* Boulder, CO, 1981.

———. *The Forgotten Few: The Polish Air Force in the Second World War,* New York, 1996.

Zawodny, J.K. *Nothing but Honor: The Story of the Warsaw Uprising 1944.* Hoover Institution Press, 1978.

———. *Death in the Forest: The Story of the Katyn Forest Massacre.* University of Notre Dame Press, 1962.

INDEX OF NAMES

Abbreviations: PN = Polish Navy
PA = Polish Army
PAF = Polish Air Force
PMM = Polish Merchant Marine
ORP = Polish Warship
HMS = Royal Navy Warship
RN = Royal Navy

Polish History Titles from Hippocrene

Jews in Poland: A Documentary History
Iwo Cyprian Pogonowski
Foreword by Richard Pipes

Originally published in 1993, this classic historical work is now available in paperback! *Jews in Poland* describes the rise of Jews as a nation and the crucial role that the Polish-Jewish community played in this development. The volume includes a new translation of the Charter of Jewish Liberties known as the Statute of Kalisz of 1264; 114 historical maps; as well as 172 illustrations including reproductions of works of outstanding painters, photographs of official posters, newspaper headlines and cartoons.

402 pages • maps, illustrations, index • 8½ x 11½ • 0-7818-0604-6 • $19.95pb • (677)

The Polish Way: A Thousand Year History of the Poles and Their Culture
Adam Zamoyski

"Zamoyski strives to place Polish history more squarely in its European context, and he pays special attention to the developments that had repercussions beyond the boundaries of the country. For example, he emphasizes the phenomenon of the Polish parliamentary state in Central Europe, its spectacular 16th century success and its equally spectacular disintegration two centuries later . . . This is popular history at its best, neither shallow nor simplistic . . . lavish illustrations, good maps and intriguing charts and genealogical tables make this book particularly attractive."

—New York Times Book Review

422 pages • 170 illustrations • $19.95pb • 0-7818-0200-8 • (176)

The Forgotten Few: The Polish Air Force in the Second World War
Adam Zamoyski

This is the story of the few who are rarely remembered today. Some 17,000 men and women passed through the ranks of the Polish Air Force while it was stationed on British soil in World War II. They not only played a crucial role in the Battle of Britain in 1940, but they also contributed significantly to the Allied war effort.

272 pages • 30 illustrations, 30 maps • 6 x 9 • 0-7818-0421-3 • $24.95hc • (493)

Forgotten Holocaust: The Poles Under German Occupation, 1939-1945, Revised Edition
Richard C. Lukas
Foreword by Norman Davies

This new edition includes the story of Zegota and the list of 700 Poles executed for helping Jews.

"Dr. Richard C. Lukas has rendered a valuable service by showing that no one can properly analyze the fate of one ethnic community in occupied Poland without referring to the fates of others. In this sense, *The Forgotten Holocaust* is a powerful corrective."
—from the foreword by Norman Davies

"Carefully researched—a timely contribution."
—Professor Piotr Wandycz, Yale University

"Contains excellent analyses of the relationship of Poland's Jewish and Gentile communities, the development of the resistance, the exile leadership, and the Warsaw uprisings. A superior work.
—*Library Journal*

300 pages • 6 x 9 • illustrations • 0-7818-0528-7 • $24.95hc • (639)

Did the Children Cry?: Hitler's War Against Jewish and Polish Children
Richard C. Lukas

Winner of the 1996 Janusz Korczak Literary Competition for books about children.

" . . . [Lukas] intersperses the endless numbers, dates, locations and losses with personal accounts of tragedy and triumph . . . A well-researched book . . ." —*Catalyst*

263 pages • 15 b/w photos, index • 0-7818-0242-3 • $24.95hc • (145)

Your Life is Worth Mine
Ewa Kurek
Introduction by Jan Karski

First published in Poland in 1992 as *Gdy Klasztor Znaczyl Zycie,* this is the story of how Polish nuns saved hundreds of Jewish lives while risking their own during World War II. This long awaited American edition includes a section of interviews with nuns and Jewish survivors which did not appear in the Polish edition.

"A welcome addition to Holocaust literature . . . deserves a wide readership." —*Zgoda*

250 pages • 5½ x 8½ • 0-7818-0409-4 • $24.95hc • (240)

Bitter Glory: Poland and Its Fate, 1918–1939
Richard M. Watt

"Admirably fair-minded and meticulous about the achievements and the disasters of the Pilsudski years."

—The New York Times

"An able political history of the Polish Republic from its reconstruction at the end of the First World War."

—The New Yorker

"An American popular historian writes objectively and well, and from a solid base in the existing literature, about Pilsudski and Poland's period of independence between the wars."

—Foreign Affairs

With remarkable skill, Richard M. Watt tells the story of the twenty-one years of freedom snuffed out by two traditional enemies of Poland.

Greatly praised by Barbara Tuchman, William L. Shirer, Alistair Horne, and J.H. Plumb for his earlier works, Richard M. Watt is noted historian and author of two other books, *Dare Call it Treason* and *The Kings Depart*. He has also written numerous articles and reviews for *The New York Sunday Times* and other periodicals. The author won the 1996 History Award of the J. Pilsudski Institute in New York.

511 pages • 6¼ x 9½ • 32 pages b & w photos • 0-7818-0673-9 • W • $16.95pb • (771)

Old Polish Legends
Retold by F. C. Anstruther
Wood engravings by J. Sekalski

Now, in a new gift edition, this fine collection of eleven fairy tales, with an introduction by Zygmunt Nowakowski, was first published in Scotland during World War II, when the long night of German occupation was at its darkest.

66 pages • 7¼ x 9 • 11 woodcut engravings • 0-7818-0521-X • $11.95hc • (653)

The Works of Henryk Sienkiewicz

Quo Vadis
Henryk Sienkiewicz
translated by W. S. Kuniczak
New Paperback Edition!
Written nearly a century ago and translated into over 40 languages, *Quo Vadis* has been a monumental work in the history of literature. W. S. Kuniczak, the foremost Polish American novelist and master translator of Sienkiewicz in this century, presents a modern translation of the world's greatest bestseller since 1905. An epic story of love and devotion in Nero's time, *Quo Vadis* remains without equal a sweeping saga set during the degenerate days leading to the fall of the Roman empire and the glory and agony of early Christianity.
589 pages • 6 x 9 • 0-7818-0550-3 • $19.95pb • (648)

In Desert and Wilderness
Henryk Sienkiewicz, edited by Miroslaw Lipinski
In traditional Sienkiewicz style, Stas and the little Nell and their mastiff Saba brave the desert and wilderness of Africa. This powerful coming-of-age tale has captivated readers young and old for a century.
278 pages • 0-7818-0235-0 • $19.95hc • (9)

With Fire and Sword
translated by W.S. Kuniczak
The first volume of the epic trilogy, this novel has been translated and adapted for the modern reader by W.S. Kuniczak. It is a sweeping saga of love, adventure, war and rebellion set in Eastern Europe during the 17th century.
"A Polish *Gone with the Wind* . . . racy, readable to a fault . . . provides the timeless joys of a good old-fashioned read. *With Fire and Sword* should have taken its place in the general literary repertory long ago beside the works of the elder Dumas, Walter Scott and Margaret Mitchell."
—*The New York Times Book Review*
1,154 pages • 6 x 9 • 0-87052-974-9 • NA • $35.00hc • (766)

The Deluge
Translated by W.S. Kuniczak

This second part of the trilogy is published in two beautifully designed volumes. It is a superb account of the Swedish War of 1655–69, which came close to overwhelming the Polish-Lithuanian Commonwealth until the Polish people rallied to the defense of Czetochowa, found new strength and faith when there was little left to hope for, and drove out the invaders. As the structural and thematic heart of Henryk Sienkiewicz's magnificent Trilogy, *The Deluge* is a masterful blend of history and imagination that illuminates the character of an extraordinary people.

"*The Deluge* is historical fiction at its best . . . This massive epic of love, war and adventure comes to life in English in an innovative modern rendering by W.S. Kuniczak . . . [it] glows with vivid imagery and unforgettable characters."

—*The Chicago Tribune*

2 volumes: 1,808 pages • 6 x 9 • 0-87052-004-0 • NA • $60.00hc • (762)

Fire in the Steppe
Henryk Sienkiewicz, in modern translation by W. S. Kuniczak

"The Sienkiewicz Trilogy stands with that handful of novels which not only depict but also help to determine the soul and character of the nation they describe."

—James A. Michener

750 pages • 0-7818-0025-0 • $24.95hc • (16)

The Little Trilogy
Henryk Sienkiewicz; a new translation by Miroslaw Lipinski

Comprised of three novellas, *The Old Servant*, *Hania*, and *Selim Mirza*, this collection will be enjoyed by the thousands of admirers of the greatest storyteller in Polish literature and the winner of the Nobel Prize for Literature in 1905.

267 pages • 0-7818-0293-8 • $19.95hc • (235)

Teutonic Knights, Illustrated Edition

Henryk Sienkiewicz; in a translation edited by Miroslaw Lipinski

"Swashbuckling action, colorful characters and a touching love story . . ."

—*Publishers Weekly*

" . . . one of the most splendid achievements of Polish literature."

—*Zgoda*

" . . . a memorable, massive, breathtaking and compulsive read."

—*New Horizon*

800 pages • illustrated • 0-7818-0433-7 • $30.00hc • (533)

All prices subject to change without prior notice. **To purchase Hippocrene Books** contact your local bookstore, call (718) 454-2366, or write to: HIPPOCRENE BOOKS, 171 Madison Avenue, New York, NY 10016. Please enclose check or money order, adding $5.00 shipping (UPS) for the first book and $.50 for each additional book.